THE CHALLENGES OF
STUDENT
DIVERSITY
IN CANADIAN SCHOOLS

Essays on Building A Better Future
for Exceptional Children

THE CHALLENGES OF
STUDENT DIVERSITY
IN CANADIAN SCHOOLS

Essays on Building A Better Future for Exceptional Children

Coordinating Editor:

Judy Lupart

Editors

Anne McKeough
Marion Porath
Linda Phillips
Vianne Timmons

Fitzhenry & Whiteside

Fitzhenry and Whiteside Limited
195 Allstate Parkway
Markham, Ontario L3R 4T8

In the United States:
311 Washington Street,
Brighton, Massachusetts 02135

www.fitzhenry.ca   godwit@fitzhenry.ca
Fitzhenry & Whiteside acknowledges with thanks the
Canada Council for the Arts, and the Ontario Arts Council for their support
of our publishing program. We acknowledge the financial
support of the Government of Canada through the Book Publishing Industry
Development Program (BPIDP) for our publishing activities.

Library and Archives Canada Cataloguing in Publication
The challenges of student diversity in Canadian schools:
essays on building a better future for exceptional students/
coordinating editor Judy Lupart.

ISBN 978-1-55041-977-1
1. Multicultural education—Canada. I. Lupart, Judy Lee
LC1099.5.C3C53 2008   370.117'0971   C2008-903770-7

Cover and interior design by Darrell McCalla
Cover image courtesy of Mark Taylor Andre
Printed and bound in Canada

1 3 5 7 9 10 8 6 4 2

CONTENTS

ACKNOWLEDGEMENTS

At the University of Alberta, we would like to acknowledge: the Faculty of Education, specifically the Offices of the Dean and the Department of Educational Psychology, Alberta Education, Edmonton Public School Board, Edmonton Catholic School District. In addition we would like to thank Lise Belzile for her administrative contribution to this Lecture Series.

The following individuals' support of the lecture series at The University of Prince Edward Island site is gratefully acknowledged: Barbara MacNutt, Manager of Literacy Initiatives, Prince Edward Island Department of Education; Myra Thorkelson, Student Services and Diversity Education Consultant, Prince Edward Island Department of Education; Jay McPhail, University of Prince Edward Island Audiovisual; and Beverly Gerg, Research Administrator for the Vice-President Academic Development at the University of Prince Edward Island. The lecture series received funding from the Department of Canadian Heritage.

In the Faculty of Education, UBC, the Offices of the Dean and External Programs and Learning Technologies and the Psycho-educational Research and Training Centre and the Vancouver School Board.

The Calgary site had several supporters (funding and in kind support). Here is the list:

Canadian Rockies Public Schools, Calgary Board of Education, Calgary Catholic School District, Golden Hills School Division, Calgary Regional Consortium, Rocky View School Division, and University of Calgary Learning Commons and Division of Applied Psychology.

Introduction

Building a Better Future for Canadian Students

Judy L. Lupart and Marion Porath

The essays in this book broadly address the complexity of contemporary schools and classrooms, as well as our need, as a Canadian society, to challenge the beliefs and practices that underpin lack of full access to, and benefit from, education. Together, the contributions acknowledge the important influences of social, cultural, linguistic, ability, academic, behavioural, gender, and sexuality differences on the lives of students and raise important questions about how this diversity is respected in educational policy and practice. The contributors challenge our thinking about how we make education meaningful for students who live in a global society — how we provide responsive, connected, and culturally congruent experiences for all learners in Canada and what we mean by "diversity." This is accomplished by focusing on learners in context, consistent with Bronfenbrenner's ecological theory.

An ecological theory developed by Bronfenbrenner and Morris (1998) provides a powerful framework for connecting the school and myriad social, demographic, cultural, environmental, political, and socio-historical influences. Their model of influences places the individual at the centre of ever-widening social and environmental influences. The model contextualizes individuals while at the same time acknowledging their uniqueness.

Affecting each individual (the learner, in this case) is a series of "progressively more sophisticated scientific paradigms for investigating the impact of environment on development". These scientific paradigms include: the microsystem, the mesosystem, the exosystem, the macrosystem, and the chronosystem.

The *microsystem* describes the environment of direct influence of family, peers, school, and neighbourhood. The *mesosystem* links the various microsystems and personal interactions with them, intertwining students' personal characteristics and their immediate environments. The *exosystem* evaluates aspects of the external environment such as community services, school boards, and governmental influences. The *macrosystem* considers the overarching influences of society and culture, and the *chronosystem,* a socio-historical sequence, examines developments that occur during a child's life.

Families, Policy, and Problems

In the present volume, the first set of essays, "Families, Policy, and Problems," addresses the complexity of beliefs and practices within our education system — specifically the challenges and issues created by acknowledging and dealing with diversity in our schools. These essays focus on the need to enable families to support their children's education and the complexity of the issues surrounding the inclusion of students with developmental disabilities into the "regular" classroom. The contributions in this section make it clear that to effect change within our education system, we must consider the levels of Bronfenbrenner's ecological model that are in close proximity to the student: the microsystem and the mesosystem, respectively.

In the introductory essay, "The Challenges of Student Diversity in Canadian Schools," Judy L. Lupart examines how, historically, students with disabilities have been relegated to the margins of Canadian schools as they were expected to meet minimal standards within a "one size fits all" system. By the 1950s and 1960s parents of exceptional students began to react against this paradigm by lobbying for special services for their children but the resulting changes caused a split between regular teachers who strove for excellence and special education teachers who aimed for equity. Lupart suggests the possibility of authentic inclusion where the best future of regular and special education are encapsulated in a unified system of education. Although this recent shift back to inclusion remedied the split "dual" system problem, teachers were overwhelmed by their changing roles and responsibilities as diverse students were brought together in one classroom. Lupart recommends that by downsizing the referral, testing, labelling, and placement activities that supported the "dual" system, the resulting cost savings can be applied to reducing pupil-teacher ratios and to options for professional advice to assist educators as they work in contexts of student diversity.

The next essay in this section, by Vianne Timmons, addresses the question "How can schools enable families?" because research has shown that positive relationships between schools and families ensure quality education for children. Families are the experts on meeting their children's needs, and schools can benefit from this expertise by forming collaborative relationships with families not only to learn from them, but also to give them appropriate supports within the home. Timmons demonstrates how a collaborative relationship can work through the development of a literacy program that addresses two issues: literacy support and basic parenting skills. Overall, Timmons stresses that schools need to recognize both the differences and the unique possibilities that exist within each family, to ensure that an appropriate approach is developed to meet their child's educational needs. Indeed, further evidence-based support for this direction is provided in the essays contributed by Doug Willms and Clyde Hertzman. In the next essay, Cam Crawford presents an overview of the current issues within inclusive education for Canadian students with developmental disabilities through an exploration of the tensions that exist between "inclusive education" and "special education" and between "excellence" and "equity." He also explains current policy issues: the identification/assessment processes for student placements and the current flaws within this system; how individual program planning works and parents' feelings of exclusion from this process; the funding/resource issues schools face and the lack of accessibility supports; the confusion school staffs feel regarding their roles and the lack of preparation they receive for teaching students with special needs; and the lack of professional development for school staff in this area. Crawford explains how key stakeholders can overcome these issues through the development of shared expectations and the establishment of a common policy approach by building on established principles. The points made by Crawford are consistent with those introduced earlier in this essay. However, his contribution reflects only certain parts of the whole, as the following section demonstrates.

Economics, Environment, and Politics of Diversity

Moving to the external exosystem of Bronfenbrenner and Morris's (1998) ecological model of social influences, the essays in the section "Economics, Environment, and Politics of Diversity" examine the political dynamics that surround diversity issues in Canada, as well as Canadian approaches to overcoming the socioeconomic inequalities and other external influences affecting the quality of education received by some Canadian students. Ben Levin stresses how important it is for researchers to understand the effect of political dynamics on social policies, focusing specifically on the education system. He gives an historical overview of Canada's past political policies that resulted in

4

the suppression of diversity through the assimilation and homogenization of this country's diverse cultures. Levin further argues how this political approach has changed over the last century, leading to the perception that diversity is an asset to be cultivated. Levin's position supports the perspective taken in the opening discussion of this essay. These political dynamics affect diversity issues within our education system, where schools have traditionally been under pressure to emphasize students' homogeneity. However, due to the change in political dynamics over the last several decades, schools have established policies promoting diversity and inclusion. While this has promoted many positive changes, the issue of diversity is complex and challenging because of the very nature of our diverse population, and Levin cautions that we have a long way to go. The more diverse a population grows, the less agreement there is about shared values. This creates a political reality where governments must try to please the majority while offending the minority. Researchers who strive to effect positive changes in social policies must understand how these political realities work.

Doug Willms' essay continues the discussion about the effects of external dynamics but moves it to the global level. He explains how Canada wants to sustain its current economic growth, while at the same time maintaining and improving its presence in the global economy. However, this requires skilled individuals with superior literacy and numeracy skills, adaptability, and the aptitude to work well within a fast-paced, team-oriented work environment. Canada wishes to produce the individuals needed through our education system. In 2003 Canada ranked second in literacy skills, sixth in mathematics, and fifth in science in the Programme of International Student Assessment (PISA). However, large discrepancies were also noticed in the scores produced by students with lower socioeconomic status (SES). To become one of the top three countries in reading achievement, mathematics, and science, Canada needs to address these inequalities. Willms also describes the Initiative on the New Economy, a research project that produced five specific strategies to raise and level the learning bar in Canadian schools. These strategies included the following actions: (1) safeguard the healthy development of infants, (2) strengthen early childhood education, (3) improve schools and local communities, (4) reduce segregation and the effects associated with poverty, and (5) create a family-enabling society. Willms concludes his essay asserting that by implementing this mix of policies, Canada can raise and level the learning bar for youths at risk and consequently maintain and improve its global economic status.

Clyde Hertzman's essay examines how the *British Columbia Atlas of Child Development* can be used as a tool to identify factors influencing early childhood vulnerabilities affecting development. Early Childhood Development (ECD) research has been difficult to interpret, given the numerous limitations of previous studies. The atlas addresses many of the previous problems of small sample size and focuses on higher-risk populations by collecting developmental outcome data from approximately 44,000 kindergarten children from across the province. Where previous studies typically examined a single or a few developmental domains, the atlas covers the full spectrum of variables, allowing broad-based, simultaneous consideration and analysis. More importantly, traditional geographical boundaries and parameters derived from traditional Census units are redefined by the entire community context and the capacity for "social care"; therefore, the data collected better describe the population and their specific vulnerabilities.

The atlas uses a strategy of mapping, which provides a visual, colour-coded representation of how different environments (i.e., socio-ecological, cultural, etc.) all intersect. Mapping allows researchers to focus on ecological correlations, where the neighbourhood is the unit of analysis, not the child. The Early Development Instrument (EDI) that is used to measure early childhood development includes five scales: (1) physical well-being, (2) social competence, (3) emotional maturity, (4) language and cognitive development, and (5) communication and general knowledge.

This unique and innovative approach can serve many purposes and can help us understand the important interacting factors influencing the exosystem of community context, the macrosystem of society and culture, and perhaps even the chronosystem of sociohistorical developments (Bronfenbrenner & Morris, 1998). First, community mapping can provide a baseline of the state of early childhood development across the province, and through monitoring changes across time, it can be used to evaluate change. Second, community mapping goes well beyond simple SES-vulnerability correlations to yield (1) fine-tuned analysis of the conditions that promote optimal human development and (2) ways in which universal access to them can be achieved. Third, this approach can be particularly useful for understanding the influences of early childhood development on special populations such as recent immigrants, those living in low-SES environments, and Aboriginal children. Finally, community mapping can help to inform community development initiatives and policy development by revealing the barriers to accessing services for families and agencies; understanding and defining the clinical, targeted, universal, and civil-society levels of interventions that are available within and across communities; and determining what mix of programs might best serve a community's needs.

The essays in this section make it clear that many complex and evolving issues need to be addressed within the Canadian education system. However, each author provides guidelines and solutions to help resolve these issues, and they all believe that positive change can result through the application of research and an understanding of the multilevel ecological dynamics involved. The contributions in this section provide a plausible framework for consideration of new and emerging conceptions of student diversity in school and society — particularly, those based on diversity, culture, and power, including diversity in exceptional learning needs. These two categories are reflected in the final two sections of this book: "Diversity, Culture, and Power" and "Diversity in Exceptional Learning Needs."

Diversity, Culture, and Power

Marie Battiste's essay opens this section, situating Aboriginal education in socio-historical context, detailing the history of educational policies that have resulted in failure for Aboriginal students. She challenges the positioning of mainstream beliefs and values over those of First Nations' families. First Nations communities value education but have had no voice in the shaping of educational policy in Canada. Often, Aboriginal youth are viewed as "the problem" when the system has actually failed to acknowledge and value their worldviews. Battiste emphasizes the fact that each child represents a "micro ethnic group"; teachers need to be aware of how that child's worldview is represented and reflected in their knowledge and learning. This requires sensitivity and openness to the familial, social, and cultural systems that envelop each child. As Battiste points out, knowledge differs when viewed from different perspectives. We need to unpack and understand diversity.

Jim Cummins' essay highlights theoretical insights and pedagogical practices that have the potential to bring Canada's linguistic and cultural diversity into our schools in meaningful ways. Cummins, like Battiste, recognizes the social, cultural, and linguistic realities that are often not addressed by Canadian schools. Also, like Battiste, he celebrates the richness of the heritages that make up the Canadian population. Moving from a

8

unidimensional concept of literacy, often taken to mean English literacy, to *multiliteracies*, allows us to understand the multiplicity of worldviews that children bring to Canadian classrooms. Cummins emphasizes pedagogy and school environments that value and support *identity investment* — the "affective bond" between students and literacy that encourages investment of personal identities into the learning process. Multiliteracies take into account cultural and linguistic diversity and social transformation and include technological literacy as a tool for knowledge generation. Cummins weaves together social constructivist pedagogy and the many influences of Bronfenbrenner's external systems on learners, providing concrete theory-practice links in the form of innovative pedagogical practices that honour cultural and linguistic diversity.

Paula S. Cameron and Blye Frank's essay also challenges us to examine different perspectives and to question the mainstream belief and value systems that have an impact on students. They quote Bernstein (1996): "The question is: Who recognizes themselves as of value [in schools]? What other images are excluded by the dominant image of value so that some students are unable to recognize themselves?" (p. 7). Cameron and Frank highlight the "complex ecosystem" of school communities, situating them in the larger social context where conventional beliefs and values often militate against acceptance and respect. For example, when heterosexuality is framed as the norm, "identity erasure" is the result for students who are identified as or who identify themselves as lesbian, gay, bisexual, transgendered, or intersexed (LGBTI). Cameron and Frank examine both the impact of larger social structures on LGBTI youth and the effects of inequity on our culture. To break this interactive cycle, we need to challenge heterosexual privilege and engage in analysis of how violent events related to sexuality occur and of how gender stereotypes contribute to this violence. In other words, an analysis of systemic bias and inequity is necessary. Cameron and Frank describe a number of in-place, school-based programs that are designed to create more equitable and accepting spaces for LGBTI youth, but they emphasize that our discussions must take place at the macrosystem level for meaningful change to take hold.

Debra Pepler and Wendy Craig address power dynamics of another sort — the power held by bullies in our schools over the children they victimize. These dynamics parallel, and result in, the marginalization of certain members of our school communities that Battiste, Cummins, and Cameron and Frank addressed. Pepler and Craig purposefully avoid the usual labels of bully, victim, and bully/victim, characterizing bullying problems as relationship problems that arise as a function of group dynamics. They use the lens of a developmental systemic perspective, and their work resonates with that in other essays in this section through its focus on the "salient systems or contexts" in which children develop. They introduce the concept of "social architecture" to describe how positive peer groups may be encouraged in schools and negative groups may be deconstructed. They emphasize that this structuring of peer group dynamics must be done within supportive school communities that provide nurturing, positive environments for children's lives in school. Equally important is the notion of "formative consequences": bullies must not only be held accountable for their actions, but also need to be supported in the development of prosocial, responsible behaviours. School- and social-system-level initiatives are described that have the potential to build strong social support networks for children affected by bullying.

Diversity in Exceptional Learning Needs

The final section of this book reveals how diversity can be taken to mean different ways of learning — sometimes reflected in the terms "exceptional learners" and "children with special needs."

Labels assigned to these learners often reflect a lack of critical analysis of what these terms actually mean for children and for pedagogy. The two essays in this section address diversity *among* "exceptional learners." John Kirby probes diversity among learners who experience difficulty learning to read, and Marion Porath explores diversity among gifted learners. Students with exceptional learning needs are also affected by mainstream beliefs and values discussed in the previous essays. Cultural and linguistic heritages, gender, sexuality, and peer relationships may marginalize students with exceptional needs; in addition, they are marked (portrayed) as different because they do not learn in "typical" ways.

John Kirby defines reading difficulties broadly, including students who are considered reading disabled and dyslexic, but also recognizing that a multiplicity of reasons underlie difficulties in learning to read. Learning to read in English is "no trivial matter" because of the lack of predictability of the sound-symbol relationship. This learning becomes even more difficult when children experience fundamental information-processing problems related to cracking the symbolic code of English. In a review of theories of reading, Kirby emphasizes the complexity of the different pathways children may take in learning to read. The implications are that we need to assess and intervene in early childhood, tailoring interventions to the needs of individual children and families. Kirby is cognizant of the microsystem supports that need to be in place to encourage families to facilitate language development. He acknowledges that parents may lack the resources, time, and/or knowledge of *how* to best support their children and that the language(s) of the home need to be attended to. These microsystem supports imply an exosystem that is committed to facilitating early language development in a seamless fashion from home to preschool to formal education. They also imply that teacher education, as well as the roles and responsibilities of teachers, need to be reconceptualized. Solid knowledge of theories of language and reading development, combined with expertise in understanding diverse pathways to learning are essential to pedagogy that provides suitable support for students who are learning to read effectively.

Marion Porath examines the diversity that is evident among learners identified as gifted, and questions the use of the single descriptor "gifted" to capture this diversity. This group of learners is highly heterogeneous, differing significantly from more typically developing learners and also differing among themselves. The latter form of diversity derives from the influences of widely varying academic profiles, creativity, gender, co-occurring disability, culture, and language. Consonant with other essays in this book, Porath emphasizes aspects of the school environment that are important in supporting all learners to realize their potential and to have their identities affirmed. To achieve such support and affirmation, critical analysis must be carried out concerning the meanings of the terms that permeate both the discourse regarding learners identified as gifted and the discourses related to other forms of diversities. We must also examine our own beliefs about teaching, learning, and children's "capacity"; analyze how we create and sustain rich learning environments; and think deeply about what it means to be educated in contemporary society. Learners who are gifted often challenge us to engage in this sort of analysis; their perspectives need to be included and honoured in our analyses and discussions.

Diversity: Whose Problem Is It?
Who Tells the Story?

All the essays in this volume share an underlying principle: that diversity is a matter for all of us to grapple with on a deep level. Diversity is not situated in individual learners but in the social and cultural practices, values, and beliefs that make up our

Canadian society. It is critical to acknowledge and celebrate the social, cultural, and imaginative capital represented in our society and in our schools as microcosms of that society and to examine deeply the entrenched values, beliefs, and practices that may work against the inclusion of this richness in social and educational contexts. These essays provide a solid framework for engaging in this examination.

The essays in this book also emphasize the need to attend to all the voices of diversity. Indigenous peoples, LGBTI youth, multicultural families, children who are victims of negative peer dynamics, and students with exceptional learning needs must be part of the conversation, and their identities and perspectives must be honoured in authentic ways.

The ideal of diversity has deep philosophical roots that can be traced to Aristotle, who believed that plurality was essential to an ideal society, and subsequently to Mill, Dewey, and Nussbaum (Moses & Chang, 2006). "Taken together, these philosophers argued that the ideal of diversity is worth wanting because it enriches a democratic society and cultivates adults who can function more effectively as citizens of a complex and connected world" (Moses & Chang, p. 9). Understanding the philosophy underlying diversity provides the framework for analysis of what diversity means in Canadian schools and why it is important.

References

Bernstein, B. (1996). *Pedagogy, symbolic control and identity: Theory, research and critique*. London: Taylor and Francis.

Bronfenbrenner, U. (1986). Ecology of the family as a context for human development: Research perspectives. *Developmental Psychology, 22*, 723–742.

Bronfenbrenner, U., & Morris, P.A. (1998). The ecology of developmental processes. In W. Damon & R.M. Lerner (Eds.), *Handbook of child psychology: Vol. 1. Theoretical models of human development* (5th ed.) (pp. 993–1028). Hoboken, NJ: Wiley.

Moses, M.S., & Chang, M.J. (2006). Toward a deeper understanding of the diversity rationale. *Educational Researcher, 35*, 6–11.

The Challenges of Student Diversity in Canadian Schools

Judy L. Lupart

For too many years, Canadian schools have been chasing the concept of a standard "one size fits all" approach within our public education systems. Although students with obvious disabilities were generally excluded from public education for the first half of the century, all others were expected to meet some sort of "minimal standard." As the public education systems grew and developed over the ensuing decades, the extent of student diversity mushroomed, and the minimum standard bar was raised higher and higher. Children with exceptional learning needs were the first group of students to be relegated to the margins of our school systems, and as educators attempted to deal with the ever-increasing expectations of society, more and more students were considered to be at risk for failure. Even though current legislation and policy in every province and territory advances support for inclusive education, actual practice is, in many respects, far from the ideal. Our institutions are organized in ways that support the majority, and those students who are different from the norm have little choice but to try to fit. These systems are not malleable enough to support all those who enter, and consequently some of our students will not be sufficiently supported to develop to their full potential. It is our contention, as it is for all the contributing authors of this book, that there are many ways that Canadian schools can better serve the needs of our diverse students. In this essay, we argue for authentic inclusive schools within an ecological framework. In the following segments of this essay, we provide a brief historical overview of progressive inclusion and promising directions for authentic inclusive education practice.

A Century of Progressive Inclusion of Students with Exceptional Needs

There has been a steady shift toward inclusion within our schools and our country over the past century; however, for the first half of the twentieth century, there was only limited educational provision for students with exceptional needs within the public education system. During the 1950s and 1960s, parents began to lobby for services for their children with exceptional needs. Advocacy groups like the Canadian Association for the Mentally Retarded (currently the Canadian Association for Community Living) and the Canadian Association for Children and Adults with Learning Disabilities became powerful influences on both the direction of future education and the growth of special education within public school systems. Services that were provided informally for children with exceptional learning needs "operated separately from the education system, with parents, volunteers, and occasionally trained teachers mostly responsible for funding, developing, and delivering instructional programs" (Andrews & Lupart, 2000, p. 33). Educational practices that were more personalized and relevant to the needs of the students emerged from these settings; these precedent-setting practices became important as public schools gradually assumed greater responsibility by creating special classes for children with exceptional needs in regular schools.

Most often these services were organized and implemented on the basis of classification and categorical distinctions.

Concomitantly, schools began to use testing and assessment procedures as the primary means of diagnosing and labelling different categories of children with special needs. Thus began a system of educational service provision for students with exceptional learning needs, recognized today as "Special Education." Andrews and Lupart (2000) describe the traditional referral, testing, labelling, placement, and programming processes as the "five-box special education approach." Importantly, this approach cut a sharp wedge in the public education services of the time and would become a sophisticated competing system of education in future decades.

Despite the fact that the "special education approach" perpetuated the isolation and segregation of students with exceptional needs, educators rationalized that students were better served in special classes. They lauded the reduced pupil-teacher ratios, as well as special teaching methods, resources, equipment, and programs particularly geared to the unique needs of each category of student. More importantly, parents and advocacy groups, jubilant at the victory of winning a place for their children in the public education system, were generally satisfied with the special education classes that were set up. In fact, special education classes and exceptional student categories in public schools proliferated throughout the country, and that trend continued until well into the 1980s.

By this time, special education had become a huge, specialized, bureaucratic system, with its own programs, services, and personnel. Students with exceptional needs were offered an extensive range of education services, including individual education programs; curriculum modifications; special devices; special classroom arrangements, counselling services, and speech/language therapy; occupational therapy/physiotherapy and other therapies; medical services; and social services. Small wonder that when school districts experienced continual funding cuts

FUNDING!

throughout the 1980s and 1990s, the special education system was in direct competition with the regular education system as both resources and personnel started to decline.

Oddly enough, the broader public commitment to the social welfare and normalization of individuals with disabilities in communities across Canada led to the demise of special education within the public education system (Friend, Bursuck, & Hutchinson, 1998; Wolfensberger, Nirge, Olshansky, Perske, & Roos, 1972). The influence of the American civil rights movement in the early 1970s and resulting federal legislation, passed in 1975 in the United States, as well as the growing Canadian social commitment to foster normalization practices for persons with disabilities and handicaps within our communities, led to significant conceptual changes in Canadian public schools. First came the tenet of "integration," the educational concept that was parallel to normalization in society. As commonly practised in schools, however, integration simply entailed the removal of students with special needs from segregated special education classrooms and placement in regular classrooms. It wasn't too long before complaints from both teachers and parents were voiced. How could we expect special education students, who had been removed from the regular education classroom, to return to the very setting where they had failed in the first place? During the 1980s, in an attempt to improve regular classroom services for students with exceptional needs, schools were required to have an individualized education program developed and approved by the child's parent(s), with all special services and curriculum modifications clearly specified and planned out beforehand. This meant that many students with exceptional learning needs would spend most of their time in a regular classroom setting with some in-classroom modification and/or some specialized pullout classes, as promulgated by the highly influential "Cascade of Services" Model (Deno, 1970). These "symbols" and "ceremonies," as

Skrtic (1996) called them, became the norm for what was generally referred to as "mainstreaming." Fashioned after U.S. special education systems, the new Canadian system placed students with special educational needs in the "least restrictive environment" and removed them from special settings and placements to more normal educational settings as soon as possible. Unfortunately, even though the services were updated and offered some regular class experience for most students, the onus was still placed on individuals with special needs to change in ways that would allow them to fit into the "one size fits all" system of regular education.

During the 1990s, a radical shift toward inclusive education movement was launched. This approach emphasized a unified system of education, in which all students could be provided with an appropriate education (Andrews & Lupart, 2000; Lupart, 1998). Adopting a platform of human minority rights, proponents argued that schools needed to change classroom instruction and educational services to meet the diverse needs of all students. If any students encountered obstacles to learning, these were to be removed and/or adjusted so as to ensure that students experienced successful learning and development. Unfortunately, this move brought with it sufficient misunderstanding and distrust that the majority of school systems became paralyzed in a battle over regular and special education funding and resources, and opportunistic administrators began to systemically close down special education classrooms under the false guise of promoting inclusive education. The ultimate paradox was that the philosophy of inclusion promoted by schools and school boards was in direct contradiction to actual practice. More and more students were identified as requiring special education, and regular classroom teachers became less tolerant of student diversity in their regular classrooms. For example, Alberta Education records show that the number of students identified as having exceptional learning needs increased from 23,701 in 1979 to 51,711 in 1992, and to 77, 700 (a record increase) in 2002. During the same period, the number of special needs categories grew from 15 to 20 (Alberta Education, 2002).

The widely adopted special education approach embraced in the 1960s has continued to be a strong element in present-day schools. Recently, educational leaders have charged that this approach simply perpetuates the isolation and discrimination experienced by students with exceptional learning needs (Andrews & Lupart, 2000; Lupart & Webber, 2002; Skrtic, 1996). In practice, this approach allowed schools and regular educators to carry on the way they always had. When certain students were considered to require something different from what was offered in regular education classrooms, they were simply "decoupled" from regular education and put in a special class with a special teacher, and not much else had to change (Skrtic, 1996). This arrangement was initially successfully practised in Canadian schools, to the apparent satisfaction of regular and special education stakeholders.

However, with increasing emphasis on inclusion and the mass return of exceptional students to regular education classrooms in the 1990s, schools verged on a state of crisis. Teachers became confused and overwhelmed about their changing roles and responsibilities. Students and parents raised concerns about a "watered-down curriculum" and the lack of services for students with exceptional learning needs. Moreover, the margins where students were considered to be at-risk in our schools spread over to nontraditional special education categories such as students from cultural minorities, students from an ESL background, and students from economically disadvantaged backgrounds (Lupart & Odishaw, 2003). Clearly, radical change in our educational systems is required to meet the growing diversity of students, and it is our position that this goal could be at least partially achieved through the adoption of authentic inclusive practices.

Promising Directions for Authentic Inclusive Education Practice

Diversity and Disability: New Perspectives

Skrtic (1991; 1996) has been a forceful critic of traditional views concerning special education and predominant views of disability. He asserts that several inaccurate assumptions underlie special education practices:

> (1) Disabilities are pathological conditions that students have. (2) Differential diagnosis is objective and useful.
> (3) Special education is a rationally conceived and coordinated system of services that benefits diagnosed students.
> (4) Progress results from incremental technological improvements in diagnosis and instructional interventions. (p. 54)

These claims are further supported by Hahn (1989), who proposed an ideological shift from the traditional view of individuals with disabilities, which he refers to as "functional limitations," to a more constructive perspective of "minority rights." He asserts that such a shift will move the onus for change from the individual with the disability to the institutions that need to adopt practices allowing persons with disabilities to acquire the same basic rights that all Canadian citizens enjoy. This shift can be achieved only through the "deconstruction" of the notion of disability and ability, as well as through the removal of all obstacles and barriers that make it difficult for many individuals to achieve their full potential.

To achieve this goal, we need to create school-based learning communities that reach beyond outdated perceptions of disability and that truly value student diversity. There must be sufficient flexibility in the ways we deploy our resources in schools to obtain maximum benefits for all students. A continuation of our standard grade-by-grade, subject-by-subject approach to regular classroom instruction is inconsistent with what we now know about the way children learn. Recognizing and celebrating student diversity will be an important element in achieving authentic inclusive classrooms.

Restructuring of Schools

The concept of merging the current separate systems of education into a unified system that can meet the needs of all students has been around for at least two decades (Andrews & Lupart, 2000; Lipsky & Gartner, 1989; Stainback, Stainback, & Bunch, 1989). The idea of reconstructing our public school systems into a unified system of education, capturing the best of both regular and special education, is appealing to many. However, finding the ways and means of actually doing this has been difficult. Many strategies and approaches have been tried, from top-down government directives and legislation to promote integration to individual classroom teachers making bottom-up changes in their design and delivery of instruction, so all students within the classroom can experience learning progress and success. The biggest challenge is for systems to align their efforts so that they are consistent with the goal of authentic inclusion. This means that government departments or ministries of education, teacher preparation programs, school boards, teacher unions, and advocacy groups all need to review their policies and practices, and if those practices run counter to the promotion of inclusion and support of student diversity, the necessary changes need to be made. Moreover, in Canada, separate provincial and territorial educational jurisdictions make it that much more difficult to share our best practices and knowledge systems and to assess how we are making progress as a country.

The Excellence/Equity Dilemma

Very few publications fully describe changes and reforms that have taken place in Canadian schools. Certainly, we can recognize Canadian leaders such as Michael Fullan, Andy Hargreaves, and Ben Levin (Fullan, 2001; Fullan & Hargreaves, 1991; Hargreaves & Fullan, 1998; Levin, 2001a, b) as key proponents of school reform in Canada, but they tend not to deal with the issues surrounding students with exceptional learning needs and equity. In a similar vein, Andrews and Lupart (2000), Lupart (1998) and Hutchinson (Friend, Bursuck, & Hutchinson, 1998) have been instrumental in advancing the ideal of authentic inclusion of students with exceptional learning needs, yet they give minimal attention to general education reforms. In an analysis that does attempt to combine regular and special education change and reform literature, Lupart and Webber (2002) concluded that changes appear to take place on two separate planes, with regular education leaders representing the ways and means to foster excellence in our schools, and special education leaders representing ways and means to foster equity in our schools. Consequently, schools have operated with one goal or the other as their focus, overlooking the possibility that both goals might be simultaneously achieved.

Publications by Skrtic (1991; 1995; 1996) and Smith and Lusthaus (1995) made a strong case for schools to promote both goals simultaneously; indeed, authentic inclusion requires it. Skrtic (1991; 1995) provided a critical analysis of professional culture and school organization and concluded that educational equity is a precondition for educational excellence. He stressed the need for schools to shed their current bureaucratic systems by encouraging teachers to invent better ways of supporting student diversity, a process he defines as "adhocracy." By increasing the professional uncertainty that student diversity creates in the school, teachers will advance their own professional growth through meeting the challenge of providing appropriate instruction for all students. Teachers and students are therefore sustained in their pursuit of lifelong learning. To support this notion, Smith and Lusthaus (1995) advanced the idea that students should, on an individual basis, demonstrate that they are making continuous progress as a result of their schooling experiences. Indicators of continuous progress stem from the abilities and talents of the student, rather than a universal minimum standard that is from the outset impossible for some students to achieve. Recognizing that all students and their learning potentials are unique will help us to achieve authentic inclusion in our future schools, where there would be no artificial age, grade, or subject barriers.

Teachers Are Key

The final area of consideration for future promise of authentic inclusion in our schools is recognizing that teachers are the key individuals in supporting the learning of every child. Teachers are the school-based professionals who have a lengthy, personal relationship with each child in their classrooms. They are the ones who take the knowledge base as it is presented in our school curricula and who chart the course for the learning success of their students. Fifty years of separate, special education instruction has shown us that every child is capable of making continual progress, no matter how limited his or her ability and no matter how small the gain. Accordingly, many special education teachers have found limited value in the precise identification and diagnosis of students. Although it might be considered simplistic by some, significant downsizing of the first four boxes of the special education approach — referral, testing, labelling, and placement — could have immediate impact for moving toward authentic inclusion. If the huge resulting cost savings were then shifted right over to the important programming box, teachers would have the supports they have been seeking in reduced pupil-teacher ratios, more flexibility, and more options for professional assistance. They would even perhaps have adequate time to carry out important collaboration and consultation with other educational professionals and parents.

Obviously, a major transformation like this isn't going to happen quickly. What has been successfully practised in regular and special education classes over the past thirty years now needs to become the knowledge base for all educators. New ways of sharing, collaborating, and learning from and with our professional colleagues as an accepted process of lifelong learning will need to be invented. Fullan (1991) nicely summed up what it will take to realize this transformation: "Educational change depends on what teachers think and do — it's as simple and complex as that" (p. 107). By including all students in their community schools and regular classrooms and by ensuring that all students are making continual progress, schools can model what an inclusive community should look like.

In summary, the paradoxes and inconsistencies in our ways and means of serving the needs of all students can be eliminated. In order to do this, we have to make choices. If we are prepared to support authentic inclusion in our schools, we must be prepared to adopt the simultaneous goals of equity and excellence. Thus committed, we must reject current school structures and procedures that perpetuate the view that education is an instrument of selective mobility; instead, structures and procedures must be seen as tools for the empowerment of all students (Marcoulides & Heck, 1990). It is equally important to recognize that schools are situated in neighbourhood communities, and as such, possibilities for improving student learning and achievement are embedded in multilevel systems that reflect our social and cultural practices, values, and beliefs.

References

Alberta Education. (1989). *Special education: Students with challenging needs*. Edmonton: Education Response Centre.

⸻ (1992). *Students with challenging needs: Updated facts and figures*. Edmonton: Education Response Centre.

⸻ (2002).

Andrews, J., & Lupart, J.L. (2000). *The inclusive classroom: Educating exceptional children* (2nd ed.). Scarborough, ON: Nelson.

Bruner, J. (1986). *Actual minds, possible worlds*. Cambridge: Harvard University Press.

Deno, E. (1970). Special education as developmental capital. *Exceptional Children, 37,* 229–237.

Edmonds, R. (1979). Some schools work and more can. *Social Policy, 9*(5), 26–31.

Fullan, M.G. (1991). *The new meaning of educational change*. London: Cassels.

⸻. (2001). *The new meaning of educational change* (3rd ed.). New York: Teachers College Press.

Fullan, M.G., & Hargreaves, A. (1991). *What's worth fighting for? Working together for your school*. Toronto: Ontario Public School Teachers' Federation.

Gardner, H. (1993). *Multiple intelligences: The theory in practice*. New York: Basic Books.

Hahn, H. (1989). The politics of special education. In D.K. Lipsky & A. Gartner (Eds.), *Beyond separate education: Quality education for all* (pp. 225–241). Baltimore, MD: Paul H. Brookes Publishing Co.

Levin, B. (2001a). Governments and school improvement. *International Electronic Journal for Leadership in Learning, 5*(9). http://www.ucalgary.ca/~iejll/levin.html.

⸻. (2001b). *Reforming education: From origins to outcomes*. London: Routledge Falmer.

Lipsky, D.K., & Gartner, A. (1989). *Beyond separate education: Quality education for all*. Baltimore, MD: Paul Brookes.

Lupart, J.L. (2008). The challenges of student diversity in Canadian schools. In J.L. Lupart, M. Porath, V. Timmons, A. McKeough, & L. Phillips (Eds.), *The challenges of student diversity in Canadian schools*. Toronto: Fitzhenry & Whiteside.

Lupart, J.L., McKeough, A., & Yewchuk, C. (1996). *Schools in transition: Rethinking regular and special education.* Scarborough, ON: Nelson Canada.

Lupart, J.L., & Webber, C. (2002). Canadian schools in transition: Moving from dual education systems to inclusive schools. *Exceptionality Education Canada, 12*(2 & 3), 7–52.

Lusthaus, E., & Lusthaus, C. (1992). From segregation to full inclusion: An evolution. *Exceptionality Education Canada, 2*(1 & 2), 1–7.

Pepler, D., & Craig, W. (2008). Peer dynamics in bullying: Considerations for social architecture in schools. In J.L. Lupart, M. Porath, V. Timmons, A. McKeough, & L. Phillips (Eds.), *The challenges of student diversity in Canadian schools.* Toronto: Fitzhenry & Whiteside.

Roeher Institute. (1994). *As if children matter: Perspectives on children, rights and disability.* North York, ON: The Roeher Institute.

Skrtic, T.M. (1991). The special education paradox: Equity as the way to excellence. *Harvard Educational Review, 61*(2), 148–206.

____. (1995). *Disability and democracy: Reconstructing (special) education for postmodernity.* New York: Teachers College Press.

Smith, W., & Lusthaus, C. (1995). The nexus of equality and quality in education: A framework for debate. *The Canadian Journal of Education, 20*(3), 378–391.

Stainback, W., Stainback, S., & Bunch, G. (1989). Introduction and historical background. In S. Stainback, W. Stainback, & M. Forest (Eds.), *Educating all students in the mainstream of regular education* (pp. 3–14). Baltimore, MD: Paul H. Brookes.

Willms, J.D. (2008). Raising and levelling the learning bar in Canadian schools. In J.L. Lupart, M. Porath, V. Timmons, A. McKeough, & L. Phillips (Eds.), *The challenges of student diversity in Canadian schools.* Toronto: Fitzhenry & Whiteside.

Willms, J.D. (Ed.). (2002). *Vulnerable children.* Edmonton: The University of Alberta Press.

Winzer, M. (1996). *Children with exceptionalities in Canadian classrooms.* Scarborough, ON: Allyn & Bacon.

Wolfensberger, W., Nirge, B., Olshansky, S., Perske, R., & Roos, P. (1972). *The principle of normalization in human services.* Toronto: National Institution on Mental Retardation.

Supporting Families to Enhance Children's Learning

Vianne Timmons

The ideal educational partnership is one where families and schools work together to ensure a quality education for children (Fan & Chen, 1999). There is significant research about ways in which schools can support children who are experiencing academic challenges. There is also considerable research about how families can support their children in their academic pursuits. Often these two areas of research are disconnected, leading to a gap in information about ways in which schools can enable families to support their children's learning. This essay explores the importance of family involvement in education and how schools can support and encourage families to support their children's learning. Henderson and Mapp (2002) state that "[w]hen schools, families, and community groups work together to support learning, children tend to do better in school, stay in school longer, and like school more" (p. 7).

Doug Willms (2004), an education researcher from the University of New Brunswick, puts it this way: "Raising and leveling the [learning] bar will not likely be achieved by any single strategy or reform. It will require a comprehensive strategy aimed at eliminating poverty, increasing provision during the early years, enabling families, and improving schools." Therefore, several questions arise: "How can schools *enable* families?" and "What are the steps schools can take to enable families?" These questions may seem easy to answer; however, schools have struggled with family and school relationships for decades. Because families are complex and relationships are complex, apparently simple solutions are often elusive.

No two families are the same; in fact, every family is unique and often quite diverse. There are single-parent families, dual-parent families, one-child families, multigenerational families, families with same-sex parents, and foster families. When people talk about families, they are often actually referring to parents. Baker (2001) indicates that "the structure of the unit [family] or its legality is less important in defining family than the functions fulfilled by the unit or the services provided" (p. 5). This statement means that the activities the family engages in are more important than the structure of the family.

For many families, supporting a child's education is a difficult endeavour. They may struggle themselves with literacy or cultural issues. Schools may be daunting places, where families are intimidated and feel undervalued and often judged. For many cultures, the extended family is as important as the core family members. It is critical for schools, teachers, and administrators to recognize that family structures are different, to understand that each family has various needs, and to take the time to get to know their students' circumstances. Paul and Simeonsson (1993) found that family needs are often misunderstood and neglected by schools. The researchers indicated that families had myriad needs, which could generally be clustered into five categories: appropriate direct educational services for children, such as homework clubs and tutoring programs; information exchange opportunities, such as sessions with an invited speaker or where teachers share their approaches to discipline or a new language arts program; resource use and advocacy preparation, especially for parents of children with special needs; parent-family home and community training programs such as family workshops and family literacy programs; and direct family intervention through parent-family consultation, support, and counselling (Simpson & Simpson, 1994). Even needs that are not particularly difficult for a school to deal with may require a coordinated effort on the part of the school (Simpson & Simpson).

Many school practitioners assume that parents are very involved, especially in elementary schools. Dunst (2002) notes, however, that family involvement in schools is limited, even at the elementary school level. He states that the "call for the adoption of family-centred practices in schools has largely gone unheard" (p. 142). In a large-scale study conducted by Vanden-Kieran (1996), the school involvement of 45,000 parents of children in elementary and secondary schools was examined. The extent of the parental involvement consisted primarily of obtaining information about volunteering opportunities in the school. Dunst describes this type of involvement as a family allied model. The family allied model focuses on transmission of information, primarily from the school to the home (i.e., information sharing, rather than involvement in decision making at the school). Information sharing includes activities such as parent-teacher interviews, newsletters sent home, and volunteer opportunities. This type of involvement is important in keeping schools running smoothly. However, serving lunches and stacking library shelves will not necessarily have direct impact on students' achievement. Schools have to look beyond volunteering, seeking out ways that parents can work directly with children. Most parents are keenly interested in playing an active role in their child's education. However, they may need some direction and support to do this effectively.

Henderson and Mapp (2002) synthesized a broad body of literature (51 studies) that looked at family and community involvement in schools. They found that the studies presented a positive relationship between family involvement and benefits for students, such as improved academic performance, better attendance, better social skills, and an improvement in behaviour. In their synthesis, Henderson and Mapp found that typical forms of family involvement, such as volunteering, attending school events, and parent-parent connections, seemed to have little effect on student achievement. This type of involvement is representative of the relationship most schools have with families. Schools assume that opportunities for family involvement can be adequately provided through parent volunteering. However, Henderson and Mapp's synthesis emphasizes the importance of the type of parental involvement. It is easy to set up volunteer opportunities where parents work in the school, supporting the running of the institution. However, it takes training and supervision to have parents work directly with the children in the school, especially if a parent's own child is involved and the school wants the work to continue after school. It has been shown that a child's learning is influenced by parental interactions like the following: when a parent discusses schooling with his or her child, supports the child's homework, provides many opportunities to read and write, and role models the valuing of literacy.

Family Attitudes toward Schools

Many families find that even minimal connection with the school is difficult for many reasons. Muscott (2002) discovered that some family members avoid school relationships due to long-standing negative experiences with schools. Timmons and Brookes (1997) found in a study on adult learning that these negative experiences were carried into adult life, and as a result, affected the parent's ability to develop a positive relationship with the child's teacher. In another study concerning literacy needs of families in rural communities, the same pattern was noted (Timmons, 2001b). One parent stated, "… [T]he principal at our school was my teacher in high school and I'm like … this little kid again. This is ridiculous! I'm an adult." The parent felt that every time she participated in parent-teacher interviews, she was placed in a powerless role. She felt that she reverted to the role of a child while the teacher and/or principal were the "all-knowing" adults. These experiences have long-lasting effects on families and can be passed on from parents to children. It is important to ensure that families have positive experiences with the school system so that their children can be influenced in a way that will motivate them to enjoy and appreciate the benefits of schooling.

Another parent spoke about the inability of the school system to relate to the issues she was facing with her child, "The guidance counsellor at school … she's a lovely lady … her children are perfect … [W]ho are you to tell me how to raise my children, or whether my problems are actually problems … [W]e're very different people" (Timmons, 2001b). The majority of teachers are successful products of an educational system that met their needs. They often do not understand the stress and tension of school failure, and parents who have experienced this stress find it difficult to relate to the teachers. Frequently, parents see the teacher as a person who has it all together, with perfect children, no problems, and a successful life. Many parents, such as the parent quoted above, feel that teachers cannot understand what it is like to raise a child who is struggling. Parents feel guilt, as if they are somehow responsible for their child's difficulties. These parents benefit significantly from positive interactions with school personnel, where they are able to view school employees as having typical lives, dealing with issues, and at times struggling. School structures generally have teachers playing an authoritarian role. As a result, teachers often worry about having their position as teacher undermined when interacting with parents. This is a difficult and sometimes complicated relationship, which teachers have to negotiate.

In a study of the literacy needs of families, conducted by Timmons (2001a), some teachers revealed prejudices toward certain families. One teacher, when asked about a child who was experiencing difficulty, stated that she had taught his father and that he had also had difficulty in school. She felt that the difficulties "ran in the family." Another teacher said, "You can ask the parents to do things, but they don't help at home. They expect the school to do everything." The mother, in this case, was desperate to obtain additional help with her child, as she had difficulty supporting her child with homework. However, the school-home relationship made the mother feel more inadequate.

Teachers who are searching for reasons why a child is struggling may place the responsibility on the parents. This blaming can lead to the school not seeking solutions or failing to work on collaborative relationships with the families. What is often needed, however, is joint problem solving between families and schools, and this must be done in a context of mutual respect. Teachers are often unaware of the impact of placing blame on families, rather than working with families. The effect is that the child suffers, labelled with a failure prophecy of which the family is unaware.

Families need to feel that they are partners with the school, but for many parents, this is not the case. Instead, a power differential or an accusatory relationship exists between home and school. To build a meaningful relationship with families, an empathetic approach must be taken by the school, and positive school-home relationships translate into higher achievement for children (Padak & Rasinski, 1993). This reason alone is enough for schools to investigate ways to improve family involvement in students' education. Having families as partners helps teachers accomplish their work. These partnerships can also transform family relationships internally. When parents have goals for their children and the school supports these goals, the child benefits greatly.

Impact of Family-Focused Programs

Willms (2002) has noted that a number of studies worldwide have consistently shown student achievement to be affected more often by family influences than by school or community. This statement reaffirms the importance of working with families — and families tend to respond positively when they are given ideas and strategies to support their children. A study looking at an adult literacy program found that adults often enter such programs to help their children (Timmons, 2001a). Generally, parents want their children to succeed in school and will support their child's learning if they know how. However, many do not know how to support their child. While teachers study for four to six years to receive teacher certification, it is rare for parents to have even one parenting course. Similarly, many parents have had the benefit of a visit from a public health nurse when their child was an infant, but that is usually the extent of the support they have received. For many families, this support is inadequate. Young parents who have not had positive parenting role models, as well as families facing financial, relationship, and/or literacy issues, require extensive support to learn how to contribute to the education of their children.

In a review of the literature on family-school partnerships, Simon (2001) found that when schools worked with parents and informed them about how to support their child's study habits, the parents worked with their children more often. This conclusion was evident with both elementary-age children and teenagers. For schools, this information means that developing respectful and informative programs will have a positive impact on children's learning.

One strategy a school can employ to begin building a collaborative relationship is to ask families what their needs are around supporting their children's learning. A survey or simple question during parent-teacher interviews can provide a wealth of knowledge that can lay a foundation for a program. The majority of parent-teacher interviews consist of a transmission of information from the teacher to the parent regarding the child's learning in the school. It is structured not as a dialogue, but as a presentation by the teacher.

This information is important and valuable for the parent to know, but so is information from the parent. A parent can provide insight into his or her child's learning, attitude, and interest in school. The parent can also identify challenges the child has with schoolwork and challenges the parent faces in supporting the child. This rich information can form the foundation of a partnership. If a teacher finds that a number of parents are experiencing similar frustrations, he or she can provide parental support for the families.

In Timmons (2001b), families that volunteered for a family literacy program identified homework as a huge issue for them. They not only felt inadequate in assisting their children with the content but were also struggling with getting their children to sit down and complete their homework. Televisions, computer games, and video games were consuming their children's time at home. During a single evening session with parents and children that focused on homework, contracts were developed between the parent and child, a homework centre was planned, and parents shared strategies focused on routines, incentives, and communication. Parents found the information provided helped them understand how to support their children. They were also reassured that other parents faced similar challenges and found the practical strategies easy to implement.

A school can also develop a program in which a teacher or a group of teachers serves as a liaison with the community. This liaison teacher or group could be the primary contact for parental and community concerns. The liaison could also be given the task of promoting meaningful family involvement in students' learning. When parents have concerns, they often do not know whom to approach. They may worry that the teacher will be upset with their child, they may be intimidated by the principal, and they may feel inadequate. Knowing that the school is designating a person specifically to support parents and assist with their concerns illustrates the school's support for families. Timmons (2001a) developed a family literacy program based on families' identified needs. In this study, families were asked what they felt they required to support their children's literacy needs, and this revealed that parents felt they required help not only with literacy skills, but also with basic parenting skills. Parents found it difficult to help their children with homework and had little support with parenting. Their children were experiencing difficulty in school and were often frustrated and angry. Parents felt inadequate to alter this attitude. When their children expressed their frustrations upon returning home from school, parents were at a loss as to how to deal with these emotions. Sessions on parenting, homework, and working with the school were essential components of the family literacy program, providing parents and children with information, support, and skills to deal with their children's struggles.

In 2001, a research program entitled "A Rural Family Literacy Approach to Improving Children's Literacy Levels" was designed and implemented in rural Prince Edward Island (P.E.I.). In the initial phase of the program, researchers conducted assessments of literacy challenges affecting children and parents in rural communities of P.E.I. Interviews were conducted with families, educators, and community leaders to determine the impact of low literacy on the families. The families in this study were able to describe their needs clearly, and the information provided became the basis of a family literacy program designed for families in rural communities throughout the province. Identified needs included strategies for reading, homework, discipline, and home and school relations. These areas were refined into themes, which were then developed into ten modules: comprehension, guided reading, fluency, decoding and phonics, literacy in and around the home, parenting and discipline, working with schools, word recognition, language experience, and homework. The families assisted with the content and format of the modules, providing excellent input and valuable feedback to the researchers. In addition, culturally appropriate resource packs were developed to complement each module. Magazine articles, tips, strategies, and question-and-answer-type resources were rewritten in plain language for home reference.

The program consisted of these ten modules, offered one night a week. The parents and children came to the sessions together, and parents worked together for the first hour on a skill while their children worked on the same skill in a separate room, each with support from a facilitator. For the next half-hour, parents and children came together and practised the skills they had learned. This model worked very well, as both the parent and the child were being taught skills and were given time to practise together.

In the fall of 2002, the program was piloted with self-selected participants. Pre- and post-reading assessment tests using the reading subtests of the Wechsler Individual Achievement Test (1992) were conducted to measure the children's reading improvements. The results indicated that the program was successful. All of the children involved showed an improvement in at least one of the areas tested. Comparisons of the reading assessment results between the original treatment group and the delayed treatment group definitely revealed that engaging in a family literacy program enhanced the literacy levels of the children involved. In all three subtests, the treatment group scored higher than their delayed treatment group counterparts. Basic reading revealed a mean 0.9 grade level increase in the treatment group as compared to a 0.3 grade level increase in the delayed treatment group. The listening comprehension subtest revealed a mean 1.6 grade level increase in the treatment group as compared to a 0.4 grade level increase in the delayed treatment group. Finally, the last subtest, reading comprehension, illustrated a mean 0.9 grade level increase in the treatment group as compared to a 0.4 grade level improvement in the delayed treatment group.

All participants in both groups were then interviewed to assess the impact of the program. Their comments and feedback were positive, and families indicated that the program made a difference in their relationships with their children. As one parent commented, "I liked that we learned together as a family." Another parent said, "I am glad now that there is a program being made available for people that need help with their kids." Two of the parents indicated that they would participate in the program again. The parents stated that the program transformed their family in a positive way. They were working more closely with the school as partners and had introduced more structure into the home (Timmons, 2003).

Timmons (2001b) found that parents want to support their children's learning. Dorfman and Fisher (2002) found that many parents are seeking direction from their children's schools about how to help their children at home, and they want to feel valued and respected. A program such as the one described above provides direction to parents in a nonthreatening way. Parents are given specific information and taught skills, which they first practise in a supportive environment and then practise with their children. One of the other outcomes of the family literacy program was the support parents gave each other. They commented on how relieved they were that other parents were experiencing similar difficulties. As the sessions progressed, parents exchanged strategies and advice. In the evaluations, they identified this mutual support as a critical component of the program's success. Lochrie (2005) states that "there is a rich literature of evaluations and research studies which suggest that family learning not only benefits children, but may also make a significant difference to the lives of adults, in terms of confident parenting, literacy, language and numeracy, life skills and combating educational inequality, poverty and social exclusion" (p. 2). A number of parents in the above family literacy program felt socially isolated, and often helpless, assuming that they were the only parents experiencing challenges. Through meeting other families, sharing concerns, and creating solutions, they felt supported and less isolated.

Cultural Diversity

Earlier in this essay, there was a discussion of families who had negative school experiences and who felt disconnected from school. Parents and families from different cultures can also feel disconnected from schools. Many families report having to deal with pressures that affect their family norms and behaviours when they immigrate (Howell, Albanese, & Obusu-Mensah, 2001). These parents report a desire for their children to do well in school and to pursue postsecondary education. In cases like this, parents feel a loss of control in relation to their children — especially when the parents themselves are struggling to learn a new language and the children seem to grasp it much more quickly. Another area that presents a challenge to immigrant families is the perceived loss of discipline. Immigrant families can have anxiety over the Western style of discipline and the amount of freedom given to children. Schools can support these families by providing tips on discipline, offering sessions where parents are brought together to discuss issues, and being open to parents' concerns.

Immigrant families feel connected to schools when their experience, language, history, and culture are honoured by the schools (Dorfman & Fisher, 2002). Collaboration is considered critical to successful family-school relationships (Parette & Petch-Hogan, 2000). One of the mistakes schools make in working with families from diverse backgrounds is assuming that all families from a certain culture share the same traits. It is important to be sensitive to cultural differences but not to assume that all families in a culture share the same cultural norms. In any culture, there are different religions, languages, and traditions.

Language is one area where families from diverse cultures can be at great disadvantage. Schools should ensure that skilled interpreters are available to support families in school meetings. Families should have a choice of a skilled interpreter, family friend, or relative. Dealing with school personnel can be intimidating, and families may wish to keep issues within a small family circle (Parette & Petch-Hogan, 2000). So in cases where a teacher or school administrator must discuss an issue with an immigrant family, the help of an interpreter will smooth the way to a better interchange. If written material is necessary for planning purposes, schools should consider having it translated into the family's native language. This accommodation increases the potential for true collaboration and shows respect for different languages.

Cummins (2004) spoke about the power of stories being translated into native languages for children to read. Literacy for children is increased by having stories written in English and the home language. Parents then have a greater opportunity to interact with their children about content, and to add information. This type of programming supports parent-child interactions, fosters pride in culture and language, and encourages sharing of experiences. Having stories and information sent home in a child's native language also shows the school's respect for the family.

In some cultures, the extended family is critical in child rearing and learning support, so schools need to be open to inviting members of the extended family to meetings and to encouraging their input. Since many immigrant families depend on extended families, especially for after-school support, schools need to be supportive and inclusive by inviting members of the extended family to attend meetings at school. In a study examining children's perceptions of health in a Mi'kmaq community, children identified aunts and grandmothers as their role models. It was evident that these women contributed significantly to the child rearing and often provided learning support (Timmons, Bryanton, McCarthy, Taylor, Critchley, & O'Donoghue, 2004). The children had connections to these women, who played an important role in child rearing and in supporting parents.

Brassett-Grundy (2002) best defines family learning as "one of the critical elements of lifelong learning" (p. 5). She describes family learning as intergenerational, since parental involvement is a necessity in a child's education. Keeping these characteristics in mind, schools can develop programs that promote family learning and support the work teachers are doing in school. Schwartz (1999) states that "family literacy programs around the country have been successful in breaking the cycle of intergenerational literacy deficiency" (p. 2). This has happened despite the fact that intergenerational literacy challenges are difficult to change, as children facing these obstacles rarely have literacy role models in their homes. In addition, in rural communities, where seasonal primary-resource jobs such as fishing and farming have historically been the dominant sources of employment, education was not critical to obtaining work. Today, however, education is critical, and children in rural communities need literacy skills to be successful in these occupations. Darling & Lee (2004) indicate that "Children of parents who lack basic literacy skills are less likely to have access to reading and writing materials at home, to have educational opportunities outside of the home, and are less likely to be enrolled in pre-kindergarten programs. They are less likely to observe role models who are reading and writing during the day" (p. 19). Parents may not be aware of how critical these activities are to enhancing their child's literacy skills.

School Models That Support Families

One family-supportive model that a number of schools in the United States have endorsed is "family centered schools" (Dunst, 2002). In this model, family centredness translates into beliefs and practices that treat families with dignity and respect. The practices are individualized, flexible, and responsive. Information sharing is undertaken so that families can make informed decisions, and parent choice is offered in relation to some educational practices. Dunst reviewed family-centred practices and found that the majority of family-school relations are family allied, rather than family centred. In a family allied model, parents are viewed as agents of the teachers. They work to ensure that their children's homework is complete and that school activities are supported. By contrast, in a family-centred approach, the family is actively involved in educational decision making. Preschools naturally tend to take a more family-centred approach to working with families, and parents of children who attend these preschools are actively involved in decision making, rather than simply being receivers of information. In secondary school, programs can be developed that are family centred and not family allied.

Smith (2004) describes one family literacy program that was developed in a secondary school. Parents and students were brought together and worked on literacy strategies. The results of this program were significant, with both adults and youth showing improved basic literacy skills, increased attendance, fewer disciplinary issues, and improved home-school relations. Family literacy can extend throughout the school life of a child and ensure that success is maintained and relationships are supported.

In some areas, there has been a move to full-service schools (Warger, 2001). In a full-service school, one can find a variety of services, such as health care and mental health services. These are delivered through a collaborative venture among the school, agency or agencies, and family. The full-service school can provide much-needed support to families, since it allows them to access expertise in several areas at one site. This type of support has proven to be very successful with parents of children with special needs. Fox, Leone, Rubin, Oppenheim, Miller, & Friedman (1999) found that in the full-service model, classroom teachers identified children who needed services and accessed them. Teachers also developed programs that benefited students with behavioural issues. Services like these may include speech therapy, physiotherapy, family counselling, after-school programs, newcomer and immigrant services, physicians, and even spiritual support. Incorporating all of these services into a school encourages families to see the school as serving them — a place where they are supported and their child is valued. For many families, taking their children to numerous appointments is a challenge, requiring time off work and transportation. Having services in the school provides relief for families and allows the whole child to be the focus.

Regardless of what model is developed to increase family involvement in children's education, the research clearly suggests that "programs and interventions that engage families in supporting their children's learning at home are linked to higher student achievement" (Henderson & Mapp, 2002, p. 25). However, some important criteria need to be in place for successful family involvement in schools. The involvement needs to be active, not passive. Epstein, Clark, Salinas, & Sanders (1997), for instance, developed an interactive homework program that involved parents in their children's schoolwork. The students who participated in the interactive homework program earned significantly higher grades in the subject in which the homework was assigned than they did in other subject areas. The study also found that older students benefited from programs like this. Activities such as weekly homework assignments that engaged family members were shown to result in better school performance and attendance.

Parent Efficacy

Parents' level of efficacy influences their ability to support their child's learning. Efficacy is described as the power to produce an effect (Parette & Petch-Hogan, 2000). For parents to have a sense of efficacy, they need the necessary knowledge and skills, and the school can have a positive influence in providing these. Bringing parents together and showing them how to be involved in their child's learning increases their sense of power. Dorfman and Fisher (2002) identified four components that are critical to a positive school-home relationship: parental aspirations and expectations, participation in school activities and programs, a home structure that supports learning, and communication with children about learning. Other researchers have supported these findings. Fan and Chen (1999) found that parental aspirations for and expectations of their children constituted an important factor in children's achievement and that these were connected with higher grades and test scores. R. Clark (1993) found that the way children spent their time at home had a significant impact on students' achievement. The research is clear on the importance of engaging families, yet many schools do not focus on the school-home relationship outside of the parent-school association.

Researchers have also examined socioeconomic patterns of parental involvement. R. Clark (1993) found that high achievers came from a variety of backgrounds. Dorfman and Fisher (2002) write that "assumptions about poor and minority parents' non-involvement [in schooling] are largely unfounded" (p. 5). Parette and Petch-Hogan (2000) note that "although children from higher-income families tend to do better in school, students of all backgrounds gain when their parents are involved" (p. 35). They state that "families of all cultural backgrounds, education, and income levels encourage their children, talk with them about school, help them plan for higher education, and keep them focused on learning and homework. In other words families can, and often do, have a positive influence on their children's learning" (p. 34).

Most schools, especially publicly run schools, have children from myriad backgrounds. To improve family-school relationships, the focus should not be solely on families considered to be in the low-income range. Improvement of family-school relationships should be a whole-school initiative, reaching out to all families. While parents in low socioeconomic situations and from minority cultures often have high expectations of their children, at times they are at a loss to provide the home structure that supports learning or they are uncomfortable about participating in school activities. Schools play a crucial role in providing a welcoming environment. They can ensure that parents feel welcomed and encouraged — especially parents who have language or cultural differences. Schools can also provide learning opportunities for families that provide information about how a family can maintain a home structure that supports learning. For new immigrants, who can feel isolated in a community because they have lost the family ties they have left behind, the school can be an instrumental connection, encouraging support networks, providing cultural and parenting information, and being welcoming. This support can be realized by visits to homes, holding cultural and family nights, having family advocates in the school, and welcoming community groups representing different cultural groups into the school.

Another way that schools can support family learning is to ensure that communication is accessible to all families. As mentioned earlier, this communication could include material translated into the students' home language. In addition, schools need to be sensitive to the literacy levels of family members. Although 40 percent of adults in Canada experience literacy challenges, school newsletters, memos, and information notices are often written in language that is inaccessible to a notable number of parents and other family members. The following two excerpts from school newsletters illustrate challenges some families may have in understanding such documents:

> Student achievement, demonstrates service to the community that is positive and verifiable, demonstrates capacity for leadership and ability to motivate others and demonstrates interest in innovation.
>
> Parents must assume much of the responsibility to ensure that students make this commitment. Parent involvement improves student achievement, promotes positive attitudes toward school and motivates students to succeed.

Teachers and school administrators may feel that they need to model competency in the English language. However, for many families, the use of complex language creates a barrier that alienates them from the school and impedes the transfer of information that is often desperately sought. Teachers and school administrators need to ensure that their communications with the home are written in plain language and are easy to understand. Families will also benefit from tips on how to support children's learning, including reasonable expectations and clear directions.

Families with Children with Special Needs

While all parents seek accurate information about their child's progress and program, this information is particularly important for the parent of a child with special needs. Parents of children with special needs often have to be in close connection with schools, and they also have "inordinate demands on their time, psychological well-being, relationships, economic resources and freedom of movement" (Brantlinger, 1991, p. 250). Given all these demands on the family, the school relationship becomes an especially important one. Schools that are family centred have the potential to help the family develop relationships and reduce family isolation. Successful family coping is often related to the level of support and high quality resources they have at their disposal (Brantlinger). Family support programs need to focus on families' strengths and listen to expressed family needs. Raising a child with significant learning needs can cause family stress and require extensive consultations. Families often feel they have to be advocating for their child constantly, a lone voice against the bureaucracy. Schools can support family advocacy by providing information about services, advocating on behalf of the child, and linking families to other families.

Schools that support families by preparing them for planning meetings, providing them with advocates, communicating with the families on a regular basis, providing workshops and supportive programs for parents, and developing opportunities for parents to network see positive school-home relationships emerge. Parents of children with special needs have often had to fight for services and resources and may approach the school with demands and very specific needs. Responding to these demands in a respectful, collaborative way will begin a positive interchange. Parents of children with special needs often have a wealth of knowledge and skill in meeting their child's needs from which the school can benefit. Therefore, treating parents as experts and being open to learning from them will not only enhance the potential of a positive school-home relationship, but parents will also contribute critical information to the school that can support the child's learning. Families of children with behavioural difficulties need special support from school personnel. These families deal with tremendous feelings of guilt and frustration in trying to meet the needs of their children. For many of these families the school may serve as a referral system. As Simpson and Simpson (1994) explain,

> Parent/family consultation, support and counseling focus on some individuals' and families' need for support programs, counseling, crisis intervention and other assistance. Few educators have the time, skills, and knowledge to independently provide services associated with addressing all needs in this area (e.g., counseling). Accordingly, educators' primary role in regard to some needs in this area may consist of assisting parents and families to obtain appropriate services, rather than directly providing them. (p. 3)

The school may then have to serve as a liaison and even as an advocate for the parents with the service provider. Many family literacy programs incorporate discipline and parenting skills as part of the curriculum. Giving parents the skills and knowledge to be effective parents contributes to their ability to encourage and support their child's literacy development. Schools that use the family-centred model adopt a no-fault policy. No family or parent is assigned blame for a student's challenges or difficulties. For parents with children who have behavioural difficulties, this approach works very well. The families become partners in the solution-finding process. School personnel work closely with the family, supporting them through close collaboration regarding the development of interventions for the child. For many parents, working collaboratively with schools does not come naturally. As a result, schools need to assume responsibility for and support families/parents in forming positive working relationships with school staff. As Simpson and Simpson (1994) indicate:

> Educators should not only be encouraged to initiate contacts and relationships with parents and to form partnerships with other professionals, but parents and families should also be assisted in learning how to work with professionals and to advocate for their children. Consistent with empowering parents and families, this process involves such activities as assisting parents and families in collaborating and interacting with professionals; understanding educational, social service, mental health, and legal procedures and protocol; knowing how to participate in various conferences (e.g. progress report, IEP); and advocating for a child or youth with a particular problem or exceptionality. (p. 5)

This type of support is important not only for families with children who have behavioural difficulties, but for all families.

Strategies That Support Family Involvement

In the family literacy program conducted by Timmons (2001a), parents identified challenges in working with their children's schools. They did not know how to approach the teacher when their child was having difficulty. They felt self-conscious and embarrassed that they did not know how to support their child's learning. A module was developed for the families, suggesting ways for parents to approach the school, what questions to ask, what information to share, and how to ask for support. A number of the parents used the strategies when approaching the school and found that they were well received. Families from diverse cultures and with different home languages also benefit from this support. Parette and Petch-Hogan (2000) encourage educators to develop a range of strategies to help families from diverse backgrounds participate in educational decision making. They recommend that trust be built with the professional, either through home visits or through working with a community liaison person. Parette and Petch-Hogan also identify time as a potential issue:

> Time is also an issue related to the functioning of the family. Families from different cultural backgrounds will view time and its relationship/importance to team processes differently from many professionals. Families may not be in time for meetings, presenting a hurdle for teams who desire to adhere to rigorous timelines necessary for planning IEP's and other school services. (p. 8)

School personnel need to be sensitive to this potential and look at flexible scheduling for meeting times. This need for flexible scheduling applies to many families. Traditional meeting times during the school day are very difficult for many parents who have jobs with little flexibility and who will lose income if they leave work during the day. Many professionals also do not have a great deal of flexible time during the day. Schools therefore need to provide different options for parents regarding meeting times, and some sessions should be scheduled during the evening hours. To partner with families in meaningful ways, schools have to be flexible and innovative in their approaches. Mothers are often the ones who are targeted/involved in school-home communication. Flexible meeting times often provide needed support to working mothers and may also encourage fathers to become more involved with their child's education.

Lamb (2004) for instance, has done research on the issue of father involvement in education. R. Clark (2005) highlights the fact that parents — and especially fathers — are spending more time with their children than ever before. Fathers are taking a more active role in the care of their children and are also reading to them and supporting their homework. Programs that target families may need to explicitly encourage father involvement in contributing to their children's attitude and success with schooling.

Schools need to be careful not to judge families on account of their children's academic difficulties. When teachers assume that families are not doing enough at home to support their children's learning, the family may not actually know what to do. Communication and a relationship that is respectful, nonblaming, and focused on supporting the child is critical for a positive family-school relationship.

Conclusion

This essay has explored a number of strategies that schools can implement to enable families to support their children's learning. The research clearly indicates that family involvement in education results in increased achievement for children. Working with families makes the educator's job easier.

Families can be involved with their children's schooling in many ways. However, schools need to recognize that families are unique and flexible approaches must be developed to meet all families' needs. Schools need to honor and respect the strengths of families and encourage recognition of diverse cultures and backgrounds. Working with families in their own language and being respectful of families' literacy levels is critical. Often, personal contact will achieve better results than a written note sent home. It is also important for schools to recognize that active family involvement is important to supporting improved outcomes. Families who are supported in assisting their children at home create environments that support their children's learning. They talk about the school day, have aspirations for their children, and model literacy skills at home. Families want to be partners in their children's education. They bring a wealth of knowledge, support, and capacity upon which schools can draw to support shared goals for children's learning. Myriad strategies and models are available to help schools support their students' families. Schools that use a family-centred approach are best able to reap the benefits of positive family, school, and community relations.

References

Baker, M. (2001). *Families: Changing trends in Canada.* Toronto: McGraw-Hill Ryerson.

Brantlinger, E. (1991). Home-school partnerships that benefit children with special needs. *The Elementary School Journal,* 91(3), 249-259. doi:10.1086/461652

Brassett-Grundy, A. (2002). *Parental perspectives of family learning.* Wider Benefits of Learning Research Report no. 2. London: London Institute of Education, The Centre for Research on the Wider Benefits of Learning. Retrieved from ERIC database (ED468441).

Clark, C. (2005, March). Father involvement and children's literacy outcomes. *Literacy Today,* 14–15.

Clark, R. (1993). Homework-focused parenting practices that positively affect student achievement. In N.F. Chavkin (Ed.), *Families and schools in a pluralistic society* (pp. 85–105). Albany: State University of New York.

Cummins, J. (2004, April). *From literacy to multiliteracies: Designing learning environments for knowledge generation in culturally and linguistically diverse schools.* Paper presented at the Building Capacity for Diversity in Canadian Schools lecture series at the University of Prince Edward Island, Charlottetown, PE.

Darling, S., & Lee, J. (2004). Linking parents to reading instruction. *The Reading Teacher,* 57(4), 382–384.

Dorfman, D., & Fisher, A. (2002). *Building relationships for student success: School-family-community partnerships and student achievement in the Northwest.* Washington, DC: Northwest Regional Educational Laboratory. http://www.nwrel.org/partnerships/cloak/booklet2.pdf

Dunst, C.J. (2002). Family-centered practices: Birth through high school. *Journal of Special Education,* 36(3), 139–47. Retrieved from http://sed.sagepub.com/cgi/content/abstract/36/3/141

Epstein, J.L., Clark, L., Salinas, K.C., & Sanders, M.G. (1997). *Scaling up school-family-community connections in Baltimore: Effects on student achievement and attendance.* Paper presented at the Annual Meeting of the American Educational Research Association, Chicago.

Fan, X., & Chen, M. (1999). *Parental involvement and students' academic achievement: A meta-analysis.* Arlington, VA: National Science Foundation, National Center for Education Statistics. Retrieved from ERIC database (ED430048).

Fox, N., Leone, P., Rubin, K., Oppenheim, J., Miller, M., & Friedman, K. (1999). *Final report on the Linkages of Learning program and evaluation at Broad Acres Elementary School.* College Park, MD: University of Maryland, Department of Special Education.

Henderson, A.T., & Mapp, K.L. (2002). *A new wave of evidence: The impact of school, family, and community connections on students achievement. Annual Synthesis.* Austin, TX: Southwest Educational Development Laboratory. http://www.sedl.org/connections/resources/evidence.pdf

Howell, N., Albanese, P., & Obusu-Mensah, K. (2001). Ethnic families. In M. Baker (Ed.), *Families: Changing trends in Canada* (4th ed.) (pp. 116–142). Toronto: McGraw-Hill Ryerson.

Lamb, M.E. (2004). *The role of the father in child development.* Hoboken, NJ: John Wiley & Sons.

Lochrie, M. (2005). Building all our futures. *Adults Learning, 16*(6), 8–11.

Muscott, H.S. (2002). Exceptional partnerships: Listening to the voices of families. *Preventing School Failure, 46*(2), 66–69. Retrieved from Academic Search Premier database (6502494).

Padak, N., & Rasinski, T. (1993). *Initiating even start programs* (Occasional Paper No. 1). Kent, OH: Kent State University.

Parette, H.P., & Petch-Hogan, B. (2000). Approaching families: Facilitating culturally/linguistically diverse family involvement. *Teaching Exceptional Children, 33*(2), 4–10.

Paul, J.L., & Simeonsson, R.J. (1993). *Children with special needs: Family, culture, and society.* Fort Worth, TX: Harcourt Brace Jovanovich.

Schwartz, W. (1999). Building on existing strengths to increase family literacy. New York, NY: ERIC Clearinghouse on Urban Education. Retrieved from ERIC database (ED431064).

Simon, B.S. (2001). Family involvement in high school: Predictors and effects. *NASSP Bulletin, 85*(2), 8–19.

Simpson, R.L., & Simpson, J.D. (1994). At-risk and disabled students: Parent and family needs. *Preventing School Failures, 39*(1), 21–26. Retrieved from Academic Search Premier database (9502081082).

Smith, C. (2004). Family learning in secondary school. *Literacy Today, 41*, 8.

Timmons, V. (2001a). Enhancing family literacy across PEI. Presented to the National Literacy Initiatives Secretariat. Unpublished manuscript.

(2001b). Families learning together: A literacy needs assessment of rural Prince Edward Island. Unpublished manuscript.

(2003) Enhancing family literacy in rural Prince Edward Island. Unpublished manuscript.

Timmons, V., & Brookes, A.L. (1997). Evaluation of the HALE Curriculum: Final report. Unpublished manuscript.

Timmons, V., Bryanton, J., McCarthy, M.J., Taylor, J., Critchley, K., & O'Donoghue, F. (2004). Building healthy Mi'kmaq communities in Prince Edward Island. Unpublished manuscript.

Vanden-Kieran, N. (1996). *Parents' reports of school practices to involve families* (Report No. 97-327). Washington, DC: U.S. Department of Education, National Center for Educational Statistics.

Warger, C. (2001). *Research on full-service schools and students with disabilities*. Arlington, VA: ERIC Clearinghouse on Disabilities and Gifted Education. Retrieved from ERIC database (ED458749).

Wechsler Individual Achievement Test (1992). San Antonio, TX: Harcourt Assessment.

Willms, J.D. (2002). *Vulnerable children: Findings from Canada's National Longitudinal Survey of Children and Youth*. Edmonton: The University of Alberta Press.

(2004, April). *Raising and leveling the bar in Canadian schools*. Paper presented at the Building Capacity for Diversity in Canadian Schools lecture series at the University of Prince Edward Island, Charlottetown, PE.

Inclusive Education for Students with Developmental and Other Disabilities: The General Situation and Implications for Advocacy and Policy Development

Cameron Crawford

This essay presents [a view of current issues] in the inclusive education of students with developmental disabilities in Canada and describes [implications] for advocacy and policy development. It points to the general importance of education — and of inclusive education in particular — to the social and economic situations of people with disabilities in Canada. The essay then addresses several key questions:

- How, or on what basis, do we know about the general educational situation of children and youth with developmental and other disabilities?

- Given the data sources and knowledge available, what are some of the key issues and challenges to furthering quality education for these students in regular schools and classrooms?

- What are some of the practical implications that parent groups, other organizations, and policymakers would do well to hold in view in their efforts to advance quality inclusive education for all learners?

*includes specific language

For context, working definitions of the terms "disability," "disability supports," "developmental disability," and "inclusive education" have been included in an appendix at the end of the essay.

Education and Inclusion Matter

Education is a cornerstone of responsible citizenship in robust and stable democracies. Since the Confederation of Canada, governments and ordinary citizens have recognized the importance of education and have made public provision for its universal availability to children and youth at the elementary and high school levels. Presently, Canada spends 3.3% of GDP on public elementary and secondary education: $39.6 billion in 2002/03 (Nault, 2004).

With increases in the level of education attained, the chances also increase that people will be integrated within the paid labour force, enjoy economic security, participate in a range of community activities, and enjoy better health and wellness overall (Crawford & Porter, 2004). People who are disabled before completing their schooling and who are educated in regular instead of special education programs, are more likely to be involved in the paid labour force later in life and to be participants in a range of community activities. This trend generally holds up regardless of the nature or severity of the disability (Crawford & Porter, 2004).

The Present Situation

Knowledge about the Present Situation of Students with Develop-mental and Other Disabilities

Several factors make it quite difficult for researchers and others to develop a clear picture of the present educational situation of students with developmental and other disabilities in Canada. These factors include Canada's size and its decentralized responsibilities for education programs and educational statistics; the lack of "rollup" of statistics for analysis at the provincial/territorial and federal levels; the lack of focus on disability in provincial and territorial administrative data systems; the lack of detailed focus on education and disability in most major statistical surveys; the cost of developing specialized surveys; problems of sampling bias in statistical and other methodologies; difficulties in generalizing on the basis of case studies and self-reported observations by parents; the scarcity of research on issues of disability and inclusive education in Canada; the infrequency of provincial/territorial evaluations; and the lack of comparability between provincial/territorial reviews of special education and other issues in education (Crawford, 2005).

The Approach Adopted in This Essay

Given that Canadians are hampered in obtaining information and knowledge about the educational situations of young people with developmental and other disabilities in this country, the remainder of this essay adopts a composite approach to providing a general picture. It draws from statistical data, expert seminars, provincial special education reviews, and other reviews and assessments. Statistical data include Statistics Canada's National Longitudinal Survey of Children and Youth (NLSCY).

One of the expert seminars drawn upon was cosponsored by The Roeher Institute and the Canadian Research Institute on Social Policy (CRISP). It focused on the state of research into inclusive education in Canada (The Roeher Institute, 2003c). The other seminar was cosponsored by The Roeher Institute and the University of Calgary. Its focus was teacher preparation and professional development (The Roeher Institute, 2003d).

Provincial reviews of special education services were also consulted (Alberta Learning, 2000; Office of the Auditor General of Ontario, 2001; Ontario Human Rights Commission,

2002, 2003 ; Proactive Information Services Inc., 1998; Saskatchewan Special Education Review Committee, 2000; Siegel & Ladyman, 2000), as was a recent pan-Canadian review of educational issues that placed some focus on the education of students with "special needs" (Tobin Associates, 2004). Other papers consulted were by researchers from Canadian universities and research organizations that have placed a focus on the education of students with disabilities. These researchers are cited throughout this essay. *→ Other researchers*

Additional Review

While there is a substantial amount of descriptive information about legislation, policies, and recommended practices (e.g., see Proactive Information Services Inc., 1998, pp. 154–203), relatively little research has been done in relation to actual classroom and administrative practice in inclusive education in Canada. Key themes that emerge from the review of the research and other sources in Canada are the tension between "inclusive" and "special" education; the "excellence-equity dilemma"; issues around vision and policy commitment on inclusion; processes for disability identification/assessment and student placement; individual program planning; parental involvement and status in the educational process; parental appeals of placement and other decisions; issues around funding, resource allocation, and resource management; issues of accessing disability supports; roles and responsibilities of school staff; and teacher preservice preparation and professional development.

Described in more detail in the following pgs.

Other important matters that are not explored in much detail in the Canadian literature or in the present essay include issues of school culture, expulsion policies, transition planning, measures for communicating and accessing information about best practices, the purpose and focus of accountability measures, student testing and evaluation, and student certification upon graduation. *other issues not being openly presented*

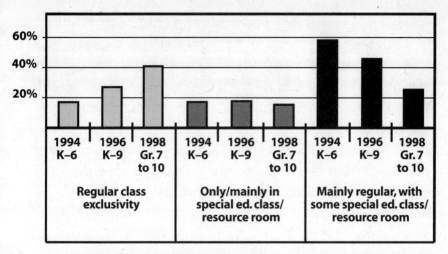

Movement towards inclusive education for pupils receiving additional
assistance because of disability, showing percentages in various
educational arrangements.

Source: The Roeher Institute based on NLSCY (1995, 1996 AAND 1998) data.

Shift to Inclusion

Statistical data from the NLSCY (above) indicate that there is an
increasing shift in recent years to regular classroom placements
for students with disabilities, and a shift away from a mix of regular and specialized placements. Yet a fairly consistent proportion of students with disabilities continues to be placed mainly or
exclusively in separate, special education classrooms (see also
Tobin Associates, 2004).

The Difficulty of "Doing Inclusive Education"
in a Special Education Context

Lupart (1998) pointed out that, while the philosophy of inclusion is becoming more widespread, "innovations have tended to
be piecemeal and fragmented" (p. 253) and the special education
model continues to prevail. Running parallel to notions of inclusion, "traditional special education programs have been fashioned according to the medical or deficit model, which assumes
functional limitations and emphasizes student classification,

Teacher training has decreased for special Ed

standardized assessment, and separate, remedial intervention" (p. 253). Given that the publicly funded special education system has been in place since the early 1960s in Canada, generations of regular educators' competence and commitment to deal with student diversity in the regular classroom have systematically decreased.

Reg ED vs. SPED over Funding.

The two models (regular and special education) have resulted in the creation of separate bureaucracies, policies, and procedures, with each system having its own funding and professional networks and incentives for maintaining the status quo (Lupart, 1998). Thus, said Lupart, "The very success of this special education model poses the greatest barrier to inclusive education" (p. 254).

② Excellence and Equity in Education

Traditionally, one goal was always pursued, however, Lupart claims that both can be achieved

The special and regular education systems evolved largely along separate paths in response to demands for change in the educational system, with special educators leading reform efforts to promote equity through progressive inclusion and the general education system focusing on excellence based on teacher development and school effectiveness (Lupart, 1998). This has led to what Lupart called the "excellence-equity dilemma" (p. 9; see also Skrtic, 1991). Lupart is of the opinion that while most schools currently focus on one goal at the expense of the other, it is possible for both goals to be pursued simultaneously.

③ Vision and Policy Commitment

Interpretation of Inclusion is open as no legislation exists.

While education policies in every jurisdiction across Canada back inclusion as a preferred option, there is a considerable distance to go to shift policies and practices from the special education model onto that footing. New Brunswick is furthest along in adopting a comprehensive model of inclusion; elsewhere, there is no legislated requirement. Accordingly, the door is open for wide

variation across local school districts and schools concerning
how they interpret and apply provincial policies on inclusion.

Winzer (1998) wrote that "philosophical acceptance ... far
outstrips commitment to implementation" (p. 231). From their
reading of teacher files, Field and Olafson (1999) concluded,
"school failure is located [by teachers] in the individual, with no
consideration of the role of institutional or social factors" (p. 74).

At recent consultations on teacher education and research
on inclusive education, The Roeher Institute found that variations in vision and policy commitment result in implementation
of inclusive practice that is highly inconsistent, even within a
given province. Practice varies widely from school district to
school district, across the English and French systems, across the
public and Catholic systems, and from school to school in the
same community (The Roeher Institute, 2003c, 2003d).

Identification/Assessment and Placement

The educational system in most jurisdictions typically requires that
students thought to have disabilities requiring services/accommo-
dations — and therefore needing dollars beyond those earmarked
for the general student population — should be formally assessed
and categorized by professionals as having specific physical, intel-
lectual/developmental, learning, emotional/behavioural, mental
health, or sensory disabilities. Once categorized as having a bona
fide disability, decisions are made about placement — that is,
whether the student will be educated entirely within the regular
classroom with or without supports for the student and regular
teacher; whether the student will be educated in a special classroom; or whether the student will be educated in arrangements
somewhere between these poles, such as in a mix of regular and
special classroom placements.

The Saskatchewan Special Education Review Committee
found that the way the notion of "most appropriate environ-

most appropriate

ervment" is currently defined leads to overemphasis on which school or classroom the student should attend, rather than on what instruction they should receive. The committee found that "[i]n some cases, students are included but separate. There is a need to see children as diverse individuals, not as students with a disability label" (Saskatchewan Special Education Review Committee, 2000, p. 93).

Status Diverse Disability

In most provinces, parents have a legislated right to be involved in the disability determination and placement process. While students in many jurisdictions *must* be diagnosed by a physician or other professional in order to receive higher levels of provincial public funding, there are exceptions to this rule, including in the Northwest Territories, where educational services for students with disabilities are reportedly based on identification of individual need rather than on categorization.

B.C

In British Columbia, Siegel and Ladyman (2000) took issue with the categorical approach to identification of exceptionality, which they maintained is insufficiently responsive to students' needs and diverts scarce resources away from directly supporting the needs of students. The researchers would rather see classroom-based, teacher-initiated assessments and immediate action rather than recourse to more formal assessments.

Alberta

Similarly, Alberta Learning's (2000) Review of Special Education took issue with categorical assessment. The committee preferred an approach different to one that uses specific labels or categories because the complex needs of some students can defy adequate description by a single label.[1] The committee made the point that the labelling process tends to focus on students' deficits while ignoring strengths, "creating an unbalanced picture of the student" that may even result in misunderstanding among people not well versed in what specific diagnostic labels mean (p. 22).

Sask

The Saskatchewan Special Education Review Committee's report (2000) asked the question "How can children's needs rather

64

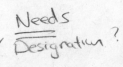

Needs
Designation?

than [categorical] designation become the basis for PPP [Personal Program Plan] development?" (p. 47). The Manitoba Special Education Review characterized the process as affecting the students themselves — "the use of labels, and focusing on the negative aspects of the student [are] detrimental to the student's future development" (Proactive Information Services Inc., 1998, p. 318).

Manitoba

The Ontario Human Rights Commission (OHRC) (2002) brought attention to problems with the labelling of students as a means of securing funding for accommodations, stating, "Some have raised concerns that the accommodation process ... and in particular the process for accessing ISA funding, encourages labelling of students ... rather than assessing the individual needs and strengths of each student (p. 18)." ("ISA" means Intensive Support Amount — that is, additional funding to address disability-specific needs in education.)

Ontario

The OHRC found that student labelling during assessment of eligibility for ISA funding may "result in pre-determining accommodation on the basis of stereotypical assumptions" (OHRC, 2002, p. 30). The commission expressed a concern that students' needs may be oversimplified, their strengths reduced by a fixed categorical designation; and their progress overshadowed by paternalistic attitudes. The commission was told that students receiving ISA funding are often referred to as "ISA kids" and are therefore "identified more by their disabilities than by their individual characteristics" (p. 31). Community Living Ontario called ISA funding "seriously flawed" and "a crude and highly suspect approach at best" (Driscoll, 2002).

Problem of over labelling

Draw to Funding can have negative outcomes

The report of Nova Scotia's Special Education Implementation Review Committee (2001) recommended a change from deficit-based assessment to identification of "both the strengths and needs of students, with a concomitant appreciation of the diversity of their strengths and needs" (p. 33), accompanied by earlier identification and assessment in order to enhance

Nova Scotia

preschool-to-school transition. In addition, the committee was of the view that assessments lead to recommendations for programming that continue to be based too heavily on a medical model of disability.

Such problems with the student "labelling" process are aggravated by assessments that are continual. Alberta's Review of Special Education (Alberta Learning, 2000) found that students are often submitted to repeated assessments. It called for a single point of entry (preferably based on a coordinated system of preschool identification and assessment), as well as for safeguards to protect the information that is collected. The committee observed that some provinces have initiated a "portfolio system" for parents to maintain and provide to school staff upon their children's entry into school. This may help to reduce service fragmentation and unnecessary reassessment. Manitoba's Special Education Review also pointed to repeated diagnoses as a problem (Proactive Information Services Inc., 1998).

For all the effort invested in the assessment process, placement decisions may be quite inappropriate. For instance, Field and Olafson (1999) noted that three of eight students in their study had been placed in resource rooms, yet "showed no evidence of learning disability in recent testing" (p. 74).

Then there is the matter of who is to conduct the assessments. The review team in Alberta (Alberta Learning, 2000) identified the shortage of qualified assessment professionals, especially in rural areas, and pointed to problematic wait lists. Similarly, Manitoba's Special Education Review cited a shortage of assessment professionals and long wait lists (Proactive Information Services Inc., 1998). Moreover, having to drive to Winnipeg for assessments was a major inconvenience for people living in isolated areas, and the review committee characterized many regions of the province as generally lacking "special needs programs and support services" (p. 319). The Nova Scotia

*Problem with
waiting periods, not
enough professionals*

Special Education Implementation Review Committee (2001) suggested that the problem of waiting periods for assessments could be addressed by hiring more assessment personnel and that the process could be improved through multisite assessments that would include the use of nonmedical assessment professionals (e.g., social workers).

Speaking more generally, Lupart (2000) found that students typically must be categorized in order to receive specialized supports and instruction; that there is often a significant time lag between referral/assessment and programming change; and that identification and testing take up an "inordinate proportion" of available funding.

*Summary
of
I.A.P.
pg. 63.*

*Same concept/diff
language*

IPP/IEP/ISSP

Individual Program Planning

Once a student is identified and placed, an individualized program plan (IPP) is typically created. (An IPP may also be called by other names, such as "Individual Education Plan (IEP)" and "Individual Support Services Plan (ISSP).") This plan usually maps out what learning progress should be made in the year; the process of evaluation and review to determine progress; and adaptations, accommodations, and other measures the student will require.

The goals set out in the IPP may serve as a basis for reporting on the progress of students who are not expected to follow the standard curriculum. For students who are expected to progress under the regular curriculum, the IPP may simply state the accommodations/ adaptations, services, and supports needed in order for the student to meet standard curriculum goals. In some provinces, however, IPPs are not needed for students with disabilities who follow the regular curriculum.

Siegel and Ladyman (2000) have pointed out that in British Columbia, IEPs tend to serve funding and auditing processes rather than the "critical planning purposes" for which they are intended. Audits are conducted to determine the classification of students and provision of programs, rather than to discover whether educational outcomes are being achieved. The researchers characterized the present system as "time consuming, expensive, and unnecessarily complicated" (p. 25), and they argued that it should be replaced by audits of programs and of student progress. They made the point that in some cases, IEPs are simply not implemented. At a recent symposium on teacher preparation cosponsored by The Roeher Institute and the University of Calgary, participants were told that regular education teachers in British Columbia are beginning to resent the pulling of supports from the classroom, and some regular teachers are unwilling to go to IEP and other meetings if they feel these won't make any positive difference in the classroom (The Roeher Institute, 2003d).

More generally in Western Canada, it was observed at the symposium that responsibility for developing IEPs has been "downloaded" to classroom teachers, who typically lack background on teaching students with disabilities and who seldom have the required 8 to 24 hours to develop an IEP. The supports that teachers need are typically not in place, and school districts have different approaches to dealing with planning issues, which have not been well researched.

The review committee in Nova Scotia (2001) rated the planning process highly in cases where principals, administrators, and teachers show strong leadership — and particularly in instances where school-based teams are strongly supported by principals. This effect was even greater for schools where principals had "resource backgrounds" — that is, experience in issues of instruction for students with disabilities. Availability of procedural planning guidelines reportedly increased the clarity of the individual planning process.

The Saskatchewan review committee (2000) expressed positive views about the Personal Program Planning (PPP) process in that province. The report indicated the importance of keeping parents and other stakeholders involved over the long term. The committee indicated that the planning process could be improved by increasing the focus on student needs for assistive technology and on transition planning. The Saskatchewan committee suggested that the Personal Program Plan be used as an accountability mechanism, with student attainment of a set of goals as the guiding indicator of student progress. The review committees in Alberta and British Columbia expressed similar views.

Parental Involvement and Status

The literature generally points to the marginal status of parents in the education of children with disabilities and the considerable time and advocacy effort that parents are required to invest. Siegel and Ladyman (2000) reported that parents in British Columbia feel "excluded from the IEP planning, that their suggestions are not seriously considered, or that the IEP agreed upon is not implemented. It was clear that parents of students with special educational needs want to be more involved in their children's education" (p. 31).

[handwritten margin note: B.C — ? To what degree? Are their requests reasonable?]

The Review of Special Education in Alberta (Alberta Learning, 2000) reported that parents might not be aware of the existence or necessity of an individualized program plan (IPP). Within the context of the strong parental choice movement in Alberta, the committee reported that "many parents of students with special needs do not have an equal choice in placement and program decisions affecting their children. Parental choice for students without special needs is more respected and accommodated than parental choice for students with special needs" (Alberta Learning, 2000, p. 32).

[handwritten margin note: Alberta]

The Saskatchewan report (2000) pointed to positive developments, where parents are involved in the individual planning process. However, the report stated that the "extent of family

[handwritten margin note: Sask]

*Sask-positve
*however varies
between District*

involvement in program planning and evaluation differs across schools and school divisions" (p. 142).

The Ontario Human Rights Commission's report (2003) described a system that requires a large amount of parental advocacy for needed educational supports for their children with disabilities. The commission quoted Ontario's provincial auditor as saying, "The ability of parents to advocate for their child is variable depending on how well informed they are about available services and supports" (p. 131).

Nova Scotia's review committee (2001) found that many parents expressed frustration with their involvement in the identification, assessment, and program planning processes. The committee recommended the use of communication logs between parents and teachers to address this problem.

Parental Appeals

Disability determination and placement decisions can be contentious, and in most jurisdictions parents have the right to appeal these decisions. Appeals processes are not without difficulties, however.

The Review of Special Education in Alberta (Alberta Learning, 2000) characterized the appeals process as "time consuming and emotionally draining, as parents must go through too many levels of bureaucracy before being able to appeal to the Minister" (p. 43). There is also a lack of information about parents' right to appeal and about what they can expect from the appeals process. The review committee in Saskatchewan (2000) found that parents are uninformed and/or unsure about their rights and responsibilities in engaging the appeal process (p. 142). Manitoba's Special Education Review (Proactive Information Services Inc., 1998) pointed to the vagueness of formal provisions around appeals and called for more publicly available detail on the process (pp. 263, 458).

During the Ontario Human Rights Commission's (2003) consultations, many groups expressed reservations about the Identification, Placement and Review Committee (IPRC) process. Many comments focused on the appeals process and the lack of an effective dispute resolution mechanism. While parents can appeal identification and placement decisions, there is no appeal process for decisions concerning specific programs and services. In addition, the existing appeals process is "cumbersome, time-consuming and overly litigious" (p. 34). Decisions on primary appeals to a Special Education Appeal Board are not binding on school boards, and the combination of primary and secondary appeals (to a Special Education Tribunal), with the addition of a possible judicial review, can last well into the school year. Whether because of delays in assessment, placement, review, or preparation and implementation of Individual Education Plans (IEPs), students may have to wait for classroom spaces to open or for Intensive Support Amount applications to be processed. All of these delays can act as disincentives for parents to seek legal appeal. While parents may not agree with identification or placement decisions and may be dissatisfied with the services their children are receiving, they may simply accept the situation because they cannot afford the additional time and effort the legal process would involve. Nova Scotia's review committee (2001) pointed to the need for measures to resolve disputes around individual planning before these escalate to the point where parents feel the need to resort to formal appeals.

Funding, Resource Allocation, and Resource Management

Key issues around funding, resource allocation, and resource management are the cumbersome process, administrative burden, and inadequacy of resource allocation in relation to student needs. Present approaches are restrictive, can include repeated assessments, and typically involve categorical approaches that create incentives for schools and districts to label students in the interests of securing additional funding.

The Roeher Institute detailed elsewhere the funding arrangements for the education of students with disabilities, which vary considerably from jurisdiction to jurisdiction (Crawford, 2005). Essentially, however, provinces use a combination of base funding for regular education plus supplementary grants or other funding measures to address the additional service and support needs of students with disabilities and other "exceptionalities."

Describing arrangements in British Columbia, Siegel and Ladyman (2000) stated that "the current funding system does not promote effective early identification and pre-referral intervention and encourages the system to spend resources on more expensive forms of assessment" (p. 25). The researchers took issue with the practice of applying targeted special education funds to cover indirect expenditures such as class size reductions and administrative costs. They also found inconsistent fiscal practices between districts and made a strong statement about schools wasting time on excessive bureaucracy. The authors suggested that school boards should consider retaining some of the presently targeted funds as a contingency to provide district- or regional-level services for specific programs. The Roeher Institute (2003d) reported the view of participants at an expert seminar on teacher preparation that the time-consuming system used to code students for the purpose of receiving funding provides incentives for schools to code as many students as possible to maximize funds (see also Crawford & Porter, 1992; Owens, 2003; People for Education, 2002).

The Review of Special Education in Alberta (Alberta Learning, 2000) characterized the process and administrative requirements around Severe Disabilities funding as too time consuming and costly. The review made the point that repeated

assessments draw funding away from direct student programming and services and suggested that districts should instead
change to a needs-based system of assessment "for programming
purposes only" (p. 15). The review argued that Alberta Learning,
in collaboration with school jurisdictions, should establish individual profiles of each district that include historical data on the
pattern of growth over the past five years of students with severe
disabilities, numbers of students with severe disabilities served,
and projections for future funding. According to the committee,
this system would have the additional benefit of providing for
smoother transitions into school, from grade to grade, and from
school to school. While the provincial ministry followed this suggestion, students must still be assessed and diagnosed for type
and severity of disability. The Alberta report also stated that
funding approvals often come too late in the school year, a problem also noted by education critics in Ontario.

In the Manitoba Special Education Review (Proactive Information Services Inc., 1998), members of the public raised the need for
more funding and increased staffing. Several respondents noted
that funding was inadequate for students assessed with Level 1
needs whose disabilities may not have been "severe" but who nevertheless may have needed various services. There was a call for
clearer and more appropriate criteria for funding levels, as children
assessed in certain categories are believed not to be receiving supports and services appropriate to their needs. Further, universality
and continuity were not being achieved; programming may have
been available in some areas of the province but not in others and
may have been provided one year but not the next. This was an
issue particularly in northern communities, where funding may not
have been portable for students who were in transition between
their home communities and regional centres.

Members of the Manitoba public echoed concerns raised in
other provinces that the amount of paperwork involved in apply-

ing (and reapplying) for funding was too confusing and time consuming and that the administrative process was taking funds away from direct service provision. Participants called for the introduction of multiyear funding for students with disabilities, and suggestions were made that Individual Education Plans should be developed for longer durations than one year. Manitoba has, in fact, introduced multiyear funding, as well as "multisystem" (i.e., intersectoral) funding for students with profound emotional/ behavioural disorders (Manitoba Education, Citizenship and Youth, 2003.

The Ontario Human Rights Commission (2002) characterized the funding system for students with special needs as "complex" and reported that, from the perspective of stakeholders, many of the problems experienced by students with disabilities in accessing education were due to funding shortfalls (2003a). A similar analysis is provided by Gibson-Kierstead and Hanvey (2001). Shortfalls may result in delays, misidentification of student needs, and a lack of necessary accommodations. The commission concluded that "while school boards have a duty to accommodate students with disabilities, the Ministry of Education needs to supply adequate funding to school boards to allow them to provide this accommodation" (OHRC, 2002). The commission stopped short of defining what constitutes "adequate" funding.

A 2002 paper by the parent advocacy group People for Education argued that funding for students with special needs in Ontario is inadequate and that criteria are too restrictive for assessing student needs. The group contended that "the Funding Formula has created a triage system of special education in which only the most needy are served" (p. 1), while children with moderate needs are put on waiting lists.

In Nova Scotia, the 2001 report of the Special Education Implementation Review Committee provided a short section on funding in the province, pointing to "the critical shortage" (p. 56) of funding for special education that the Funding Review Work Group had noted since 1996. The report indicated that the shortage affects all students, not only students with special needs. It recommended that the system receive additional infusions of revenue.

Disability Supports

Young people may need various disability supports (see appendix for definitions) to enable them to participate as valued equals in regular education arrangements. Present arrangements for the delivery of disability supports are complex. Essentially, however, provincial ministries responsible for health, education, children and families, and social services are all involved, as are Indian and Northern Affairs Canada and provincial authorities responsible for First Nations.[2]

With few exceptions, people interviewed and surveyed for recent Roeher Institute research indicated that such supports are vitally important (The Roeher Institute, 2002, 2004). In its public policy efforts, the Council of Canadians with Disabilities (1999) has consistently placed emphasis on issues of disability supports since 1999. Key themes on disability supports that emerge from the literature on education are the inadequacy and inconsistency of provision, lack of coordination, delays, and unsuitability to students' needs in many cases. Statistics Canada (2003) recently reported that cost is the major factor accounting for why people with disabilities in many cases lack the supports they need.

With reference to the adequacy and coordination of support services, the Alberta review (Alberta Learning, 2000) found that "there are not enough personnel to provide services and little overlap between systems in practical application ... Services for students with special needs are not being provided in an integrated system of program delivery" (p. 36). In the Executive

Summary of its 2000 report, the Saskatchewan Special Education Review Committee noted the inconsistency of support services and programs across schools and school divisions that result from overreliance on school boards for policy interpretation. The committee contended that a more centralized approach would yield greater consistency across the province and greater understanding of and adherence to the philosophical position and goals of SaskEd. In addition to emphasizing the need for continuing innovation in the provision of disability supports, the committee suggested that service provided across multiple schools and jurisdictions needs to be improved and supported through the building of local capacity. Similar measures at the policy/system and school levels are needed in order for coordination to work — namely, shared policies and strategies, funding and other resources so that policies can be carried out, and in-service training and professional development so stakeholders can learn how systems and groups can work together.

Manitoba's Special Education Review (Proactive Information Services Inc., 1998) found a shortage of professional services needed to support the education of students with disabilities in areas such as mental health, speech/ language, and occupational and physical therapy. Parents who participated in Manitoba's review reported that access to services and supports declines in relation to student age (see also Crawford, 2004). While this presents a greater problem in rural/isolated regions, the challenge persists even in Winnipeg. In addition to the regular range of disability-specific supports that may be needed by students, many recommendations brought attention to a need for more Aboriginal staff and for ESL and other programming that would be "more sensitive, fair and educationally relevant to the needs of First Nations students, their families and communities" (p. 335).

Although Ontario's policy, legislative, and program infrastructure is quite extensive, the Ontario Human Rights

Commission (2003) reported that "stakeholders continue to express concerns ... [and] report that special education practices and procedures in school settings at the local level are not consistent with the Ministry of Education's own directives ..." (p. 14). These inconsistencies show up, for example, in barriers to physical accessibility in multilevel schools without elevators and ramps, inaccessible washroom facilities and play areas, and inaccessible laboratories and other learning facilities. The commission pointed to insufficient access to necessary accommodations (e.g., classroom supports, adaptive technology, speech-language pathologists, and alternative-format materials) because of delays in the creation of Individual Education Plans that may not, in any event, reflect student needs or that may be ignored altogether. Children may not be able to begin the school year with their peers or they may be able to attend only part time due to the lack of appropriate supports and accommodations. In some cases, students lose substantial school time as a result of disputes concerning appropriate accommodations (OHRC, 2002). Students whose behaviour may disrupt the classroom environment are reported as particularly affected by "rigid expulsion policies" (OHRC, 2002, p. 16). An indicator of the effects of these problems is the Grade 10 literacy test, in which 60% of students identified as having special needs failed, compared to 25% of other students (OHRC, 2003).

People for Education (2002) reported regional inequities in Ontario in terms of access to psychologists, social workers, and speech-language pathologists. These inequities are most pronounced in the north and southwest areas of the province, with particular difficulties in remote and rural areas. The inequities are aggravated by the general decrease in access to such supports across the province since the 1999–2000 school year. People for Education's characterization of the present system as one of "triage" is backed up by an observation from Ontario's provincial auditor that backlogged cases are dealt with according to a triage system, with the less "serious" cases having a waiting period of between six to twelve months if they are dealt with at all (OHRC, 2003). The commission quoted the provincial auditor as saying, "Service decisions are being made based on budgetary considerations, and there is no basis for either school boards or the Ministry [of Education] to evaluate the appropriateness of the service cut-off points currently in place" (as cited in OHRC, 2003). It is not uncommon that parents who can afford to will pay privately, out of pocket, for specialized education services in order to bypass waiting lists.

Nova Scotia's Special Education Implementation Review Committee (2001) recommended "interagency collaboration with community resources" (p. 33) and services, as well as a more team-oriented approach to supporting students with disabilities overall. Such an approach would be enhanced if school districts were to address the shortage of qualified professional supports, such as school psychologists and qualified resource staff, and the difficulties families face in accessing the professional supports that are in place.

Roles and Responsibilities of School Staff

The research literature points to role confusion concerning who is, or should be, responsible for educating students with disabilities: regular teachers, para-educators/teacher assistants, or both in some kind of collaborative arrangement. The research also raises questions about the competence and knowledge of teachers and teacher assistants in this area.

Teaching assistants can be detrimental if they create relationships with individual students that separate those students from the rest of the class. The Roeher Institute's (2003e) work to assess the inclusivity of special needs education policy addressed this issue in one of its benchmarking questions, "Is there a requirement that specialist resources are used to train and improve the capacity of teachers to meet their students' needs rather than [provide] direct support of students?" (tables in section III Policy Scan, rows on Professional Development and Specialist Resources). Hill (2003) discussed research on infrequent teacher interactions with students with disabilities. Interactions increased when an instructional assistant was more than two feet away from the student. Assistant "hovering" may result in the separation of students with disabilities from their classmates and interference with peer interactions. This hovering behaviour is more common among assistants who understand their role in the classroom to be that of having prime responsibility for inclusion and the academic success of the student with a disability and the expert regarding a particular student (Giangreco, Edelman, Luiselli, & MacFarland, 1997).

Siegel and Ladyman (2000) reported the concern of parents in British Columbia that "teachers have relinquished their responsibilities for the education of their children to teacher assistants" (p. 18) and that the number of teaching assistants in British Columbia rose from 1,630 to 6,508 between 1990 and 1999, a Canada-wide trend. Hill (2003) reported that despite the widespread use of instructional assistants, this practice is one of the least studied issues in special education. Siegel and Ladyman found that the training of teacher assistants is no better than that of teachers when it comes to disability awareness.

It has been reported of Saskatchewan that para-educators are doing most of the teaching of students with disabilities in that province (The Roeher Institute, 2003d). While the law requires that people who are qualified in special education do the teaching, para-educators are not required to take courses and often do not have enough days away from the job for professional development. In addition, classroom teachers are not receiving much pre- or in-service training on how to work with para-educators.

Some parents reported that children with disabilities were doing better when teacher assistants were on strike. To improve the situation of para-educators, the Saskatchewan Special Education Review Committee (2000) recommended the development of clear role and responsibility descriptions for teacher associates.

Weber and Bennett (1999) in Ontario reported a real-life instance of the role of the teaching assistant:

> A flurry of October transfers meant that Justin's grade three class suddenly acquired a new teacher only a week before his situation was scheduled for special review by an Identification, Placement and Review Committee (IPRC).
>
> The new teacher wisely allowed the full-time assistant in grade three to work with the school's resource teacher in putting together the documentation for the IPRC. The EA was experienced and held in high regard in the school, and she had worked with Justin for the past two years. Perhaps most important, she was one of the few adults who understood and managed his behaviour effectively.

This quotation illustrates two major points. On the positive side, it shows how different staff members worked together to accommodate this student's needs. Less positively, it shows that there were few adults who really understood the student's behaviour and that multiple staff can experience difficulties in responding to student needs in the absence of the "expert" teaching assistant.

While much depends on how educational assistants carry out their roles and not merely on the number and availability of such assistants, the Alberta review (2000) found that more educational assistants are required for schools to assist in delivering programs and that more professionals are needed to act as liaisons between home and school. Similarly, Nova Scotia's review committee recommended increasing the number of teacher assistants and the use of floating substitute teachers to facilitate teacher involvement in program planning in the early weeks of each year.

Winzer wrote of the operating context in education as one of "ever increasing demands" (1998, p. 231) on teachers — for example, increased student variability and diversity, new management problems, increased resource and time restraints, larger class sizes, additional responsibilities and demands for accountability, diffuse obligations, formalization of curricula and testing, and the knowledge explosion. Lupart (2000) provided a list of "gaps and limitations" in educational arrangements for students with "exceptional learning needs" (p. 7) that concretize the problems outlined by Winzer (1998). The limitations are:

• school systems are ambiguous about regular class teachers being responsible for the learning progress of students with exceptional learning needs;

• regular class teachers are not adequately prepared and are not provided with adequate supports to manage inclusive classrooms;

• regular class teachers do not have sufficient time to consult with parents and special education teachers; and

• knowledge of the needs of students with disabilities is low among administrators.

It is not surprising that Lupart found that teachers are generally not modifying their practices to accommodate the individual learning styles of students.

Teacher Pre-Service Preparation and Professional Development

A recurring theme in the literature concerning teacher preparation for addressing issues of diversity, disability, and inclusion in regular classrooms is that very little systematic provision is being

81

made for this in Canada. There are exceptions to the rule, but existing programs tend to be dependent on the leadership of individual staff working for school districts and universities, and there is always the chance that a good program will be "here today, gone tomorrow." There are also insufficient professional development days, insufficient resources for professional development, and insufficient incentives for educators to pursue preservice training and upgrading on issues of inclusion and diversity (The Roeher Institute, 2003d).

As Siegel and Ladyman (2000) have stated, "Many of the teachers currently employed in British Columbia's schools have not had the benefit of formal preparation for working with students with special educational needs. Indeed, many teachers expressed the view that they feel they do not have the knowledge they need to work with such students" (p. 17). That opinion was echoed at the consultation on teacher education cosponsored at the Roeher Institute–University of Calgary seminar on teacher education in March 2003 (The Roeher Institute, 2003d). Participants in that consultation indicated that there is a need in British Columbia to offer courses that will help teachers deal with what they are already doing, instead of providing professional development courses that are "add-ons." Fragmentation of ministry and district support for professional development is reportedly making teachers desperate for information. Itinerant teachers are not as available as previously to provide even the most basic information to educators on instructional issues, and the positions of well-trained, specialist support teachers are being eliminated. People moving into the specialist teacher role may have very little background on issues of disability and inclusion and tend to move on to other positions once their preferred job postings become vacant. While in some cases they may become department heads, they tend to lack the expertise needed to help the other teachers, and this is resulting in considerable frustration for regular educators.

Concerning people doing sessional work at the University of British Columbia, it was reported, "There is no real consistency. The courses depend on who's teaching and the overall approach is very haphazard (The Roeher Institute, 2003d, p. 4)." This was acknowledged as a problem in other jurisdictions as well.

The Campus Alberta Inclusive/Special Education Initiative (CAISEI) (2002) referred to the "merging" of the regular and special education systems in Alberta, and to the trend of specialized programming being provided in regular rather than segregated settings. These and other developments have driven changes in the education of future teachers, including the provision of "special needs–related" instruction for all school staff, rather than only for special education teachers. CAISEI holds the opinion, however, that "professional development opportunities at Alberta universities have not kept pace with the growing demands" (p. 3). This has been the case particularly for professionals practising in rural and isolated areas and for those with personal and family obligations that prevent them from undertaking rigidly scheduled professional development courses.

The University of Calgary has had some success in designing a program that integrates academic knowledge with experience in the field, although secondary school teacher candidates reportedly still do not have much exposure to students with disabilities. At the University of Alberta, all education students must take a general course on "special needs," which includes information about inclusive practice. However, according to a participant at the Roeher Institute–University of Calgary symposium on teacher preparation, "Piling course on course hasn't done much to ensure that people have the knowledge needed for actual use" (The Roeher Institute, 2003d, p. 5).

Members of the public who participated in Manitoba's Special Education Review (Proactive Information Services Inc., 1998) reported that "clinicians, teachers, resource teachers, and support staff need increased training and professional development." However, this was considered to be a less urgent issue in Winnipeg and Brandon. Teacher preparation in Manitoba involves a two-year, post-degree program. Students take six credit hours in educational psychology, which includes a focus on how to modify the curriculum and other measures for a diverse range of learners. The Roeher Institute (2003d) reported that "the challenge is to safeguard this course work because it gets put in and taken out of the teacher preparation program; there is pressure for future teachers to learn the [regular] curriculum instead of perceived 'add-ons' like educational psychology" (p. 2). The province also offers a post–Bachelor of Education Special Education Certificate, which focuses mainly on adaptations. However, neither teachers nor teaching assistants are required to obtain this certificate, even if they intend to work with students with disabilities (The Roeher Institute, 2003d).

Ontario's provincial auditor found that "efforts to ensure that all teachers had [a strong foundation in special education service delivery] were not sufficient" (Office of the Auditor General of Ontario, 2001, p. 141), although a number of significant reforms were underway. The lack of relevant knowledge may be exacerbated by the high rate of teacher turnover in the current and next few years, resulting in "fewer experienced teachers ... available to meet students' needs and to act as mentors to the many new teachers entering the system" (p. 141). This was reported as a problem in British Columbia, as well (The Roeher Institute, 2003d). The Ontario auditor indicated that the "amount and nature of practical classroom experience that Ontario teachers are required to have prior to graduation" (p.142) is less than in other jurisdictions. The auditor also pointed out that Ontario places less focus on issues of disability than do other jurisdictions, which a review of other reports suggests is generally neither major nor of particularly high calibre.

In response to findings that teachers want more post-degree information on issues of disability, Nova Scotia's review committee (2001) recommended that improved professional development be provided through the Department of Education. Increased funding would strengthen the department's delivery capacity, and such funding would ideally be an integrated component of special education policy implementation.

A recurring theme in the Nova Scotia report (2001) is the general lack of teacher knowledge about the specifics of disability and disability-related needs. Issues of professional development and preservice training, especially for teachers, are cited throughout the document. Also at issue is the knowledge of paraprofessionals such as teacher assistants, "unqualified" resource teachers, and the "fragmenting [of]resource positions to 'top off' teacher assignment schedules, especially at senior high schools" (p. 43).

Future Directions: Implications for Advocacy

Key Challenges to Be Addressed

The review of the research found that it is difficult to move inclusive education forward in the special education policy and program framework that continues to prevail in Canada. There is a tension between efforts to achieve excellence and equity in education, a tension that some researchers believe can be reconciled. While the vision of inclusion is held out in most jurisdictions, there is wide variation in the interpretation and application of provincial policies by local school boards and schools. As a result, actual implementation is inconsistent from place to place; between Catholic, public, and private systems; between French and English systems; and even between schools within the same system and community. Considerable time, energy, and resources are expended in assessing and labelling students as having bona fide disabilities that meet funding criteria. While individualized education plans are often developed, the process is time consuming, teachers tend to lack the required expertise, and there is no guarantee that the plans will accurately reflect student needs — let alone drive instructional practices and evaluations of student progress and teacher performance. Parents tend to have marginal involvement in the formal educational process, although they usually possess a wealth of insight and information on the specifics of their children's needs and strengths. Parents may not know about appeals processes, and they can face various disincentives to using those processes. Additional funding tends to be highly restrictive and difficult to secure, involving major time and effort by educators, parents, and others. The disability-specific supports and other measures needed to further the education of learners with disabilities are often inadequate, uncoordinated, and difficult to secure. These supports and measures may also come on stream too late in the school year to foster the learning and broader participation of students with disabilities.

There is confusion and uncertainty about whether the classroom teacher or the educational assistant/teacher assistant has prime responsibility for educating students with disabilities; roles for effective collaboration need to be clarified. Teachers tend to have only minimal exposure to issues of disability in preservice training and limited opportunities and incentives to develop their knowledge and skills in this area through ongoing professional development. These factors together create considerable challenges for teachers who may be philosophically supportive of moving an inclusion agenda forward but who often feel hampered and ill prepared to do so effectively.

A Framework of Shared Expectations: Key Stakeholders and Measures Needed

Arguably, greater focus needs to be placed on supporting regular teachers so they can succeed in their efforts to bring quality education to all learners (see Tobin Associates, 2004, pp. 57–58). The discussion in this section is drawn from *Supporting Teachers: A Foundation for Advancing Inclusive Education* (Crawford & Porter, 2004). To further an agenda of inclusion and quality in education, key stakeholders need to support teachers in a variety of ways. These stakeholders and the roles they should play are summarized below.

Governments

In order to support teachers, provincial and territorial governments need to develop a legislative framework for education, with a coherent focus on the inclusion of all learners in regular schools and classrooms. Adequate funding needs to be allocated to make inclusion successful for teachers, students, and parents. Governments also need to show leadership by establishing and modelling interdepartmental cooperation (e.g., between education, health, and social services) in fostering full inclusion and educational excellence for all learners.

Ministries of Education

In support of teachers, ministries of education could establish funding approaches that have focused, dedicated revenue streams for inclusion but without requiring categorical approaches that involve labelling and stigmatizing students while burdening classroom teachers with extra administration.

Ministries should ensure the provision of in-service and professional development, and they should encourage and recognize teachers' efforts to undertake professional development. Ministries of education can require teacher candidates to develop basic skills for dealing with diversity in the classroom in order to be certified. Ministries can clearly articulate the broad directions and standards for professional training. Standards can, in turn, inform the efforts of teacher training institutions, including universities.

In curriculum development, some focus should be placed on diversity and inclusion, and the learning of positive messages about people of diverse abilities, family backgrounds, and cultures should be facilitated. Learning resources should be accessible, and they should support the place in society held by people with disabilities and others from diverse backgrounds and cultures. Ministries should develop clear, well-communicated policy statements that establish inclusion as the practice norm; disseminate practical guidelines for implementation; and make available best-practice documents and e-resources.

Parents

Parents can support classroom teachers by engaging in constructive partnerships with them. This involves establishing high but realistic expectations about the learning and development of their children, helping teachers better understand the particular needs and strengths of their children, reinforcing the teachers' efforts in their homes, and facilitating complementary activities for their children's development in the community. Parents can share information and knowledge about instructional strategies and other supportive measures that have worked well with their children and with teachers.

Parent Associations and Advocacy Groups

Like individual parents, parent associations and advocacy groups can support classroom teachers by engaging in constructive partnerships. This can involve holding high but realistic expectations for the learning and development of all students. These associations can collaborate with teachers' organizations to jointly sponsor, lead, and provide instruction for in-service development for teachers and school administrators. Parent and advocacy organizations can extend formal recognition for exemplary practice and can draw attention to it through newsletters, symposia, and conferences. They can help develop positive public focus and attention to issues of inclusion through their dealings with the media and political leaders. They can facilitate knowledge networking and best-practice initiatives, and they can engage in policy development, curriculum development, and advocacy.

University-based Teacher Education Programs

University-based teacher education programs can develop curricula that prepare teacher candidates for diversity and inclusion in regular classrooms. They can insist that all teacher candidates meet basic competency standards on inclusive practices in order to graduate. They can provide ongoing professional development (e.g., inservice and e-learning) for teachers and leadership training in inclusion for district and school administrators, so these professionals can extend the competencies they gained in preservice training.

Universities should also conduct research on inclusive school and classroom practices; advocate for evidence-based practice; and establish incentives for new researchers to place a focus on issues of inclusion in education. Ideally, university programs should facilitate critical discourse and engage in partnerships with ministries of education, teacher associations, parent and professional groups, and other universities. Universities have a key role to play in diffusing knowledge about current research on inclusive education by translating the research and other knowledge into readily accessible language and formats for practical use in schools and classrooms.

Other Professionals

Other professionals such as social workers, psychologists, speech and language specialists, public health nurses, and personal support workers also have roles to play in supporting teachers. They can collaborate with teachers, administrators, and others who are involved in the lives of young people who may be facing complex challenges. They can apply their knowledge to help address teachers' challenges in the classroom. They can develop new strategies to facilitate inclusion and focus on reducing the use of segregated practices.

School Districts

School districts should provide leadership and policy support, articulating clear standards and expectations for administrators and teachers. They also need to communicate a commitment to support teachers in their efforts to bring quality education to all learners. As they support teachers, school districts can provide professional development on best practices and link policy to practice through evaluations of school, administrator, and teacher performance. They should provide adequate resources and support to schools and advocate with ministries of education to ensure that the funding and other necessary measures are in place. District-level human resource considerations should include adequate instructional planning time, so that teachers can gear their instructional strategies to the strengths and interests of all learners.

The School-based Team

At the school level, the principal and other school-based team members should establish a positive, supportive, and welcoming climate for all students. They should also welcome and engage in effective partnerships with parents. School leaders should encourage, support, and reward teachers' professional development efforts and cultivate the model of teacher as "lifelong learner." Leaders should establish mutual support among teachers by creating a climate and work routines that favour teamwork and collaboration. They should ensure effective use of resources, focus the attention of teachers on effective instructional strategies, and ensure that classrooms are effectively organized for quality instruction. For their part, educational assistants/ teacher assistants and classroom teachers should find ways of collaborating so that the regular teachers have prime responsibility for educating all students but with the additional insights and expertise that EAs/TAs often bring to the table.

Teachers' Associations

Teachers' associations should develop policies that encourage and support effective practices for inclusion. They can sponsor and provide training, and like ministries of education, universities, and family/advocacy organizations, they can disseminate knowledge and information, broker knowledge networks, and foster effective practice initiatives. They can establish and maintain partnerships with parents, ministries of education, other professional groups, and universities. They can reinforce the model of teacher as "lifelong learner" and can advocate for professional development, good instructional materials, and other supports for teachers. Teachers' associations can engage in positive public relations on issues of inclusion and can complement the work of family and advocacy organizations to attract public focus and attention to inclusion through the media and in transactions with political leaders.

Concerted Efforts by All Stakeholders

If key stakeholders were to engage in the efforts outlined in this section of the essay, regular classroom teachers would find themselves much better prepared and supported to bring quality education to all learners in inclusive settings.

Toward a Common Policy Approach: Building on Established Principles

At various federal/provincial/territorial (FPT) tables, considerable work has been done to forge consensus across governments concerning key social policy issues. A policy framework for inclusive education based on shared pan-Canadian goals could build on the objectives, values, and principles embedded in FPT agreements. The Roeher Institute has discussed these agreements in considerable detail elsewhere (2003f).

Shared objectives consistent with objectives in FPT agreements include fostering the full and active participation of all children and youth with disabilities in regular schools and educational programs and in society more generally; supporting and protecting children and youth with disabilities most in need; and ensuring healthy, safe, and nurturing environments for children and families.

Shared values consistent with the language in FPT agreements include:

• all children can learn;

• the entitlement of all children to equality, fairness, human rights and dignity;

• shared responsibility between families and society at large for public education programs;

• recognition of the distinct roles and responsibilities of governments, teachers, administrators, families, children/youth with disabilities, communities, voluntary organizations, business, labour, and Aboriginal peoples; and

• inclusion in regular education schools and classrooms with the instructional and other supports necessary for children to develop to their fullest potential.

Key *service principles* in FPT agreements that could be nuanced to focus on the inclusive education of children and youth with disabilities are:

• every child's right of access to reasonably comparable, regular education and related support services throughout Canada, irrespective of disability status;

• availability of affordable educational and related support services based on need, not ability to pay;

• flexibility and responsiveness of educational services and disability-specific supports;

• parental control and choice in identifying the educational and support preferences and needs of their children with disabilities;

• efficiency and transparency of eligibility determination for disability-specific support services;

• high-quality, effective, safe, and person-centred educational and support services;

• program features across jurisdictions that do not require residency requirements or impose other barriers to accessing inclusive public education or related support services;

• cultural and gender sensitivity of inclusive programming; and

• fair appeals and dispute resolution for parents who feel their children have been unfairly treated or denied the educational or support services that they require.

Administrative principles that appear in present FPT agreements or that figure in proposals that have been advanced include:

• collaboration, coordination, and harmonizing of efforts between stakeholders in inclusive education;

• flexibility for provinces/territories to determine their own service and other priorities;

• sustainability and affordability of the education system for present and future generations;

• stability and predictability of funding;

- accountability through public reporting by governments in view of commonly accepted indicators of program effectiveness;

- knowledge generation and information sharing on good practices; and

- citizen input in designing inclusive programs and in reviewing outcomes.

Conclusion

Education matters to the general health, well-being, income security, and citizenship of Canadians. If properly implemented, education programs that include students with disabilities in regular classrooms and schools can more effectively deliver positive social and economic outcomes than arrangements that label, segregate, and stigmatize students.

While Canadians face many challenges to gaining information and knowledge about how students with disabilities are faring in primary and secondary education arrangements, there is an increasing shift to regular classroom placements for students with disabilities. A small yet fairly consistent proportion of students with disabilities, however, are mainly in special program placements. Despite progress in moving toward more inclusive education arrangements, it is difficult to move that agenda forward in the special education policy and program framework that continues to prevail across Canada.

Many considerations and efforts are required to support teachers so they can advance inclusive, quality education for all learners. A significant, positive difference could be made by a pan-Canadian policy framework consistent with the objectives, values, and principles outlined in this essay, backed up by investments and other measures to bring about the outcomes outlined above (under "A Framework of Shared Expectations: Key

Stakeholders and Measures Needed"). Such an approach would go a considerable distance in ensuring that teachers have the supports they need to bring quality education to *all* learners in regular schools and classrooms and that children and youth facing various challenges — including developmental and other disabilities — would receive the educational and other support services they need to thrive as valued learners with their age peers in inclusive arrangements.

NOTES

Cameron Crawford, past president of The Roeher Institute and presently Director of Research and Knowledge Management, Canadian Association for Community Living, wrote this essay. Shawn Pegg, staff researcher at The Roeher Institute, conducted background research.

1 In research concerning arrangements in Ontario, Weber and Bennett (1999) relate in an ethnographic study how various professionals within and beyond the education system had labelled a particular student as "autistic, ADHD, learning disabled, cerebrally dysfunctional and mentally disabled."

2 For high school students and working-age people, ministries responsible for labour market services are involved, as are workers' compensation programs; the Vocational Rehabilitation program of the Canada Pension Plan Disability benefit; and private and employer-based insurers and employers, in both the public and the private sectors.

REFERENCES

Alberta Learning. (2000). *Shaping the future for students with special needs: A review of special education in Alberta. Final report, November 2000.* Edmonton: Alberta Learning. **http://www.learning.gov.ab.ca/k_12/ special/SpecialEdReview/SpEdReport.pdf** (accessed December 10, 2004).

American Psychiatric Association. (1994). *Diagnostic and statistical manual of mental disorders* (4th ed.). (DSM-IV). Washington, DC: American Psychiatric Association.

Artiles, A.J. (2000). The inclusive education movement and minority representation in special education: Trends, paradoxes and dilemmas. Keynote speech given at International Special Education Congress, University of Manchester. http://www.isec2000.org.uk/abstracts/keynotes/artiles.htm (accessed January 24, 2004).

Barnes, C., Mercer, G., & Shakespeare, T. (1999). *Exploring disability: A sociological introduction.* Cambridge: Polity Press.

Bradley, E.A., Thompson, A., & Bryson, S.E. (2002). Mental retardation in teenagers: Prevalence data from the Niagara region, Ontario. *The Canadian Journal of Psychiatry, 47,* 652–659. http://www.cpa-pc.org/Publications/Archives/CJP/2002/september/bradley.asp (accessed December 10, 2004).

British Columbia Ministry of Children and Family Development. (2001, October). *Discussion paper on community living services.* Victoria: Ministry of Children and Family Development.

Bunch, G. (1997). From here to there: The passage to inclusive education. In G. Bunch & A. Valeo (Eds.), *Inclusion: Recent research* (pp. 9–23). Toronto: Inclusion Press.

Campus Alberta Inclusive/Special Education Initiative (CAISEI). (2002). *Collaborative Alberta university programming in inclusive/special education: Concept paper.* http://psych.athabascau.ca/html/CAISEI/Concept_Paper_Nov_26.doc (accessed December 10, 2004).

Council of Canadians with Disabilities. (1999, November). *A national strategy for persons with disabilities: The community definition.* Winnipeg: Council of Canadians with Disabilities.

Crawford, C. (2004). *Gathering momentum: Mobilizing to transform community living in B.C.* Toronto: The Roeher Institute.

(2005). *Scoping inclusive education for Canadian students with intellectual and other disabilities .* Toronto: The Roeher Institute.

Crawford, C., & Porter, G.L. (1992). *How it happens: A look at inclusive educational practice in Canada for children and youth with disabilities.* North York: The Roeher Institute.

(2004). *Supporting teachers: A foundation for advancing inclusive education.* Toronto: The Roeher Institute.

Driscoll, J. (2002, October 9). Community Living Ontario lashes special education funding formula. *Community Living Leaders.* http://www.communityliving.ca/Daily_News/2002/Oct_02/oct_09.htm (accessed December 10, 2004).

Dyson, A. (1999). Inclusion and inclusions: Theories and discourses in inclusive education. In H. Daniels & P. Garner (Eds.), *World yearbook of*

education 1999: Inclusive education (pp. 36–53). London: Kogan Page
Limited.

Fawcett, G. (2004). *Supports and services for adults and children aged 5–14
with disabilities in Canada: An analysis of data on needs and gaps.*
Ottawa: Canadian Council on Social Development.

Field, J.C., & Olafson, L.J. (1999). Understanding resistance in students at
risk. *Canadian Journal of Education*, 24(1), 70–75.

Giangreco, M.F., Edelman, S.W., Luiselli, T.E., & MacFarland, S.Z.C. (1997).
Helping or hovering? Effects of instructional assistant proximity on students with disabilities. *Exceptional Children*, 64, 7–18.

Gibson-Kierstead, A., & Hanvey, L. (2001). Special education in Canada.
Perception, 25(2). **http://www.ccsd.ca/perception/252/specialed.htm**
(accessed December 10, 2004).

Hansen, J. (2001). *Each belongs.* Hamilton, ON: Hamilton-Wentworth
Catholic District School Board.

Hill, C. (2003). The role of instructional assistants in regular classrooms: Are
they influencing inclusive practices? *The Alberta Journal of Educational
Research*, 49(1), 98–100.

Horwitz, S.M., Kerker, B.D., Owens, P.L, & Zigler, E. (2000, December). *The
health status and needs of individuals with mental retardation.* New
Haven: Department of Epidemiology and Public Health; Yale University
School of Medicine; Yale University, Department of Psychology.
**http://www.specialolympics.org/Special+Olympics+Public+Website/
English/Initiatives/Research/Health+Status+report.htm** (accessed
December 10, 2004).

Lipsky, D.K., & Gartner, A. (1999). Inclusive education: A requirement of a
democratic society. In H. Daniels & P. Garner (Eds.), *World yearbook
of education 1999: Inclusive education* (pp. 12–23). London: Kogan Page
Limited.

Lupart, J. (1998). Setting right the delusion of inclusion: Implications for
Canadian schools. *Canadian Journal of Education*, 23(3), 251–265.

(2000, April). Students with exceptional learning needs: At-risk, utmost.
Paper presented at the Pan-Canadian Education Research Agenda
Symposium: Children and Youth at Risk, Ottawa. **http://www.cmec.ca/
stats/pcera/symposium2000/lupart.en.pdf** (accessed December 10, 2004).

Manitoba Education, Citizenship and Youth. (2003b). *Special needs funding
support guidelines.* **http://www.edu.gov.mb.ca/ks4/specedu/funding/
index.html.**

Nault, F. (2004). *Summary public school indicators for the provinces and territories, 1996–1997 to 2002–2003* (pp. 12, 25). Ottawa: Statistics Canada (Culture, Tourism and the Centre for Education Statistics Division).

Nind, M., Shereen, B., Sheehy, K., Collins, J., & Hall, K. (2004). Methodological challenges in researching inclusive school cultures. *Educational Review, 56*(3), 259–270.

Nova Scotia Special Education Implementation Review Committee. (2001). *Report of the Special Education Implementation Review Committee.* http://www.ednet.ns.ca/pdfdocs/studentsvcs/seirc/seircss.pdf (accessed December 10, 2004).

Office of the Auditor General of Ontario. (2001). Special education grants to school boards (Section 3.06). *2001 Annual Report.* Toronto: Government of Ontario.

Ontario Human Rights Commission. (2002). *Education and disability: Human rights issues in Ontario's education system — Consultation paper.* Toronto: Ontario Human Rights Commission.

(2003). *The opportunity to succeed: Achieving barrier-free education for students with disabilities — Consultation report.* Toronto: Ontario Human Rights Commission.

Owens, D. (2003). *Gaming the system: Special education funding in Manitoba.* Winnipeg: Frontier Centre for Public Policy.

People for Education. (2002). *Special education and the funding formula: Emergency service only.* Toronto: People for Education. http://www.peopleforeducation.com/reports/spcialed/spcialed.PDF (accessed December 10, 2004).

Proactive Information Services Inc. (1998). *The Manitoba special education review: Final report.* Winnipeg: Proactive Information Services Inc. http://www.edu.gov.mb.ca/ks4/specedu/seri/legislation.html (accessed December 10, 2004).

The Roeher Institute. (2002). *Moving "In Unison" into action: Towards a policy strategy for improving access to disability supports.* Toronto: The Roeher Institute.

(2003a). *Not enough: Canadian research into inclusive education. Final report.* Toronto: The Roeher Institute.

(2003b). *Not enough: Canadian research into inclusive education — Summary report.* Toronto: The Roeher Institute.

(2003c). *Seminar on research into inclusive education.* Toronto: The Roeher Institute.

(2003d). *Seminar on teacher preparation for inclusive education.* Toronto: The Roeher Institute.

(2003e). *Analysis of special needs education policies in Canada using an inclusion lens.* Toronto: The Roeher Institute.

(2003f). *Federal transfer options for expanding access to disability supports.* Toronto: The Roeher Institute.

(2004). *Improving the odds: Employment, disability and public programs in Canada.* Toronto: The Roeher Institute.

Saskatchewan Special Education Review Committee. (2000). *Directions for diversity: Enhancing supports to children and youth with diverse needs.* **http://www.sasked.gov.sk.ca/admin/pub_pdf/committee.pdf** (accessed December 10, 2004).

Siegel, L., & Ladyman, S. (2000). *A review of special education in British Columbia.* Victoria: British Columbia Ministry of Education. **http://www.bced.gov.bc.ca/specialed/review/report/review.pdf** (accessed December 10, 2004).

Skrtic, T.M. (1991). The special education paradox: Equity as the way to excellence. *Harvard Educational Review, 61,* 148–206.

Statistics Canada (2002). *Participation and activity limitation survey: A profile of disability in Canada, 2001 — Tables.* Ottawa: Minister of Industry.

Statistics Canada. Housing, Family and Social Statistics Division (2003). *Participation and Activity Limitation Survey, 2001: Disability Supports in Canada, 2001.* Ottawa: Minister of Industry.

Tobin Associates. (2004). *Quality education for all young people: Challenges, trends, and priorities* (Report of Canada). Ottawa: Council of Ministers of Education, Canada. **http://www.cmec.ca/international/unesco/ 47th-ICE-Report.en.doc** (accessed January 24, 2004).

UNESCO (United Nations Educational, Scientific and Cultural Organization). (1994). *The Salamanca statement and framework for action on special needs education.* Paris: UNESCO.

U.S. Department of Health and Human Services. Administration for Children and Families. (2004). *Frequently asked question: What is the prevalence and incidence of intellectual disabilities?* **http://faq.acf.hhs.gov/ cgi-bin/acfrightnow.cfg/php/enduser/std_alp.php?p_cat_lvl1=69** (accessed December 10, 2004).

Weber, K., & Bennett, S. (1999). *Special education in Ontario schools* (4th ed.). Thornhill, ON: Highland Press.

Willms, J.D. (2002). *Vulnerable children: Findings from Canada's National Longitudinal Survey of Children and Youth*. Edmonton: University of Alberta Press.

Winzer, M.A. (1998). The inclusion movement and teacher change: Where are the limits? *McGill Journal of Education, 33*(3), 229–251.

APPENDIX: DEFINITIONS

Disability

For several years, The Roeher Institute has defined "disability" as one or more limitations in carrying out activities of daily living and in participating in the social, economic, political, and cultural life of the community. Such limitations may arise from:

• a physical, sensory, intellectual, emotional, or other personal condition such as a long-term health problem;

• societal stereotypes about such human conditions; or

• ways of organizing social, economic, and built environments that, in their effects, exclude or impede the participation of people with such conditions. (The Roeher Institute, 2002, p. 5)

This definitional approach is a synthesis of traditional biomedical and more contemporary social models of disability (e.g., Barnes, Mercer, & Shakespeare, 1999).

Disability Supports

More than 2 million Canadians have a disability and need one or more human, technological, or other supports so they can overcome limitations in carrying out activities of daily living and in participating in the social, economic, political, and cultural life of the community (Fawcett, 2004; The Roeher Institute, 2002; Statistics Canada, 2003). Typically, such supports include human assistance and aids/devices for participation in education, employment, leisure, and various other activities, e.g., accessible transportation; modified curricula or individualized instructional strategies; accessible workstations, classrooms, and features in the home environment; modified computers and other equipment; attendant service to help the person with a disability get ready for school in the morning, occasionally throughout the day, and at home in the evening; assistive devices such as mobility and communication aids at home, at school, and in other situations (The Roeher Institute, 2002, pp. 5–6).

Developmental Disability

Definitions of the term "developmental disability" are contested ground. For instance, IQ cutoffs can range from 70 to 75, and there is variation in whether environmental factors are taken into account (e.g., availability of support systems) and whether measures of adaptive behaviours or etiology (familial/cultural and organic) are factored into the definition. Horwitz, Kerker, Owens, and Zigler (2000) provide a helpful discussion. Generally, definitions connote long-term conditions with onset before 18 years involving significant cognitive limitations and affecting adaptive functioning in everyday activities that most people can carry out without major difficulty. While the terms "developmental delay" and "intellectual disability" are technically distinct from other "developmental disabilities" (see American Psychiatric Association, 1994), the terms are often used interchangeably.

Prevalence estimates of intellectual disability vary from about 0.7% to about 3% of the general population (Bradley, Thompson, & Bryson, 2002; British Columbia Ministry of Children and Family Development, 2001; Horwitz et al., 2000; Statistics Canada, 2002; U.S. Department of Health and Human Services, 2004).

Inclusive Education

Approaches to, and definitions of, "inclusive education" can also vary (Nind, Shereen, Sheehy, Collins, & Hall, 2004). Common threads are the need for school-wide approaches, the belief that all children can learn, the need to develop a sense of community, services based on need rather than location, natural proportions of students with disabilities, attendance of children with disabilities at neighbourhood schools, supports provided in regular rather than separate education, teacher collaboration, curriculum adaptations, enhanced instructional strategies, and a concern for standards and outcomes. However, definitions vary regarding the extent to which students with disabilities would ideally be placed in the regular education classroom (e.g., part-time, full-time), and emphases can differ, with some approaches focusing on the transformation of individual school cultures and others emphasizing broad-level systems change (Lipsky & Gartner, 1999, as cited in Artiles, 2000).

Dyson (1999, as cited in Artiles, 2000) has argued that varying definitions and goals contribute to discourses that run along the lines of ethics (e.g., justice and equality demand inclusion), efficacy (e.g., separate education is no more beneficial than inclusive approaches), and the practicalities of realizing inclusion (e.g., the politics of systems change, funding requirements, regulatory regimes, knowledge resources needed, dimensions of school culture, and professional practice implications).

The Roeher Institute has been using a working definition of inclusive education that is based on an approach developed in 2003 in Fredericton, New Brunswick, by a panel of knowledgeable educators, education administrators, government officials, researchers (university based and other), family members, and community advocates who are familiar with issues of disability, education, and inclusion (The Roeher Institute, 2003c). This approach is consistent with the vision of inclusion as set out in the *Salamanca Statement* (UNESCO, 1994), which has helped shift the focus of international actions in education toward inclusive approaches and away from instituting separate arrangements for students with disabilities.

Refocusing the Fredericton definition slightly to emphasize the role of the teacher, inclusive education can be defined as arrangements where the teacher has the instructional and other supports that are needed to:

• welcome and include all learners, in all of their diversity and exceptionalities, in the regular classroom in their neighbourhood school with age peers,

• foster the participation and fullest possible development of all learners' human potential, and

• foster the participation of all learners in socially valuing relationships with diverse peers and adults. (Crawford & Porter, 2004)

It is understood that any child, regardless of whether he or she has a disability, may need individualized attention and support from his or her teacher, in order to address difficulties with the curriculum on any given day. However, where such support is needed outside the regular classroom, in an inclusive system, this would be for as brief a period of time as possible, and the out-of-classroom support would be accompanied by an active plan to reintegrate the student into the regular classroom as soon as possible — with appropriate supports for the teacher and the student (Crawford & Porter, 2004).

As explained more fully by Crawford & Porter (2004), this approach addresses inclusion on multiple levels: classroom, school, community, and system (i.e., legislative, policy, regulatory, and funding arrangements) and takes into account the need for clear vision based on values and ethics, as well as for advocacy, political support, and other pragmatic measures.

The emergence of inclusive education in Canada is discussed elsewhere (Bunch, 1997; Hansen, 2001; The Roeher Institute, 2003b). Essentially, however, the inclusive education model challenges the cornerstones of the special education model by contending that the rights of and benefits to learners with disabilities who are included in regular classroom environments outweigh the challenges to teachers inherent in such a situation. Inclusion advocates tend to argue that, with the support of properly trained resource teachers and other supports, regular class-room teachers should be able to work effectively with all students. Academic and social achievement have actually been found to be higher in regular education with mixed groupings of students of different abilities from diverse backgrounds (Willms, 2002). It is also possible for students without disabilities to benefit from being educated in the company of peers with disabilities (The Roeher Institute, 2003a).

The Politics of Diversity

Ben Levin

In many ways, the history of educational politics in Canada is the history of diversity issues. This essay takes an inclusive perspective that suggests that population diversity is an asset that ought to be encouraged and developed rather than suppressed, while recognizing the challenges implicit in such a statement. For purposes of this essay, diversity is defined as including the full range of differences among people relevant to their education, including but not limited to gender, socioeconomic status, ethnicity, language, immigration status, and disability. Politics encompasses the range of macro and micro, official and unofficial processes that occur in organizations and society concerned with the distribution of power, benefits, and costs. However the main focus of the discussion is on the ways in which governments in Canada have tried to respond to diversity issues.

The most difficult issues in Canadian educational history have largely been related to how schools would respond to the population diversity that has always characterized Canada, even before the country came into being as a single political entity. Disagreements about the roles of language and religion in schooling, and the extent to which a single system of education could be imposed, have been among the most heated political issues throughout Canadian history. Compromises over and protections for religion and language in schools were at the heart of the bargain of Confederation in the 1860s. The Manitoba Schools Question in the 1890s created a national crisis and may have changed the outcome of a key national election. Nor have these issues receded in more recent years. The full funding of Catholic schools in Ontario in 1984, the change in the Quebec system from religious to linguistic in the 1990s, and the constitutional amendment concerning religious schools in Newfoundland in 1996 show the continuing prominence of these issues.

In recent years educational concerns about diversity have broadened beyond the longstanding issues of official languages and religions. The appropriate organization and governance of Aboriginal education, in First Nations and in urban areas, has been a subject of growing concern, especially since 1970. The declaration of Canada as a multicultural society marked increasing attention being paid to Canada's large immigrant and ethnic minority population. The rise of feminism throughout the twentieth century brought a focus on creating equal opportunities for girls and women. And the normalization movement beginning in the 1960s, followed by a great deal of political lobbying and litigation, brought many controversies about how to accommodate the needs of people with disabilities. In all these cases we have witnessed a great deal of conflict over what schools ought to do and how they ought to do it. No matter what one's views on these various issues, it would be impossible to write a history of Canadian education without giving questions of diversity a prominent place.

A Sorry History of Intolerance

Although diversity issues have always been prominent in Canadian education, for most of our history the record in terms of recognizing and accommodating difference has ranged from dubious to shameful. Discrimination in various forms has been a fundamental feature of life in Canada (as in most other countries). One can hardly begin to speak about the so-called "education" of Aboriginal people in Canada, whose treatment was, through most of our history, at best totally inadequate. The waves of immigrants who arrived before the First World War were seen as half-savages, needing to be civilized by being assimilated to Anglo-Saxon orthodoxies. The rights of minority francophone populations were systematically ignored or even abrogated; it is only in the last twenty-five years or so that most of the country has recognized the rights of the linguistic minority, and then often only under duress or as a result of court decrees. Many children with disabilities were denied education altogether. As recently as the 1950s, even left-handedness was seen as a deviation to be stamped out. In other words, most of the history of Canadian schooling is much more an effort to eliminate diversity than to encourage or support it.

The pressures for homogenization of the Canadian population have been substantial, and until quite recently, unrelenting. However, it is important to understand the sources and nature of these pressures lest we succumb to the temptation of seeing them as simply the actions of bad people, a perspective that is not useful if we are to improve our current situation.

It is possible to identify at least two kinds of pressures for homogenization and assimilation in education in both the past and the present. The first was political. Governments tend to appeal to the popular and the powerful, and most of the time in most places, there is more support for the maintenance of the social status quo, even if it is unsatisfactory to many, than for changes in the social order that will result in more power or privilege for the marginalized and excluded. This is a fundamental element of politics that should not be ignored and cannot be wished away. Support for the status quo is often strong even among those who have suffered from it. The children and grandchildren of immigrants, for example, may be highly supportive of efforts to restrict further immigration. Governments in Canada have been, in many instances, active perpetrators of discrimination rather than inclusion.

At the same time, we should recognize that our institutions, including schools, have also been sources of pressure for homogenization. It is simply much easier in large institutions to treat people as if they were all more or less the same or, alternatively, to marginalize people seen as different or to treat them as if their problems were their own fault. Thus, in the history of schooling, there are many instances of educators arguing to keep out those who were different or to provide them with an inferior form of education, on grounds of language, ethnicity, geography, gender, or other factors. Women and Aboriginal people were excluded because they were seen as incapable of benefiting from advanced education. Canadian universities had quotas on Jews in professional schools as late as the 1940s. Even today the credentials of immigrants often remain unrecognized, excluding them from full participation in Canadian society.

Diversity as a Political Issue Today

Gradually, over the last century, perspectives on diversity have been changing. The reasons for this are undoubtedly complicated, involving evolving ideas of human interaction and dignity, as well as changing patterns of migration and of political participation. The worldwide growth of attention to human rights that has accompanied and partly resulted from the monstrous crimes and abuses of the last century has also had an impact, leading to new legal structures and growing ability of various minorities to assert their places in society. Looking back over a century, it seems clear that there has been a sea change in our general acceptance of diversity, though, as will be clear shortly, we are still far from any golden age of inclusion.

Canada today has large and growing population diversity. With one of the world's higher rates of immigration, much of it made up of visible minorities, Canadian cities especially have become very diverse. The Aboriginal population has not only grown rapidly but has also increased significantly in its political sophistication and ability to exert itself. Thus, many Canadians have been brought face to face with the realities of population diversity to an extent rarely matched in our history.

Just as importantly, diversity is now seen as a potentially valuable political resource. Immigrants to Canada, as well as our Indigenous people and our official linguistic minorities are all much better educated than was the case a century ago. People who are better educated are more aware of their rights and more able to act to protect themselves and make the case for their full and equal participation in society. Various minority communities have become more politically active, and their support and votes are therefore of interest to more politicians — witness the significant number of elected officials from various minority communities in various parts of Canada. Political processes have, at least in some cases, become more open to diverse points of view and a range of participants. It is no longer thought unreasonable to translate key documents into multiple languages or to provide interpretation for non-English speakers or to recognize out-of-the-mainstream customs and traditions at mainstream events.

A variety of legal and structural supports for diversity and inclusion have also gradually been put into place over the last several decades. The official declaration of Canada as a multicultural society, the advent of the Charter of Rights and Freedoms, provincial human rights legislation, and the growing number of court cases setting out the rights of minorities are among the important instances in which diversity is being officially recognized. Within education these developments have had important effects in many areas, such as creating governance structures for

Aboriginal and francophone education and creating legal and institutional bases for special education and inclusion. These structures are far from settled or universally accepted, but at the same time there appears to be no going back to the days of a monolithic, assimilationist version of schooling.

While minorities now play a much more active role than in the past and the official recognition of diversity has increased substantially, we should not pretend that there is broad consensus on these issues. Canadian public opinion on diversity is itself quite diverse. There continues to be substantial public concern about levels of immigration and substantial support from at least some sectors for policies that limit diversity and support assimilation. Opposing immigration, for example, or expressing concern about the so-called "extra rights" of Aboriginal people are still views that have strong support in many parts of Canada. Diversity continues to evoke fears among some people. The fact is, as Heath (2001) has put it, "The exercise of human reason, under conditions of freedom and equality, tends to generate more — not less — disagreement about the ultimate aims of life". Such disagreement is necessarily uncomfortable and will be resisted by many people.

The net result of these changes is, overall, positive but not unfailingly so. Clearly there have been some positive developments and real progress. In almost every area it is possible to point to important improvements. The development of inclusion as a fundamental principle of special education has been hugely important; many children who used to be excluded from schooling or segregated within it are now included in mainstream provision with evident benefits to them. Minority language provision has improved dramatically, not only for official minorities, but also for all the heritage language communities in Canada. Many more Aboriginal students are completing high school and participating in postsecondary education than used to be the case, and more and more school systems are recognizing that they need to pay attention to Aboriginal education issues. It is also important to keep in mind that the education system is more equitable than most other social systems — much more so than the labour market, for example.

At the same time, it is clear that much remains to be done. The outcomes of schooling continue to be quite inequitable, and students' economic, ethnic, and linguistic backgrounds continue to predict those inequalities to an undesirable degree. Socioeconomic status continues to be the single most powerful predictor of educational and other life outcomes (Levin, 2004b). Data from the School Achievement Indicators Program, operated by the Council of Ministers of Education, Canada (reports are available at cmec.ca) show that francophone students outside Quebec are not doing as well as their Anglophone peers. Every available indicator demonstrates that Aboriginal students are not achieving at average Canadian levels. The number of children being referred to special education continues to grow. We may not agree on what equity is or how we would know when we had arrived at an equitable state, but we can surely recognize that we are not currently there. As noted already, however, there is substantial conflict over whether particular policies and strategies have been helpful, and even more conflict over what should happen next.

Factors Supporting Improvement

In thinking about where we are and what might happen next, it is worth probing further into the factors that have led to the improvements just described. When one looks at the history of minority education, whatever minority one might consider, several conclusions can be drawn.

First, much has depended on strong advocates for equity and diversity. Attention to children with special needs came in

111

(1) Advocates
(2) Legal Structures

large part because advocates, often but not only parents, worked relentlessly and often against official indifference if not opposition, to create change. The advent of some self-governance in education for First Nations and for francophones is similarly the result of endless work by leaders in those communities, often over very long periods of time. Where would we be in regard to gender equity had there not been so many women ready to endure much in order to make the case for the needs and rights of women? Everywhere one looks, advocates play a vital role. It is important to remember that those now considered heroes or heroines were at one time largely seen as nuisances and troublemakers.

A second important conclusion concerns the vital role of legal structures in Canada — especially that of the courts interpreting the Charter of Rights and Freedoms — in the extension of equity and inclusion. It is no accident that supports and protections for diversity and inclusion have been extended considerably since 1982. One can point to a vast number of court decisions that have reminded us of our obligations to minorities. To take just one example, francophone education in English Canada would have nowhere near its current strength without a whole series of court decisions. Although the political system is, in my opinion, much more open to diverse views than it once was, not everything can be left to the political process, because in the end elections depend on majorities. The protection of minorities does require commitment to a constitutional and legal system, although the ongoing legitimacy of that system can be ensured only through support from the political system.

What can we say about the role of educators and the education system in these debates and conflicts? Clearly some educators have worked hard for the extension of equity and inclusion. Many leaders in various movements supporting diversity were educators. Many special educators have been powerful advocates for children who had few others to speak for them. Much of the leadership in many minority communities is made up of people who were originally teachers.

Yet in other ways the education system has played an ambiguous role in relation to issues of diversity. I have already noted the degree to which schools, as large institutions, embody a strong tendency towards uniformity and the suppression of difference. The school system did not readily embrace mainstreaming or minority language education or more emphasis on the needs of Aboriginal students. In too many schools and classrooms, expectations remained too low, offending language was not quickly cleaned up, and the needs and voices of the marginalized were not adequately recognized. In some cases the rhetoric was right but the practice did not follow. The language may not have been oppositional. Instead, objections may have been couched more in terms of inadequate resources, but the net effect was still to make it more difficult to achieve goals related to inclusion and diversity.

Central Issues concerning Diversity Policy in Education

From a political point of view, issues of diversity continue to raise serious difficulties. These difficulties can be described through several questions or problems: To what extent can we accommodate highly divergent views and values in a single public education system? What is the relationship between equity and equality or, to put it another way, how much and what kinds of differences in educational approaches and outcomes are acceptable? To what extent does diversity imply separate delivery and governance systems and how can diverse systems be accommodated? In other words, what choices will be given to which people? And finally, how does attention to diversity affect outcomes? Does focusing on difference make things better or worse? In raising these problems, my intent is not to explicate them from a conceptual or philosophical standpoint, a task that is beyond my powers, but to try to illustrate the political issues they engender.

Perhaps the most central challenge related to diversity has to do with how the education system responds to the range of beliefs and values in society. The historical direction, as already described, has tended toward recognizing the legitimacy of a range of ideas and practices and trying to find a place for them in the school system. Not all differences, however, can be reconciled. Some groups or cultures have beliefs and practices that are simply unacceptable to others. The challenges are evident in many contemporary situations. Ryan (2003) describes the dilemmas facing school principals in highly diverse communities concerning issues such as whether boys will be allowed to talk with girls in unchaperoned settings or how the school will respond to pupils who have fundamentalist religious beliefs. Educators may have great difficulty when they encounter beliefs that severely limit the role of women, for example, or that are strongly supportive of corporal punishment or reject some important element of school curriculum such as the teaching of evolution. How does the school system maintain its own important values in relation to equity or the welfare of children without being perceived as attacking those who think differently? What happens when these differences run up against the legal system — for example, in an area such as different ideas about what constitutes child abuse? And how is the response of the education system affected by important larger social dynamics, such as the increasing fear and suspicion of some minorities arising from various contemporary international developments?

While there is broad acceptance of tolerance as an important value to be taught and supported by schools, Holmes (1998), among others, has argued that the limited or negative virtues of tolerance and respect for others do not provide sufficient basis

too much diversity ?

for a strong and coherent community. Important positive values must also be widely shared. Is it even truly possible to have a society that is broadly accepting of real diversity in views and practices, or must such acceptance necessarily be largely at the margins, where it does not threaten mainstream beliefs in any significant way? Indeed, given ongoing fears and suspicions about differences, we may be seeing a backsliding away even from previously held positions of tolerance.

In education, debates about diversity also take place in the context of the focus on equity. Many educators have struggled for many years to advance the idea that all children can be successful and that great and ongoing differences in outcomes among various groups — whether gender, ethnic, linguistic, or socioeconomic — ought to be seen as problems to be overcome. The idea that schools should offer quite different kinds of curricula to different students smacks of segregation and raises the concern, supported by a great many examples, that "separate," whatever the rhetoric, usually turns into "unequal" (Osborne, 1999).

Yet at least one strand in thinking about diversity advocates increasingly separate provision, such as single-sex classes or Aboriginal schools or Black-focus schools, on the grounds that mainstream institutions are unlikely to serve the needs of some groups adequately. These issues provoked a heated and sustained public debate in Winnipeg a decade ago when the Winnipeg School Division, responding to strong community pressure, created two Aboriginal-focus schools as part of its provision. Edmonton hosts a significant number of schools aimed at particular religious and ethnic minorities. Girls-only classes have been started in a number of schools and communities, usually creating quite a bit of debate and some opposition.

Of course, schools have always had their program streams, and they have always had some kinds of segregated provision, whether these were academic tracks in high schools or French

[margin note: Separate turns to unequall]

Immersion programs or segregated programs for students who were thought to have various handicaps. One difference is that in the new proposals for separation, people are asking, by and large, to do something on their own, rather than being refused entry by others. Still, to some who fought hard for decades for integrated public schools, these developments are difficult to accept or understand. Whatever one's position on the specifics, these are controversial approaches that raise difficult issues about what we mean by public schooling.

When schools are differentiated by the kinds of students they target, further questions arise immediately about standards and accountability. If Aboriginal students, as an example, would benefit from having their "own" schools within the public system, does this have any implications for curriculum and achievement standards? Should the same curriculum expectations apply, or do separate programs also imply separate evaluation standards? If the latter, how does one guard against the old problem of "separate and unequal," such that separate systems are resourced less well or hold lower expectations for students or provide credentials that do not have wide acceptance?

The status of minority language education in Canada provides a good example of the politically charged environment created by demands for more control over schooling from a segment of the population. As noted, almost every development to strengthen francophone schooling outside Quebec has been the result of court decisions. Many of these moves were politically controversial and would not have occurred without legal direction. In Manitoba in 1983 and 1984, the government's efforts to strengthen legal protection for French in Manitoba's laws and services resulted in the province's worst political crisis in decades and almost led to the government's defeat, as the Opposition was able to whip up a huge amount of public resentment. Other examples could also be cited, such as the heated dispute in British

Columbia over the use of books in schools that depicted same-sex couples with children.

The political volatility of diversity issues is certainly not confined to education, and may actually be much more muted there than in other sectors. One has only to consider the vociferous opposition in some quarters to immigration or to the desire of various immigrant communities to maintain their languages, or the highly aroused feelings — on many sides — around the situation of Aboriginal people in Canada to see that these questions elicit great passions.

Realities of Politics

In trying to manage diversity issues in education, governments face the same pressures as in any other difficult policy area.[2] Governments are concerned about trying to satisfy as many people as possible. That is how they become elected and stay elected, and that is what democratic politics is about. Nor, we can be assured, would we be happier if governments did not care about getting elected. The calls for "political will" are usually calls for governments to do something that we like but most people do not. When governments do something that others like but we do not, we call it "ideology" or "political correctness." The nature of politics is such that for governments, what people believe is much more important than what may actually be true. Voters count more than experts.

Pleasing people is hard enough at any time, but it is important to remember that voters do not need to be either well informed or consistent in their views. There is nothing to stop people from wanting several contradictory things at the same time, and then wanting a different set of things next week. And while that is happening, governments also have to deal with all the events and pressures that crop up unexpectedly, changing everyone's plans (take SARS or "Mad Cow disease" as examples). There is never enough time to think through issues as clearly and fully as one might want. These are some of the reasons that government often equivocates on issues and positions. Where clarity is sure to make a significant number of voters very unhappy, it's understandable that one might not want to be crystal clear.

At the same time, everything governments do is subject to a high degree of scrutiny, including an Official Opposition whose goal it is to put things in as bad a light as possible, and the media, who often seem to have much the same purpose. These unrelenting efforts to depict government decisions as negative are one reason behind today's cynicism and disillusionment about politics.

These general aspects of politics are exacerbated by some dimensions that are particularly applicable to issues of diversity. As already noted, many issues concerning diversity are deeply felt and arouse strong emotions, whether or not people are at all well informed on the matters in question. The sense that someone else is somehow gaining some kind of privilege is one of those things that tends to rankle most of us quite a bit, and that is precisely the dynamic that is often set off by efforts to accommodate diversity in education.

In many cases, too, the differences are difficult to bridge. People see the world in quite different ways, and they may see the issues in terms of a zero-sum game — if you win, I lose. This is always a recipe for political trouble. The increasing presence and political sophistication of many identity groups makes it impossible to ignore their issues, but these same issues are often used as wedges by those in political opposition to mobilize unhappiness with a government.

Finally, we are living at a time when the essential lubricant of politics — money — is in relatively short supply. Thanks to a steady diet of pressure for tax cuts and attacks on the public sector, public spending has shrunk as a share of our national wealth, making it more difficult for governments to satisfy opponents by giving everyone something. That is one reason why governments are not unhappy to have the courts give them orders. This gives them a reason for action without having to own the decision.

What Governments Try to Do

Given the complexity of the challenges and the constraints on possible solutions, what options are available to governments? As usual, government is a matter of trying to find ways to satisfy as many people as possible at least to some degree, while offending as few as possible and especially trying not to arouse strong emotions that can set difficult political dynamics into action. In writing this, I'm reminded of a cartoon that shows a group of people debating an issue. The caption reads: "We've got to give the appearance of changing direction without giving the appearance of changing principles in a way that won't be dismissed as cosmetic." While many people find this humorous, it is often what politics demands, referred to as "building a big tent," where many different people can find something they like. Governments try to adopt policies that are acceptable to most people or sometimes policies that are least likely to set off extremely strong opposition. Yet given the dynamics already described, no Canadian government can proceed as if diversity were not an important issue or without recognizing differences in the way people want and need to be treated. The trick is to frame these differences in ways that do not raise the suspicion that someone is being given particularly favourable treatment.

Often political dynamics lead to governments' giving their supporters less than what they want and expect. Indeed, it is often strong supporters who are most unhappy with a government because it does not act as decisively or quickly as they desire. Only in unusual cases do governments deliberately take on highly divisive issues — generally in order to demonstrate to supporters that they will act decisively and thus strengthen their core support, and sometimes when their ideological beliefs are particularly strong. Though highly visible, these approaches actually affect only a small minority of issues.

A further requirement for governments is to try to keep expectations manageable. Everybody wants things from governments, generally more things than can be delivered, even if they were all mutually consistent, which they never are. So a common strategy is to try to keep expectations modest and not to promise too much. Delivering more than people expected is almost always better politics than delivering less, even if the "more" was in relation to very modest goals. I was told early in my involvement in politics that it was far better to have 50 people in a room made for 40 than to have 250 in a room that holds 500; the former looks like success, the latter like failure.

Current Government Strategies Concerning Diversity

What are Canadian governments, federal and provincial, doing to try to manage diversity issues in education? A short and honest answer would be that they are struggling with how to recognize and respect diversity without unduly alienating too many people. On the whole, education policy in Canada has been moving, slowly and falteringly, toward greater accommodation of diversity, including more differentiation in provision and more choice for parents and students. Legislation and policy related to special education have been shifting gradually toward greater recognition of a variety of student needs and more attention being paid to the wishes of parents in making placement decisions. At the same time, some efforts have begun to try to prevent too many students from being identified as special. Provinces are increasingly attempting to gather data on student outcomes that take into account background. In this way, they can at least be aware of whether students from various backgrounds are all making reasonable progress. However, even the process of identifying and classifying students and families by ethnic or linguistic origin has been controversial, with special dispensation required in most cases from human rights commissions before such data can be collected.

Most provinces now have some form of parent choice of schools, though it is generally rather weak. Multiculturalism and the recognition of differences among ethnic and linguistic groups have been given increasing recognition, even though much confusion remains about how these ideas should be manifested in schools (Joshi & Johnson, 2004). Most provinces also have a variety of forms of provision, including minority language schools, other school programs aimed at particular ethnic or linguistic groups (such as Hutterite or Aboriginal focus or Black focus or bilingual schools), and some recognition and public funding in most provinces for at least a number of forms of private (independent) schooling. Especially in urban settings quite a few schools have some form of specialized program and draw students from outside their immediate area. For example, students in Winnipeg can choose bilingual programs in Hebrew, German, or Ukrainian, French Immersion, Advanced Placement, International Baccalaureate, vocational, multi-graded, music-intensive, sports-focused, Aboriginal, and others. Home schooling has also received increasing official recognition. In fact, Canada has considerable diversity in education provision in comparison with many other countries — especially the United States — even though our official policies in this area are often rather weak (Riffel, Young, & Levin, 1996).

At the same time, governments in Canada are aware that these changes are to some extent problematic. As already noted, political pressure for greater uniformity in education is also significant. The pressure to avoid too much differentiation comes from several different sources. Many conservatives do not like a highly differentiated school system, but many who would describe themselves as being on the political left also uphold an ideal of a single public school system in which children from all parts of society meet and mix. Hence, the opposition to school choice policies. Whether schools in Canada or anywhere else were ever places where everyone mixed or where some general public interest was developed and protected is, in my view, doubtful, but the idea is still ideologically and politically powerful. So while policies provide or at least recognize greater diversity in some respects, in other ways — such as uniform curricula and more centrally determined standards and practices — governments are actually promoting homogeneity.

Governments are naturally criticized for both kinds of policies. Some see greater attention to diversity as leading to a balkanization of Canadian society with dangers to social cohesion and national unity. Others believe that the school system remains in essence hegemonic in its favouring of the mainstream and essentially hostile to the needs and aspirations of most minorities. The debates, such as those over the wearing of a kirpan by a Sikh student or a hijab by a Moslem student or the accommodation of traditional Aboriginal ceremonies or discussion of which holidays should be recognized and celebrated, remain, in many cases, highly charged.

These contradictions are typical of most fields of public policy as governments struggle with how best to balance contradictory or incommensurable values. In the case of education, the struggle is between the recognition of difference, the desire for social cohesion, and the concern that different treatment should still be equitable. There is no simple way to maximize all these values at the same time.

What Educators Might Do

Like many other ordinary citizens, educators tend not to recognize the contradictions and dilemmas facing policy makers. We, too, are likely to call for greater "political will" to do what we think is right without taking all the contradictory pressures into account. So one essential requirement is to recognize that the political issues surrounding diversity, at all levels of education, are complicated and sometimes contradictory. Rather than pushing for simple solutions, we need to recognize the intractability and contentiousness of many of the issues and be a little more modest in our expectations of governments, just as we want them to be reasonable in their expectations for schools.

A second implication for educators is the need to be better at managing conflict. Given diversity in people's ideas and views, there will continue to be conflict about school policies and practices. In much of our approach to education management, we tend to see conflict as something to be avoided. Yet conflict can, under the right conditions and with good management, be part of a process of learning and mutual accommodation. Indeed, that is what we must have if we are to avoid other, much worse alternatives, such as suppression of some people by real internal political strife and violence. Canada is probably as good as any country in the world at managing diversity in opinions without violence, but of course we could still do better. There are numerous techniques for managing conflict effectively, mainly involving various learning and negotiating skills; these need to be developed and encouraged among educators so that we are better able to deal with the difficult, even intractable divisions that are very likely to lie ahead.

At the same time as we work to improve conflict management skills, it will be vitally important for educators to reach out to communities of various kinds. Much conflict starts from lack of understanding and can be avoided if we know more about each other in various ways. These contacts have to extend beyond the "3 Ds" of a surface multiculturalism (dress, dance, diet) to take on some of the more difficult issues connected with very different values and approaches to education. Such discussion is not easy. It requires commitment and patience. It also means that one has to be willing to listen attentively and to respond to real concerns in real ways. This does not mean always doing what parents or community members want, of course, but it does mean taking their ideas seriously and trying to work toward mutually agreeable approaches. It also means recognizing that schools have not always been and are not today always in the right. Schools and educators do understand, increasingly, the importance of community connections, but for the most part, this work remains a relatively low priority and something to be done as time and resources permit. (This often translates into the work not being done at all.)

It will be important, however, not simply to seek accommodation or to avoid conflict, but also to try to maintain a focus on doing what is right and just. Of course, ideas about justice vary from person to person and group to group, but educators have a particular role to play in trying to make the discussion of difference and conflict an educational process — that is, one concerned not just with a resolution, but also with advancing ideals such as inclusion.

While I was in government, I was often visited by people or groups looking for something — usually funding or a policy change. I often made this response to such requests: When you ask for something for yourself, you join a long line of others. I was much more interested when people came to ask for something for somebody else, something in which they did not have the same kind of direct interest. That type of request made me listen. In education we frequently purport to be speaking on behalf of children (though often without ever asking the children), but the altruism often rings hollow. Speaking on behalf of others more than ourselves is always a good political strategy.

What Researchers Might Do

I conclude this essay with some suggestions for academics and researchers concerning issues of diversity and inclusion. My first suggestion is that while advocacy is legitimate — indeed vital — it has to be informed advocacy. Very few researchers, in my experience, have much idea of how politics and government really work, yet we often feel quite justified in criticizing what the political system produces. Such criticism is, as I've already pointed-ed out, our right as citizens. Citizens do not have to be well informed or reasonable. Researchers, however, should regard it as a requirement to be both. That means that we should know whereof we speak when we make pronouncements on policy issues. We have to be willing to face the evidence, as it exists, even when it does not neatly line up with our preferences — as it often does not. We have to be prepared to change our minds in the face of new information and to try to understand how others might see things differently. Many of us do these things, and very well, but such approaches are far from universal.

Much research on education policy focuses on critique, pointing out the limitations and weaknesses of current policies. All policies have weaknesses — in implementation if not in conception. While critique is both legitimate and important, it is not enough. Criticism without proposals for change is insufficient and can even be irresponsible insofar as it contributes to increasing cynicism about politics and government. Nor is it adequate to put forward proposals for change that have little or no public support and hence are simply not available to elected governments. "Making everyone do what I think is right" is not a viable political program.

To affect policy, researchers also need to understand that governments are not convinced primarily by studies but by political processes (Levin, 2004a). To affect policy, researchers need to speak to citizens and voters — primarily through the various organizations of what is called civil society — as a way of bringing ideas into the political debate. Ideas have resonance as they are picked up, adopted, and adapted by political participants. Policies will improve as voter understanding improves with consequent implications for what is acceptable to politicians and governments. This is slow work, but there are no substitutes for it, and it ought to be one of the critical functions of academics.

Living with Diversity

Living with diversity is the great social challenge of the twenty-first century. Humans have a long history of suspecting, mistreating, and even murdering those who are different. Examples of this still surround us today. Ironically, when we accuse people of "behaving like animals." they are usually doing something that is particularly human. While schools are not involved in that kind of violence — indeed, are often leading in much more positive directions — as the early part of this essay shows, educators are not immune to intolerance either. There are no easy answers to the question of how we overcome these deeply rooted human tendencies. We will have to struggle forward, to discover ways in which we can be different, yet live together amicably. We will have to find new ways to resolve differences without violence. Scholarship and research can and should help advance this goal.

NOTES

1 These issues are sketched here only very briefly. A much fuller treatment can be found in Levin (2005).

REFERENCES

Heath, J. (2001). *The efficient society: Why Canada is as good as it gets.* Toronto: Viking.

Holmes, M. (1998). *The reformation of Canada's schools: Breaking the barriers to parental choice.* Montreal: McGill–Queen's University Press.

Joshi, R., & Johnson, L. (2004). Multicultural education in the United States and Canada: The importance of national policies. Paper presented to the American Educational Research Association, San Diego, April.

Levin, B. (2004a, October 17). Making research matter more. *Education Policy Analysis Archives, 12*(56). http://epaa.asu.edu/epaa/v12n56/.

(2004b). Students at risk: A review of research. Report to The Learning Partnership. **http://www.thelearningpartnership.ca/Progress_Report/Progress_Report2004en.pdf.**

(2005). *Governing education.* Toronto: University of Toronto Press.

Osborne, K. (1999). *Education: A guide to the Canadian school debate.* Toronto: Penguin.

Riffel, J., Young, J., & Levin, B. (1996). Diversity in Canadian education. *Journal of Education Policy, 11*(1), 113–123.

Ryan, J. (2003). *Leading diverse schools.* Dordrecht: Kluwer.

Raising and Levelling the Learning Bar in Canadian Schools

J. Douglas Willms

O ver the past decade there has been an increasing demand for strong literacy skills to facilitate participation in the new economy, and this trend is likely to continue (Dickerson & Green, 2004; Machin, 2001; Statistics Canada & OECD, 2005). The development of a healthy, highly skilled labour force is considered critical to employment and sustained economic growth. In addition to literacy and numeracy skills, the new economy also places a premium on the ability of individuals to adapt quickly to change, solve problems, and improve technological and organizational processes (Bailey, 1997). It requires workers who are healthy, both physically and mentally, and who can work productively as part of a team. Like most countries, Canada is concerned with the integration of its youth into the labour market. It set two goals as part of the 2002 Innovation Strategy: (1) that Canada become one of the top three countries in mathematics, science, and reading achievement and (2) that all students who graduate from high school achieve a level of literacy sufficient to participate in the knowledge-based economy. To reach these milestones, Canada must raise levels of literacy, especially for those from lower socioeconomic backgrounds.

In 2001, the Social Science and Humanities Research Council of Canada launched a five-year research program, the

Initiative on the New Economy (INE), aimed at helping Canadians adapt successfully and benefit from the new economy. The Canadian Research Institute for Social Policy (CRISP) at the University of New Brunswick was funded under the INE program to develop a collaborative research program. This program brought together a multi-disciplinary team of researchers to focus their research and training efforts over a four-year period on a single question: *"How can we raise and level the bar?"* or specifically *"How can we improve the learning, behaviour, and health outcomes of our youth, while reducing inequalities associated with family background?"* The program has also received support from the New Brunswick Department of Education and the Canadian Institute for Advanced Research (CIAR). The program of research is being carried out by a national network of 30 scholars dedicated to research on the development of children and youth. It is organized around five themes: (1) safeguarding the healthy development of infants; (2) strengthening early childhood education; (3) improving schools and local communities; (4) reducing segregation and the effects associated with poverty; and (5) creating a family-enabling society. This essay provides background on the program and presents some of the early findings.

The Learning Bar

Canada has been participating in the Programme for International Assessment (PISA) since it began in the spring of 2000. PISA is a study of the literacy skills in reading, mathematics, and science of 15-year-old youth in each participating country. The PISA assessments of knowledge and skills differ from previous international school assessments in that they are not based on school curriculum common to participating countries; rather, they assess the kinds of general literacy skills that youth will need when they enter postsecondary education and the labour market. The survey includes an extensive background questionnaire that is completed by students. It covers issues pertaining to their family background, their engagement in literacy activities at home and at school, and their school and classroom experiences. The survey also includes a school questionnaire completed by the school administrator, which covers various aspects of school resources and features of the school, as well as classroom learning climate. The first international report, *Knowledge and Skills for Life: First Results from the OECD Programme for International Student Assessment (PISA) 2000,* (Organisation for Economic Co-operation and Development, 2001), provided a comparison among countries in student performance in reading, mathematics, and scientific literacy. Willms (2006) has examined how performance in these domains is related to students' family background and the features of the schools students attend.

Canadian 15-year-old youth fared exceptionally well on the PISA 2000 and 2003 assessments compared with students in other OECD countries. In the 2000 assessment, which emphasized reading skills, Canada ranked 2nd in reading literacy among OECD countries, 6th in mathematics, and 5th in science. It maintained that position in the 2003 PISA. Generally, Canada has improved its international standing in international assessments over the past decade and is now among a group of seven or eight top-scoring countries in the world.

These results suggest that the Innovation Strategy milestones are within reach. If Canada improved its score by 15 points in each domain over the next decade and assuming that other countries have scores similar to those of the year 2000, Canada will be in first place in reading, second place in mathematics, and third place in science. However, these are not the most important goals. Despite Canada's success in international comparisons, large inequalities in achievement are associated with socioeconomic status, and there is a disproportionate number of students compared with other countries with very low literacy scores —

at levels 1 and 2, which is at the bottom end of the PISA literacy distribution (Willms, 2004). This is of great concern because a high proportion of adults with low levels of literacy skills can be a barrier to long-term macroeconomic growth (Coulombe, Tremblay, & Marchand, 2004).

Socioeconomic gradients are a useful policy device for shifting the emphasis of evaluation toward issues concerning inequalities associated with socioeconomic status, gender, and ethnicity. A socioeconomic *gradient* simply describes the relationship between a social outcome and socioeconomic status for individuals in a specific jurisdiction, such as a school, a province or state, or a country (Willms, 2003a). In PISA, for example, the social outcomes might be reading literacy or student engagement. Socioeconomic status (SES) refers to the relative position of an individual or family on a hierarchical social structure, based on their access to, or control over, wealth, prestige, and power (Mueller & Parcel, 1981). The most important indicators of SES in educational research include the level of education of students' parents, the prestige of the parents' occupations, and family income. In many studies, however, it is difficult to collect data on family income; therefore, measures describing possessions in the home are used as a proxy.

Figure 1 shows the socioeconomic gradient for reading performance for Canada, based on PISA 2000 data. The vertical axis has two scales: the left-hand scale is the continuous scale for reading performance, which has a mean of 500 and a standard deviation of 100 for all students in participating OECD countries. The right-hand axis depicts the five reading levels, which are described in *Knowledge and Skills for Life*. The horizontal axis is family SES, which is a statistical composite derived from a factor analysis of five factors describing family background: the prestige of the parents' occupations, the level of education of the parents, a measure of wealth pertaining to material possessions in

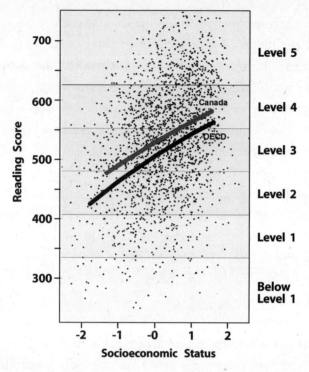

Figure 1: Socioeconomic Gradient for Reading Performance

the home, a measure describing access to educational possessions in the home, and a measure of culturally related possessions in the home, such as musical instruments and books of poetry. The five factors contribute approximately equally to the SES composite. The measure was scaled to have a mean of zero and a standard deviation of one at the student level for OECD countries.

Socioeconomic gradients comprise three components: their level, their slope, and the strength of the outcome-SES relationship. The *level* of the gradient is defined as the expected score on the outcome measure for a person with average SES. The level of a gradient for a country (or for a province or state, or a school) is an indicator of its average performance, after taking students' socioeconomic status into account. The level of the Canadian gradient is 527. The *slope* of the gradient indicates the extent of inequality attributable to socioeconomic status. Steeper gradients indicate a greater impact of SES on student performance — that is, more inequality — while more gradual gradients indicate a lower impact of SES — that is, less inequality. The slope of the Canadian gradient is 36.9 (in the centre of the data), which indicates that the expected reading performance increases by about 37 points for a one standard deviation increase in SES. The *strength* of the gradient refers to the proportion of variance in the social outcome that is explained by SES. If the strength of the relationship is strong, then a considerable amount of the variation in the outcome measure is associated with SES, whereas a weak relationship indicates that relatively little of the variation is associated with SES. The most common measure of the strength of the relationship is a measure called R-squared, which for Canada in this case is 0.11.

The gradient line is drawn from the 5th to the 95th percentile of the SES scores for a particular population. For Canada, the 5th and 95th percentiles are 1.25 and 1.56, respectively; 90 percent of Canadian students fall within this range. The average SES for Canada is 0.27, or about one-quarter of a standard deviation above the OECD average. The 5th and 95th percentiles for all OECD students are -1.71 and 1.55, respectively. These are the small black dots above and below the gradient line. They show that there is considerable variation in reading performance at all levels of SES.

The term "learning bar" is used by the research team as a metaphor for the socioeconomic gradient. The central question facing most schools and countries is "How can we raise and level the learning bar?" Increasing educational performance and reducing inequalities among students from differing socioeconomic backgrounds can be achieved in a number of ways. There is no best "policy mix" for a school district or province; it depends on a number of economic, social, and political issues. The aim of the research program, however, is to provide some direction as to what kinds of interventions and policies are most likely to be successful. The program is organized around five strategies described below.

Strategy 1. Safeguard the Healthy Development of Infants

The course of brain development from conception to age one is rapid and extensive — much more so than previously believed — and it is heavily influenced by an infant's environment (Carnegie Corporation of New York, 1994). A newborn has billions of neurons, which, during the course of development, form connections called synapses. These synapses are formed in response to environmental stimuli, and while this is occurring, many of the neurons that are not being used are pruned away. This process of synapse formation and neuron pruning is often referred to as the "sculpting" or "wiring" of the brain. Moreover, there are critical periods, especially during the first three years, when particular areas of the brain are sculpted (Cynader & Frost, 1999; McEwan & Schmeck, 1994). Research on the biological systems of animals suggests that infants receive signals from their environment which alter and become embedded in certain physiological and neurobiological systems, thereby affecting later cognitive development, behaviour, and health (Liu et al., 1997; Nelson & Panksepp, 1998; Suomi, 1997, 1999). That is, the differential social experiences of infants "get under the skin" (Barr, Beek, & Calinoiu, 1999). From this perspective, neither heredity nor environment is all important; it is their interaction that matters. The research on children's early language development emphasizes the importance of this interaction. Children begin hearing sounds *in utero,* during the third trimester of pregnancy (DeCasper et al., 1994). Soon after they are born, they can distinguish the sound of their mother's voice from that of other women (Kisilevsky et al., 2003). During their first year, children can perceive and attend to different sounds, and they begin to learn the words of their native language (Werker & Tees, 2002). At about 12 months, most children say their first recognizable word, and soon thereafter there are several words in their spoken vocabulary. Although the growth in vocabulary for most children is rapid and exponential (Huttenlocher et al., 1991), not all children develop language at the same rate. The rate of growth depends on their exposure to language in the home and to the quality of interactions with their parents (Hart & Risley, 1995). The longitudinal research by Tremblay and his colleagues also supports the importance of understanding how environmental factors interact with genetics. Their work examines the course of physical aggression during the early years (Tremblay et al., 2004). In a study that followed children from 17 to 42 months, they found that children could be classified into three groups: children with little or no aggression (28% of the sample of 572 children); children with a modest rise in aggression (58%), and children with a high and rising level of aggression (14%). Children whose mothers had displayed antisocial behaviours during high school, had early pregnancies, or had smoked during pregnancy were more likely to have children in the last, most aggressive group. Moreover, children who display aggression at an early age are more likely to display violent behaviours during adolescence (Broidy, Nagin, & Tremblay, 1999; Nagin & Tremblay, 1999). Côté and her colleagues have conducted similar research based on the National Longitudinal Survey of Children and Youth (NLSCY) and have found similar patterns (Côté, Vaillancourt, LeBlanc, Nagin, & Tremblay, 2006). The Learning Bar research team is following two veins of research. One is using data from Canada's National Longitudinal Survey of Children and Youth (NLSCY) to ask, *"What risk and protective factors during pregnancy and infancy best predict the developmental trajectories that lead to good performance at school entry?* The early results suggest that while socioeconomic factors play an important role, it is also possible to identify a number of family parenting practices and neighbourhood factors that are important. Dubois and Girard (2005), for example, studied the protective role of breast feeding on children's health and its relationship to daycare attendance during the first five years of life. They found that the positive effects of breast feeding on health persist up to the second year of life, even in the presence of daycare attendance. Breast feeding reduced the number of antibiotic treatments given to children entering daycare before two-and-a-half years of age. The study also indicated that children who were most vulnerable could be protected by breast feeding and by being taken care of in a familial setting, especially before three years of age The second vein of research is concerned with the kinds of interventions that tend to be successful in improving developmental outcomes during infancy. For example, Letourneau and her colleagues have launched a program investigating the protective effects of a support program for mothers experiencing post-partum depression. Her research builds on that of Stewart (2000), who has found that support for mothers who are experiencing post-partum depression, in the form of regular visits from women who have previously experienced post-partum depression, holds great promise for treating the illness. Other team members are interested in replicating the work of Olds and his colleagues, who have shown that home visitation programs, combined with parent training and support, have long-lasting effects on a wide range of children's outcomes, including children's language and speech development, behaviour, and health (Olds et al., 1997, 1998).

Strategy 2. Strengthen Early Childhood Education

In Canada, the number of children being cared for outside the home in various types of care arrangements has been increasing steadily for the past 25 years (Kohen, Hertzman, & Willms, 2002a). Research on the quality of early childcare provision has emphasized three factors: low child-to-adult ratios, highly educated staff with specialized training, and the availability of facilities and equipment to provide stimulating activities (Arnett, 1989; Howes, Phillips, & Whitebrook, 1992; Lazar et al., 1982; Phillips, 1987). These are the dimensions of quality that distinguish "day-cares," with their custodial function, from early childhood development (ECD) centres, which emphasize growth in children's development. Studies in Canada (Goelman & Pence, 1987); the United States (Burchinal, Roberts, & Nabors, 1996; McCartney, 1984; Peterson & Peterson, 1986), and Sweden (Andersson, 1989, 1992) have demonstrated that the quality of care offered in ECD centres affects children's linguistic, cognitive, and social competencies. Moreover, research based on the NLSCY suggests that children from low-income families who attend either regulated or unregulated ECD centres have, on average, stronger vocabulary skills at ages four and five than those cared for at home, either by parents or a relative (Kohen, Hertzman, & Willms, 2002a).

These findings are consistent with the research demonstrating the importance of the quantity and quality of parental speech. However, the research on early childhood has not adequately explicated what "quality care" is or determined the critical elements of quality learning environments for preschool children. We do not know the extent to which we can alter growth trajectories. For example, is it feasible to identify early — at 24 months, for example — the children who are growing at a rather slow pace and then intervene in a significant way to increase their rate of growth? The research team's work under this theme has three guiding questions:

1. What is the earliest age at which one can reliably detect differences in the developmental trajectories of preschool children's language and cognitive skills and in their behavioural development?

2. What are the critical elements of a quality learning environment during the early years?

3. Can we alter growth trajectories by altering environments?

Research based on the NLSCY demonstrates that many factors present in the early years of children's development affect their later success at school. Linguistic development in the preschool years, for example, is a strong predictor of how well children do in school. A child who is rarely spoken to, or read to, in the early years often has difficulty mastering language skills later in life. Those children who have more educated mothers have a substantial advantage, and for those who do not, benefits can come from the stimulus of quality childcare and preschool education (Willms, 2002).

Borge, Rutter, Côté, and Tremblay (2004) examined the prevalence of physical aggression among Canadian two- and three-year-olds, using data from the NLSCY. They found that children attending daycares were less likely than their counterparts cared for at home by their mothers to display physical aggression. However, these effects were evident only for children in high-risk families once the children's family background was taken into account.

Hertzman et al. (2002) have used the Early Development Instrument (EDI) (Janus & Offord, 2000) to map childhood vulnerability around the city of Vancouver based on the school district where children live. The EDI asks kindergarten teachers to rate their students on a number of measures of school readiness. Their research provides a baseline of the state of early child development, its social and economic determinants, and the resources available for children aged zero to five in Vancouver. They show that threats to healthy childhood development are found across the entire socioeconomic spectrum, although at increasing intensity as one goes from areas with high to low average income. Willms and Beswick (2005a, 2005b) developed a skills-based assessment tool called the Early Years Evaluation (EYE), which is being used in national evaluations sponsored by the World Bank in Jordan and the Dominican Republic and in a study of children's school progress in emerging literacy skills in 26 schools in New Brunswick. The EYE is based on a framework that comprises five domains:

1. awareness of self and environment (general knowledge),

2. social skills, behaviour, and approaches to learning,

3. cognitive skills,

4. language and communication, and

5. physical development (gross and fine motor skills).

The EYE has two parallel instruments: a teacher-based assessment that can be completed online or in paper-and-pencil format (following a "rate-by-trait" approach) and a direct assessment administered by an independent assessor. The assessment requires teachers to rate children's skills (e.g., "Can this child recognize less familiar animals such as tiger, elephant, octopus, and penguin?"), which places higher demands on teachers' knowledge of their students than rating scales that simply ask teachers to make subjective ratings of students' abilities (e.g., "How would you rate this child's ability to tell a story?" ... poor to excellent).

A number of studies of the EYE with Canadian samples have found it to be highly reliable, with reliability coefficients ranging from 0.90 to 0.96 across the five subtests. In addition, scores on the language and communication and cognitive skills subtests are strongly correlated with scores on the *Wechsler Individual Achievement Test — Word Reading Subtest (WIAT)* and two subtests of emerging literacy skills assessed with the

Dynamic Indicators of Basic Early Literacy Skills (DIBELS). Because the EYE is skills based, it can be used to identify children who may need extra help in developing their reading and numeracy skills. Data can also be aggregated to the community level to monitor changes in developmental outcomes over time.

Strategy 3. Improve Schools and Local Communities

The influential 1966 report on educational inequality in the United States (Coleman et al., 1966) suggested that "schools do *not* make a difference": the researchers found that relatively little variation in schooling outcomes was attributable to the schools children attended after the socioeconomic background of students' parents had been taken into account. This report spawned numerous studies of school effectiveness aimed at uncovering whether schools did indeed differ in their "added value" (Scheerens, 1992). During the 1970s and 1980s, researchers made marked improvements in the quality of educational achievement tests, sampling methods, and the statistical models used to study school achievement (Gray, 1989; Haertle, 1986; Willms, 1992). The research stressed the importance of using both individual- and school-level data to estimate school effects using multilevel techniques (Raudenbush & Bryk, 2002; Raudenbush & Willms, 1995). It also found that analyses of student *growth* based on individual growth trajectories provide an accurate and powerful means to assess the effects or added value associated with schools (Willms & Jacobsen, 1990).

During the 1990s, researchers placed greater emphasis on understanding *why* schools differed in their added value. The research showed that some of the differences among schools were attributable to measurable aspects of "school climate," such as teacher-student relations and the disciplinary climate of the school, which can be influenced by teachers' and principals' policies and practices (Bryk, Lee, & Smith, 1990). It also indicated that student performance was higher in schools that practised heterogeneous grouping and team teaching (Lee & Smith, 1993) and in schools where there was a higher level of parental involvement (Ho & Willms, 1996). The research during this period also strived to situate teaching resources and practices within their cultural context. It emphasized the importance of the dynamics of authority and power among students, teachers, and administrators in hierarchically organized schooling systems (e.g., Apple, 1990; McNeil, 1986; Mehan, 1992).

This research contributed to the efforts of educators who argued that schools needed to be "restructured" in ways that enabled them to be more supportive, and they also needed to have a stronger orientation toward achieving success for all children (Fullan, 1992; Levin, 1987; Madden, Slavin, Karweit, & Livermon, 1989). Over the past two decades, a number of restructuring models have been implemented in several countries. They emphasize prevention over remediation, a highly contextualized curriculum with strong components in reading and language, parental participation, and site-based governance structures (Borman, Hewes, Overman, & Brown, 2002; King, 1994).

At this juncture, we need a much better understanding of the nature of children's growth trajectories in academic achievement. The research also needs to be broadened to include other schooling outcomes, such as student engagement in school, behavioural disorders, and physical and mental health. We also need analyses that describe variation among jurisdictions in their growth trajectories: for example, do students in provinces that have consistently scored lower in studies like PISA fall behind gradually year to year or are there particular stages in children's school careers when they fall behind.

Also, relatively few of the programs aimed at restructuring schools have been subject to careful evaluation, and we do not know the extent to which children's growth trajectories can be deflected through efforts to change school structure and teacher practice.

Three of the guiding questions of this program of research are:

1. To what extent do schools and provinces differ in their growth trajectories of schooling outcomes in academic achievement, student engagement, and behaviour?

2. What are the critical elements of school reform that alter children's growth trajectories?

3. When, and for how long, should one intervene to alter children's growth trajectories?

Willms' (2003b) analysis of the PISA data revealed a high prevalence of student disaffection in most countries, gauged by their sense of belonging at school and their school participation. On average, about one-quarter of all students in OECD countries had a low sense of belonging, while about one-fifth had very low participation. However, the measures of engagement were not strongly correlated with reading or mathematics performance. Schools that are best at limiting student disaffection include those where students come from more advantaged homes, but also those with a strong disciplinary climate, good student-teacher relations, and high expectations, regardless of social composition. Schools where students feel a sense of belonging also tend to achieve lower absenteeism. Willms argued that student engagement should be viewed as an important schooling outcome in its own right, as it is related to students' ability to work with others and function in a social institution. It also affects their short- and long-term aspirations.

Strategy 4. Reduce Segregation and the Effects Associated with Poverty

Nearly all school systems are segregated along socioeconomic lines: there are schools that predominantly serve children from poor family backgrounds, while others serve children from relatively well-to-do backgrounds. A useful index of segregation is the proportion of variance in socioeconomic status (SES) between schools, which theoretically can range from zero for a completely desegregated system, in which the distribution of SES is the same in every school, to 1.0 for a system in which students within schools have the same SES score but the schools vary in their average SES (Willms & Paterson, 1995).

Among OECD countries, the index of segregation ranges from 0.12 for Finland, Norway, and Sweden, to 0.51 for Mexico. Canada's level of segregation is 0.19, which is considerably lower than that of the United States, at 0.27. In non-OECD countries the level of segregation tends to be higher, typically around 0.50 (Willms, 2006). Some segregation stems from residential segregation (especially in cities) and between urban and rural areas. Often, however, the level of segregation is exacerbated by specific features of a schooling system. These include private schools, the streaming of students into vocational and academic programs, and "open enrolment" policies that allow parents to choose schools outside their designated catchment area. Other types of school choice programs, such as language-immersion programs, magnet schools, and charter schools can also contribute to socioeconomic segregation. Research in the United States and the United Kingdom suggests that educational policies that promote greater parental choice may increase segregation, because parents with more resources are more likely to exercise choice (Echols & Willms, 1995; Lee, Groninger, & Smith, 1994).The contexts of schools with higher average socioeconomic status tend to have several advantages. For example, in most countries such schools are more likely to have higher levels of material and human resources — more computers or better-trained teachers, for example. Schools of higher average socioeconomic status are also more likely to have an atmosphere that is conducive to learning — fewer disciplinary problems, higher expectations for academic success, and greater parental support, for example (Willms, 2006). Peer effects also occur when bright and motivated students work together. Consequently, when students are segregated, either between classes or tracks within schools, or between schools within a community, students from advantaged backgrounds tend to do better, while those from disadvantaged backgrounds tend to do worse. This important relationship was evident in every country that participated in PISA (Willms, 2006).

Segregation seems to be especially harmful for disadvantaged students; thus, the term "double jeopardy" (Willms, 2003a). Relatively little work has been done to examine the effects of school composition on behavioural or health outcomes, such as conduct disorders or depression. Willms (2003b) found strong contextual effects associated with students' sense of belonging at school and their levels of truancy. Two important factors that give rise to composition effects are the disciplinary climate of the classroom and teacher-student relations. We expect, therefore, that contextual factors may be especially important for health and behavioural outcomes. We are also interested in the broader effects of segregation in local communities. For example, research based on the NLSCY indicates that children from lower socioeconomic backgrounds are less likely to participate in arts and recreation programs (Donnolly & Coakley, 2002; Offord, Lipman, & Duku, 1998).

The guiding questions for this theme are:

1. To what extent does the average ability or socioeconomic status of the school or classroom a child attends affect his or

her growth trajectories in cognitive, behavioural, and health outcomes?

2. What are the mechanisms by which poverty and welfare status in particular are markers of inferior outcomes of children and youth?

3. To what extent and under what conditions do mainline arts and recreation programs attempt to include marginalized children into their programs?

4. What are the critical life skills that help youth cope with segregated environments?

Research by Kohen et al. (2002b) on neighbourhood effects in Vancouver suggests that children whose family backgrounds put them at risk but who live in mixed-income neighbourhoods tend to be protected compared to their counterparts in low-SES neighbourhoods. The findings suggest that mixed neighbourhoods lead to lower levels of developmental vulnerability than economically segregated poor neighbourhoods. Tremblay, Ross, and Berthelot (2002) have found that health regions exert a modest but significant effect on individuals' health status, and analyses of the Canadian Community Health Survey data have suggested that neighbourhoods within the city of Montreal exert an even larger influence on health status than does the health region (Ross, Tremblay, & Graham, 2004).

Strategy 5. Create a Family-Enabling Society

The primary message of the NLSCY research on vulnerable children is that the quality of children's environments within their families, their schools, and their local communities has a great effect on children's cognitive and behavioural development and on the prevalence of childhood vulnerability:

> This finding requires us to shift our thinking from childhood vulnerability as being a problem stemming from

poverty and single parenting to vulnerability as a problem arising from the environments in which children are raised. It requires us to focus less on ameliorating risk factors to creating environments that support children's development.

The research indicates that the important factors are parenting skills, the cohesiveness of the family unit, the mental health of the mother, and the extent to which parents engage with their children, and that these features affect and are affected by the neighbourhood, the school, and the wider community. The social policy mandate is much broader, therefore, than simply offering parenting programs, increasing counseling for adolescents and parents, or building more parks and playgrounds. We need to envisage a family-enabling society and renew social policy such that families and communities receive the support they need to raise their children. (Willms, 2002, p. 366)

At the outset of the research on childhood vulnerability, we hypothesized that low socioeconomic status would be strongly related to childhood outcomes and that most of its effects would be *mediated* by family environmental factors such as parental depression, family functioning, parenting style, and the extent to which parents engaged with their children. However, the findings clearly indicated that the relationships between SES and these environmental factors were relatively weak; SES and environment acted almost independently of each other in their effects on childhood outcomes.

These findings are consistent with the classic work of Furstenberg et al. (1999), who found that many low-income parents work very hard at managing their children's use of time so as to minimize children's risks and to maximize their development. At a micro level, we need a better understanding of the factors that shape family life (Fussell & Gauthier, 2003). One way to investigate questions about family life is through a detailed study of how parents and children spend their time. Time use is related to each of the family environmental factors, and there is considerable evidence that parents' time use is related to children's developmental outcomes (Amato & Rivera, 1999; Cooksey & Fondell, 1996; Thomson, Hanson, & McLanahan, 1994). The manner in which children use their time is also related to their developmental outcomes and may partially explain differential outcomes for youth from differing socioeconomic and ethnic backgrounds (Sayer, Gauthier, & Furstenberg, 2004). Moreover, time use is a construct that can be measured reliably and is amenable to intervention.

The research program has four guiding questions under this theme:

1. Can family factors explain some of the geographic variation in childhood outcomes observed in PISA and in the NLSCY?

2. What is the amount and the nature of time spent with children by mothers and fathers?

3. What are the determinants of children's structured and unstructured time?

4. What roles do income, parental education, parenting style, and neighbourhood environment play in shaping the time use of mothers and fathers?

Gauthier et al. (2004) provide estimates of time spent by parents on childcare activities since the early 1960s. Building on earlier work, especially the research of Bianchi (2000), and Sayer, Bianchi, & Robinson (2004), the authors used 24-hour time use diaries from 16 industrialized countries to discern whether mothers and fathers really are spending more time with their children. The results suggest that despite the time pressures confronting today's families, parents appear to be devoting more time to children than they did 40 years ago. Mothers continue to devote more time to childcare than fathers, but the gender gap has been reduced. The consistency of these results across countries suggests a global trend toward an increase in parental time investment in children.

Strohschein's (2005) study of children of divorced families provides a good example of the power of analyses based on longitudinal data. Using the NLSCY data, she examined the trajectories of children's anxiety and antisocial behaviours for children who were living with their two biological parents in 1994. By 1998 some of the children's parents had divorced, while the majority remained married. She found that even before a marital breakup, the children whose parents later divorced exhibited higher levels of anxiety/depression and antisocial behaviour than those whose parents remained married. Moreover, the pre-divorce levels of family functioning explained some of the differences, and average levels of antisocial behaviour decreased when marriages in highly dysfunctional families were dissolved.

Concluding Remarks

The PISA results suggest that Canadian youth are faring quite well in their academic achievement. However, there are still large inequalities associated with family background. One of the important themes in the research for this INE program is that if we are to raise the learning bar, we must do so by levelling it. This means adopting strong policies and programs that will improve the outcomes of our most vulnerable youth. Another theme is that we need a comprehensive strategy that focuses not only on schools, but also on families and communities. Our most promising strategies for improving performance and reducing inequities are multi-faceted, and these begin at birth. Raising and levelling the bar will not likely be achieved by any single strategy or reform. It will require a comprehensive approach aimed at safeguarding the healthy development of babies, strengthening early childhood programs, reducing poverty and segregation, enabling families, and improving schools.

149

NOTE

The author is appreciative of funding from the Social Sciences and Humanities Research Council for its support of the collaborative research program *Raising and Levelling the Bar in Children's Cognitive, Behavioural and Health Outcomes* (Grant Number 512–2003–1016) and for support from the Canadian Institute for Advanced Research. He also appreciates support from members of the research team who contributed to the proposal for the INE grant and from Stacey Wilson-Forsberg for comments on earlier drafts of this article.

REFERENCES

Amato, P.R., & Rivera, F. (1999). Paternal involvement and children's behavior problems. *Journal of Marriage and the Family, 61*, 375–384.

Andersson, B.E. (1989). Effects of day-care on cognitive and socio-emotional competence of thirteen-year-old Swedish children. *Child Development, 63*, 20–26.

(1992). Effects of public day-care: A longitudinal study. *Child Development, 60*(4), 857–866.

Apple, M. (1990). *Ideology and curriculum.* New York: Routledge.

Arnett, J. (1989). Caregivers in day-care centers: Does training matter? *Journal of Applied Developmental Psychology, 10*, 541–552.

Bailey, T. (1997). Changes in the nature of work: Implications for skills and assessment. In H.F. O'Neil (Ed.), *Workforce readiness: Competencies and assessment.* Mahwah, NJ: Lawrence Erlbaum Associates.

Barr, R.G., Beek, P.J., Calinoiu, N. (1999). Challenges to nonlinear modelling of infant emotion regulation in real and developmental time. In G.J.P. Savelsbergh, H. van der Maas, & P. van Geert (Eds), *Non-linear developmental processes* (pp. 15–37). Amsterdam: Elsevier Science Publishers.

Bianchi, S. (2000). Maternal employment and time with children: Dramatic change or surprising continuity? *Demography 37*(4), 401–414.

Borge, A.I.H., Rutter, M., Côté, S., & Tremblay, R.E. (2004). Early childcare and physical aggression: Differentiating social selection and social causation. *Journal of Child Psychology & Psychiatry & Allied Disciplines, 45*(2), 367–376.

Borman, G.D., Hewes, G.M., Overman, L.T., & Brown, S. (2002). *Comprehensive school reform and student achievement: A meta-analysis.* Baltimore: Johns Hopkins University, CRESPAR.

Broidy, L.H., Nagin, D., & Tremblay, R. (1999). The linkage of trajectories of children's externalizing behaviours to later violent and non-violent delinquency. Paper presented at the Biennial Meeting of the Society for Child Development, Albuquerque, New Mexico.

Bryk, A.S., Lee, V.E., & Smith, J.B. (1990). High school organization and its effects on teachers and students: An interpretative summary of the research. In W.H. Clune & J.F. Witte (Eds.), *Choice and control in American education: Vol. 1. The theory of choice and control in education*. London: Falmer Press.

Burchinal, M.R., Roberts, J.E., & Nabors, L.A. (1996). Quality of center child care and infant cognitive and language development. *Child Development, 67*, 606–620.

Carnegie Corporation of New York. (1994). *Starting points: Meeting the needs of our youngest children*. New York: Carnegie Corp.

Coleman, J.S., Campbell, E.Q., Hobson, C.J., MacPartland, J., Mood, A.M., Weinfeld, F.D. & York, R.L. (1996). *Equality of Educational Opportunity*. Washington, D.C.: Government Printing Office.

Cooksey, E., & Fondell, M.M. (1996). Spending time with his kids: Effects of family structure on father's and children's lives. *Journal of Marriage and the Family, 58*, 693–707.

Côté, S., Vaillancourt, T., LeBlanc, J.C., Nagin, D.S., & Tremblay, R.E. (2006). The development of physical aggression from toddlerhood to pre-adolescence: A nation wide longitudinal study of Canadian children. *Journal of Abnormal Child Psychology, 34*(1), 68–82.

Coulombe, S., Tremblay, G.F., & Marchand, S. (2004). *Literacy scores, human capital, and growth across fourteen OECD countries*. Ottawa: Statistics Canada.

Cynader, M.S., & Frost, B.J. (1999). Mechanisms of brain development: Neuronal sculpting by the physical and social environment. In D.P. Keating & C. Hertzman (Eds.), *Developmental health and the wealth of nations* (pp. 153–184). New York: Guilford Press.

DeCasper, A.J., LeCanuet, J.-P., Busnel, M.-C., Granier-Deferre, C., & Maugeais, R. (1994). Fetal reactions to recurrent maternal speech. *Infant Behavior and Development, 17*, 159–164.

Dickerson, A., & Green, F. (2004). The growth and valuation of computing and other generic skills. *Oxford Economic Papers, 56*(3), 371–406.

Donnolly, P., & Coakley, J. (2002, December). The role of recreation in promoting social inclusion. In *Perspectives on social inclusion*. Toronto: Laidlaw Foundation.

Dubois, L., & Girard, M. (2005). Breast-feeding, day-care attendance and the frequency of antibiotic treatments from 1.5 to 5 Years: A population-based longitudinal study in Canada. *Social Science & Medicine, 60*(9), 2035–2044.

Echols, F.H., & Willms, J.D. (1995). Reasons for school choice in Scotland. *Journal of Education Policy, 10*(2), 143–156.

Fullan, M. (1992). *Successful school improvement: The implementation perspective and beyond.* Buckingham: Open University Press.

Furstenberg, F.F., Jr., Cook, T., Eccles, J., Elder, G.H., Jr., & Sameroff, A. (1999). *Managing to make it: Urban families in high-risk neighborhoods.* Chicago: University of Chicago Press.

Fussell, E., & Gauthier, A.H. (2003). Introduction: Dimensions of children's inequalities. *Journal of Comparative Family Studies, 34,*331–320.

Gauthier, A.H., Smeeding, T.M., & Furstenberg, F.F., Jr., (2004). Are parents investing less time in children? Trends in selected industrialized countries. *Population & Development Review, 30*(4), 647–671.

Goelman, H., & Pence, A. (1987). The impact of day care, family and individual characteristics on children's language development. In D. Phillips (Ed.), *Predictors of quality child care.* NAEYC Monograph Series. Washington, DC: National Association for the Education of Young Children.

Gray, J. (1989). Multilevel models: Issues and problems emerging from their recent application in British studies of school effectiveness. In D.R. Bock (Ed.), *Multi-level analyses of educational data* (pp. 127145). Chicago: University of Chicago Press.

Haertle, E.H. (1986). Measuring school performance to improve school practice. *Education and Urban Society, 18*(3), 312–325.

Hart, B., & Risley, T.R. (1995). *Meaningful differences in the everyday experience of young American children.* Baltimore: P.H. Brookes.

Hertzman, C., McLean, S., Kohen, D., Dunn, J., & Evans, T. (2002). Early development in Vancouver: Report of the Community Asset Mapping Project (CAMP). Vancouver: Human Early Learning Partnership.

Ho, S.-C., & Willms, J.D. (1996). The effects of parental involvement on eighth grade achievement. *Sociology of Education, 69,* 126–141.

Howes, C., Phillips, D.A., & Whitebrook, M. (1992). Thresholds of quality: Implications for the social development of children in center-based child care. *Child Development, 63,* 449–460.

Huttenlocher, J., Haight, W., Bryk, A., Seltzer, M., & Lyons, T. (1991). Early vocabulary growth: Relation to language input and gender. *Developmental Psychology, 27*(2), 236–248.

Janus, M., & Offord, D. (2000). Readiness to learn at school. *Canadian Journal of Policy Research, 1*(2), 71–75.

Kisilevsky, B.S., Hains, S.M., Lee, K., Xie, X., Huang, H., Ye, H.H., Zhang, K., & Wang, Z. (2003). Effects of experience on fetal voice recognition. *Psychological Science, 14*(3), 220–224.

King, J.A. (1994). Meeting the educational needs of at-risk students: A cost analysis of three models. *Educational Evaluation and Policy Analysis, 16*(1), 1–19.

Kohen, D., Hertzman, C., & Willms, J.D. (2002). The importance of quality child care. In J.D. Willms (Ed.), *Vulnerable children: Findings from Canada's National Longitudinal Study of Children and Youth* (pp. 105–120). Edmonton: University of Alberta Press.

Kohen, D.E., Brooks–Gunn, J., Leventhal, T., & Hertzman, C. (2002). Neighborhood income and physical and social disorder in Canada: Associations with young children's competencies. *Child Development, 73*(6), 1844–1860.

Lazar, I., et al. (1982). Lasting effects of early education: A report from the Consortium of Longitudinal Studies. *Monographs of the Society for Research in Child Development,* Series No. 195, *47*(2–3).

Lee, V.E., Groninger, R.G., & Smith, J.B. (1994). Parental choice of schools and social stratification in education: The paradox of Detroit. *Educational Evaluation and Policy Analysis, 16*(4), 434–457.

Lee, V.E., & Smith, J.B. (1993). Effects of school restructuring on the achievement and engagement of middle-grade students. *Sociology of Education, 66,* 164–187.

Levin, H.M. (1987). Accelerated schools for disadvantaged students. *Educational Leadership, 44*(6), 19–21.

Liu, D., Diorio, J., Tannenbaum, B., Caldji, C., Francis, D., Freedman, A., Sharma, S., Pearson, D., Plotsky, P.M., & Meaney, M.J. (1997). Maternal care, hippocampal glucocorticoid receptors, and hypothalamic-pituitary-adrenal responses to stress. *Science, 277,* 1659–1662.

McCartney, K. (1984). Effect of quality of day care environment on children's language development. *Developmental Psychology, 20*(2), 244–260.

McEwan, B., & Schmeck, H. (1994). *The hostage brain.* New York: The Rockefeller University Press.

McNeil, L.M. (1986). *Contradictions of control: School structure and school knowledge.* New York: Methuen/Routledge & Kegan Paul.

Machin, S. (2001). The changing nature of labour demand in the new economy and skill-biased technology change. *Oxford Bulletin of Economics and Statistics, 63,* 753–776.

Madden, N.A., Slavin, R.E., Karweit, N.L., & Livermon, B.J. (1989). Restructuring the urban elementary school. *Educational Leadership, 46(5),* 13–18.

Mehan, H. (1992). Understanding inequality in schools: The contribution of interpretive studies. *Sociology of Education, 65,* 1–20.

Mueller, C.W., and Parcel, T.L. (1981). Measures of socioeconomic status: Alternatives and recommendations. *Child Development, 52,* 13–30.

Nagin, D.S., & Tremblay, R. (1999). Trajectories of boys' physical aggression, opposition, and hyperactivity on the path to physically violent and non-violent juvenile delinquency. *Child Development, 70,* 1181–1196.

Nelson, E.E., & Panksepp, J. (1998). Brain substrates of infant-mother attachment: Contributions of opoids, oxytocin, and norepinephrine. *Neuroscience and Biobehavioural Reviews, 22(3),* 41–54.

Offord, D., Lipman, E., & Duku, E. (1998). *The arts and community programs: Rates and correlates of participation.* Ottawa: Applied Research Branch, Human Resources Development Canada.

Olds, D.L., Eckenrode, J., Henderson, C.R., Kitzman, H., Powers, J., Cole, R., Sidora, K., Morris, P., Pettitt, L.M., & Luckey, D. (1997) Long-term effects of home visitation on maternal life course and child abuse and neglect: Fifteen-year follow-up of a randomized trial. *Journal of the American Medical Association, 278(8),* 637–643.

Olds, D.L., Henderson, C.R., Cole, R., Eckenrode, J., Kitzman, H., Luckey, D., Pettitt, L.M., Sidora, K., Morris, P., & Powers, J. (1998). Long-term effects of nurse home visitation on children's criminal and antisocial behavior. *Journal of American Medical Association, 280(14),* 1238–1273.

Organisation for Economic Co-operation and Development (OECD). (2001). *Knowledge and skills for life: First results from the OECD programme for international student assessment (PISA) 2000.* Paris: OECD.

Peterson, C., & Peterson, R. (1986). Parent-child interaction and daycare: Does quality of daycare matter? *Journal of Applied Developmental Psychology, 7,* 1–15.

Phillips, D.A. (1987). Quality in child care: What does the research tell us? *Research Monographs of the National Association for the Education of Young Children* (Vol. 1). Washington, DC: NAEYC.

Raudenbush, S.W., & Bryk, A.S. (2002). *Hierarchical linear models: Applications and data analysis methods* (2nd ed.). Thousand Oaks, CA: Sage.

Raudenbush, S.W., & Willms, J.D. (1995). The estimation of school effects. *Journal of Educational and Behavioral Statistics, 20*(4), 307–335.

Ross, N.A., Tremblay, S., & Graham, K. (2004). Neighbourhood influences on health in Montréal, Canada. *Social Science and Medicine, 59,* 1485–1494.

Sayer, L.C., Bianchi, S.M., & Robinson, J.M. (2004). Are parents investing less in children? Trends in mothers' and fathers' time with children. *American Journal of Sociology 10*(1),1–43.

Sayer, L.C., Gauthier, A.H., & Furstenberg, F.F. (2004). Educational differences in parents' time with children: Cross-national variations. *Journal of Marriage and the Family, 66*(5), 1152–1169.

Scheerens, J. (1992). *Effective schooling: Research, theory, and practice.* London: Cassell.

Statistics Canada and the Organisation for Economic Co-operation and Development. (2005). *Learning a living: First results of the Adult Literacy and Life Skills Survey.* Ottawa and Paris: Statistics Canada and the Organisation for Economic Co-operation and Development.

Stewart, M. (2000). *Chronic conditions and caregiving in Canada: Social support strategies.* Toronto: University of Toronto Press.

Strohschein, L. (2005). Parental divorce and child mental health trajectories. *Journal of Marriage & Family, 67*(5), 1286–1300.

Suomi, S. J. (1997). Early determinants of behaviour: Evidence from primate studies. *British Medical Bulletin, 53,* 170–184.

(1999). Developmental trajectories, early experiences, and community consequences: Lessons from studies with rhesus monkeys. In D. Keating and C. Hertzman (Eds.), *Developmental health and the wealth of nations: Social, biological, and educational dynamics* (pp. 185–200). New York: Guilford Press.

Thomson, E., Hanson, T.L., McLanahan, S.S. (1994). Family structure and child well-being: Economic resources vs. parent socialization. *Social Forces, 73,* 221–242.

Tremblay, R.E., Nagin, D.S., Séguin, J.R., Zoccolillo, M., Zelazo, P.D., Boivin, M., Pérusse, D., & Japel, C. (2004). Physical aggression during early childhood: Trajectories and predictors. *Pediatrics, 114*(1), 43–50.

Tremblay, S., Ross, N.A., Berthelot, J.-M. (2002). Regional socio-economic context and health. *Health Reports, 13,* 33–44.

Werker, J.F., & Tees, R.C. (2002). Cross-language speech perception: Evidence for perceptual reorganization during the first year of life. *Infant Behavior & Development, 25*(1).

Willms, J.D. (1992). Monitoring school performance: A guide for educators. Lewes: Falmer Press.

(2002). Implications of the findings for social policy renewal. In J.D. Willms (Ed.), *Vulnerable children: Findings from Canada's National Longitudinal Survey of Children and Youth* (pp.359–377). Edmonton: The University of Alberta Press.

(2003a). *Ten hypotheses about socioeconomic gradients and community differences in children's developmental outcomes.* Ottawa: Applied Research Branch, Human Resources Development Canada.

(2003b). *Student engagement at school: A sense of belonging and participation.* Paris: Organisation for Economic Co-operation and Development.

(2004, October). *Reading achievement in Canada and the United States: Findings from the OECD Programme for International Student Assessment.* Report prepared for Human Resources and Skills Development Canada.

(2006). *Learning divides: Ten policy questions about the performance and equity of schools and schooling systems.* Montreal: UNESCO Institute for Statistics.

Willms, J.D., & Beswick, J.F. (2005a). *Early years evaluation: Direct assessment* (rev. ed.). Fredericton, NB: Canadian Research Institute for Social Policy.

(2005b). *Early years evaluation: Teacher assessment* (rev. ed.). Fredericton, NB: Canadian Research Institute for Social Policy.

Willms, J.D., & Jacobsen, S. (1990). Growth in mathematics skills during the intermediate years: Sex differences and school effects. *International Journal of Educational Research, 14*, 157–174.

Willms, J.D., & Paterson, L. (1995). A multilevel model for community segregation. *Journal of Mathematical Sociology, 20*(1), 23–40.

Guide to *The British Columbia Atlas of Child Development*

Clyde Hertzman, Paul Kershaw,
Lori Irwin, and Kate Trafford

I n the fall of 2004, British Columbia became the first jurisdiction in the world to produce population-based maps of early child development. Community mapping of early child development was undertaken in British Columbia by the Human Early Learning Partnership (HELP) in order to assist the province and local communities in recognizing and addressing the challenges they face in fulfilling the objectives of the National Children's Agenda. Early child development was measured using the five scales of the Early Development Instrument (EDI): physical health and well-being; social competence; emotional maturity; language and cognitive development; and communication skills and general knowledge based upon the recognition that these domains of early child development have lifelong impacts on health, well-being, behaviour, and learning skills.

By kindergarten age, significant preventable inequalities in development already reveal themselves among Canadian children. For instance, data from the National Longitudinal Survey of Children and Youth from the late 1990s (Willms, 2002) showed a *gradient* in the risk of receptive language delay, increasing *gradually* from the children of the 10% highest-income Canadian families (5.2% delayed) to the poorest 20% (approximately 26% delayed). This pattern of gradually rising vulnerability with declining socioeconomic status is seen, for most developmental outcomes and frames, as the challenge for early child development in Canada and many other societies. The implication is that although those at the bottom of the socioeconomic spectrum are "most at risk," nonetheless "most of the children at risk" are spread more thinly across the more numerous middle class. If we want to make a meaningful improvement in the state of early child development, we must find ways to create "universal access to the conditions for healthy child development."

By kindergarten age, development has been influenced by factors at three levels in society: the family, the neighbourhood or local community, and the broader social/economic/political environment. At the level of the family, the qualities of stimulation, support, and nurturance in intimate circumstances matter. These qualities, in turn, are influenced by the resources that families have to devote to child raising (represented by income); by their style of parenting; and by their tendency to provide a rich and responsive language environment (often, but not always, associated with parental levels of formal education). At the level of the neighbourhood, children growing up in safe areas, where the community is "cohesive" in relation to children — where it mobilizes resources formally (creates programs) and informally (treats its children as if they belong there) — are less likely to be vulnerable in their development than children from similar family backgrounds living in unsafe and noncohesive neighbourhoods. Children who have stable neighbourhood environments during their early years also tend to develop better than children whose place of residence is constantly changing. Similarly, children from family backgrounds with multiple developmental risk factors will do better growing up in mixed socioeconomic neighbourhoods than in poor ghetto areas. Finally, at the level of society, access to "quality" programs matters. This includes the full range of childcare, family support, and family strengthening programs; public health programs for high-risk children and for vision, hearing, and dental health; and broader social safety net functions, such as parental leave and housing programs. Thus, the state of child development in any society is an "emergent property" of a complex of factors, many of them modifiable, at the intimate, civic, and societal level, which influence each child in unique combinations. Here, we document five uses of community mapping of the Early Development Instrument (EDI) based on our population-based assessments in British Columbia, Canada.

1. monitoring the state of ECD at the level of the population,

2. judging resilience of communities in supporting child development,

3. evaluating change in ECD over time,

4. understanding the state of ECD in special populations, and

5. informing community development and policy for ECD.

Monitoring the State of Early Childhood Development (ECD) at the Level of the Population

Early Development Instrument work began in British Columbia in the Vancouver school district in February 2000, and all school districts had completed at least one population-based EDI evaluation by 2004. This province-wide collection of EDI data has been used to establish a baseline estimate of the state of early child development and school readiness, against which future progress will be evaluated. These data provide a unique opportunity to advance our understanding of early child development as a population health issue by going beyond the current literature in a number of ways. Most studies:

1. rely on relatively small samples of children for whom outcome data is available;

2. focus on high-risk populations, particularly low-birth-weight children or very poor families in inner-city American urban environments;

3. explore neighbourhood settings defined by the convenience of Census survey boundaries, rather than community divisions that reflect the perceptions of diverse groups of local residents;

4. examine only one or two developmental domains; and

5. employ a theoretically compelling, but still narrow, understanding of the neighbourhood characteristics that influence development.

The analyses featured in the Atlas overcome problems 1 and 2 by collecting developmental outcome data from nearly 44,000 kindergarten children from all walks of life across the province; distance themselves from problem 3 by engaging local constituents in the definition of neighbourhoods and then organizing 2001 Census data accordingly; transcend problem 4 by measuring physical health and well-being, social competence, emotional maturity, language and cognitive development, and communication skills and general knowledge; and go a long way to overcoming problem 5 because population-level outcome data facilitate exploratory modelling to identify which of roughly one thousand Census SES variables co-occur significantly with favourable and worrisome development patterns across neighbourhoods.

The EDI provides information that can be interpreted both backwards and forwards in time. The primary direction of interpretation for the purposes of ECD is backwards. That is, the results of the EDI can be interpreted to provide an understanding of the qualities of early experience that children in a given area had from birth to kindergarten entry. However, the EDI can also be interpreted prospectively, in that the results frame the challenges that families, schools, communities, and governments will have in supporting their children's development from kindergarten onward. The EDI asks kindergarten teachers to fill out a detailed checklist about each child in their class based on five scale measures of development. The results allow us to make observations about average outcome levels and rates of vulnerability for the under-five population in a given geographic area. Each child's EDI assessment is analyzed so that the child receives a score between 0 and 10 for each scale. A score of 10 means that the kindergarten child is doing all the things he or she should be doing, all of the time, in relation to the given scale, whereas a score of 0 means he or she is not doing any of them at any time. More than on average outcomes, however, we have focused on levels of childhood vulnerability within different domains of child development. For each EDI scale, there is a score, somewhere between 0 and 10, that serves as a "vulnerability threshold." Children who fall below that score are said to be vulnerable in that aspect of their development. The appropriate interpretation of vulnerability is that the child is, on average, more likely to be limited in his or her development on the identified EDI scale than a child who receives scores above the cutoff. Since the EDI is not an individual diagnostic, EDI vulnerability cutoffs facilitate analysis of groups of children, rather than individual children. In other words, it is a meaningful use of the EDI to say something like:

> 20% of children in neighbourhood A are vulnerable in their physical development, whereas only 5% are vulnerable in neighbourhood B.

The approach to neighbourhood mapping that we developed quickly became a popular standard for British Columbia. Our approach, which we have refined over the past several years, involves mapping child development according to the neighbour-hood of residence of the child, rather than the Census unit, school catchment area, or school attended. By creating neigh-bourhoods of 40 children or more, we ensure statistical stability and anonymity in the results. Since interneighbourhood variation is examined in EDI scores, the data create an opportunity to iden-tify the influence of socioeconomic and community factors on child development. Mapping provides a visual summary of early childhood development trends in the interests of making complex social science and population health data meaningful to broad audiences. Colour maps depict information about the many inter-secting environments in which families live and young children grow, including socioeconomic, natural, cultural, programmatic, and policy environments as they interact in and across neighbour-hood, community, regional, and provincial geographies. In this regard, maps invite observers to contemplate a broad understand-ing of early development that transcends the boundaries of any single policy envelope — such as education, health, child care, welfare, or justice — to see how the interrelations between all of these areas influence children before they reach age 6.

When mapping information at the provincial level, we have relied primarily on school district boundaries to demarcate one region or community from another. This approach corresponds with local early childhood development coalition activities, which tend to be organized around school district boundaries as well. There are 59 geographically distinct school districts in the province, such that every point in the province is in exactly one geographic school district. The 59 school districts vary signifi-cantly in their geographic size and population. New Westminster is the smallest district, just 18 square kilometres, compared to the largest district, Stikine, which is over 145,000 square kilometres. Stikine's vast size is home to fewer than 2,000 people, however, as is the Nisga'a district. By contrast, nearly 550,000 people call

Vancouver's 392 square kilometres home, making this city the most populous urban centre in the province.

The provincial maps display the proportion of vulnerable children in the 59 geographic school districts *of residence*, as measured by each of the five scales of the EDI. All children, whether or not they attend school in their home district, are accounted for in the district *where they live*. In other words, for the purposes of the EDI, school districts are serving as residential areas, not as administrative areas. Children going to independent or on-reserve schools are accounted for in the geographic school district where they live. Similarly, in the rare cases where children live in one school district but go to school in another district, EDI evaluations are completed by the kindergarten teacher where they go to school but are accounted for in the school district where they live. The reason for this is that children spend their first five years of life in families and communities that influence their development. Since the primary focus of the EDI work is to reflect upon the quality of those early experiences, mapping children according to where they live best serves this purpose. The Atlas illustrates how the 59 school districts on all provincial maps are colour coded according to "quintiles"[1] of vulnerability. That is, the 12 (59/5 equals approximately 12) school districts with the smallest proportion of children least vulnerable in their physical development are coloured dark green. This is followed by the second-lowest-vulnerability group in light green; the middle group in neutral yellow; the second-highest-vulnerability group in light brown; and the most vulnerable in dark brown.

Most of the determinants of early child development are found at the level of the family and neighbourhood. Moreover, family types differ by neighbourhood, as does the level of access to quality programs and services. Therefore, the most important population aggregation of the EDI is at the level of the neighbourhood. The literature about the effects of neighbourhoods on child development most frequently relies on data that are reported using Census boundaries or other administrative units of analysis (Burton & Jarrett, 2000, p.1117). The convenience of Census or other survey boundaries comes with costs, however, including the fact that Census boundaries often do not match local perceptions of neighbourhood divisions. In response, HELP has worked closely with communities to benefit from local knowledge in determining neighbourhood boundaries that more accurately reflect the lived experience of a diverse range of people who reside in the area. Local ECD coalition representatives were invited to draw lines on maps of their area to signal the presence of perceived divides in their community. While some local coalitions opted to maintain the Census or another existing boundary system, others opted for dramatically different breakdowns than those employed for survey data collection.

The need to protect the confidentiality of individual information prevented HELP from using the precise neighbourhood boundaries proposed by locals in some communities with very modest populations. Some perceived neighbourhoods were home to too few kindergarten children (typically fewer than 40), and thus there was a risk of revealing private information about residents. Working within this constraint, the initiative taken by local coalitions to establish neighbourhood boundaries that reflected community perceptions resulted in the identification of 469 neighbourhoods across the province. The HELP mapping team then digitized the local maps and built them into a province-wide file. The team shared this file with Statistics Canada and contracted the statistical agency to perform a special run of B.C. Census data that disaggregated information by the 469 neighbourhoods, instead of by the more traditional Census boundaries.

Judging Resilience of Communities in Supporting Child Development

Socioeconomic status (SES) is used to describe the social and economic characteristics of a given unit of analysis: for example, a child's family, neighbourhood, school district, or province. Some of the most common SES variables include income, employment, education, ethnicity, and language. Research confirms that it is important to pay close attention to SES when looking at school readiness. For instance, Hertzman et al. (2002, p. 3) observe that

> In Canada, inequalities in child development emerge in a systematic fashion over the first five years of life, according to well-recognized factors: family income, parental education, parenting style, neighbourhood safety and cohesion, neighbourhood socioeconomic differences, and access to quality child care and developmental opportunities. By age 5, a "gradient" in early child development emerges, such that, as one goes from the families with the lowest to highest incomes, least to most parental education, and least to most nurturing and interactive parenting style, the average quality of early child experiences increases.

Until about 10 years ago, research about the relationship between SES and child development focused mainly on the social and economic conditions of the *family household* in which a child grows. Drawing on data from the National Longitudinal Survey of Children and Youth, Willms (2002) has quantified this relationship in Canada. The selection of household social and economic conditions that he measures generally accounts for less than 10% of the variation between child outcomes, whether measured in terms of physical, behavioural, or cognitive development (pp. 99–100). Thus, while the family SES gradient is important in understanding early development, the data are clear that risks to healthy child development are found across the entire socioeconomic spectrum. Even though the rate of vulnerability increases as one descends the socioeconomic ladder, the majority of developmentally vulnerable children reside in Canada's much more numerous economically secure homes (Keating & Hertzman, 1999).

Following on work by Brooks-Gunn and her colleagues in the United States (e.g., 1993), as well as a number of more recent Canadian studies (e.g., Boyle & Lipman, 2002; Curtis et al., 2004; Kohen et al., 2002), we focus on the socioeconomic status of neighbourhoods to explore what role it plays in child development. This literature provides considerable evidence that the geography of opportunity has a significant statistical impact on a child's development irrespective of the SES of the child's household. While statistically significant, however, the neighbourhood effect is typically reported to be modest, accounting for between 5% and 10% of the variance in child outcomes (Burton & Jarrett, 2000, p. 1119) or less (Kohen et al., 2002).

Our interest in the relationship between SES and *neighbourhood* rates of vulnerability differs importantly from many of the existing studies. These examine the influence of socioeconomic status on *individual* children living within single households that are, in turn, rooted within neighbourhoods, in order to separate out the family SES effect on a particular child from the neighbourhood effect. Our EDI mapping activities deliberately depart from this analytical strategy by featuring maps that illustrate ecological correlations, because this information is especially useful for policy-making purposes. While the majority of policy aims to improve the lived experience of individuals, the levers and legislation available to communities and governments cannot typically engage directly with individual circumstances. Instead, when designing policy, they must grapple with generalizations about the families that live in communities. EDI average scores and vulnerability rates thus present population health data at a level of abstraction that is valuable for policy and intervention.

Although socioeconomic status is by no means the only factor influencing development, the finding that family and neighbour-hood social gradients mediate early child outcomes has significant policy implications. If we wish to make a meaningful improvement in the state of early child development in British Columbia, or in any other jurisdiction, we must find ways to create universal access to the conditions for optimal development irrespective of where children and their caregivers live and of the social groups in which they belong. This line of analysis has it roots in the African proverb "It takes a village to raise a child." Implicit in this state-ment is an assumption that the community context in which chil-dren grow influences their development. Put simply, the assump-tion is that the *village* nurtures. Child development is not just a reflection of private parenting patterns or of the resources that individual families have to invest in their children. It also reflects the broader social dynamics and institutions through which the entire citizenry organizes itself economically, culturally, socially, and so on. These broader community conditions and practices create an environment for "social care" that matters when it comes to raising healthy, happy children who have the potential to thrive as they mature. A now classic review article by Jencks & Mayer (1990) helps to unpack the social care thesis by considering the multiple ways in which neighbourhood settings may impact early development. They focus on five patterns of influence:

1. *Neighbourhood resources.* Child outcomes are related to the level of resources available in communities, especially publicly provided or subsidized resources like community centres, parks, and childcare.

2. *Collective socialization.* Child outcomes relate to the social ties between community residents that facilitate the

collective monitoring of children relative to shared neigh-bourhood norms and practices, as well as providing positive role modelling. Neighbourhood characteristics, such as poverty, residential instability, lone parenthood, and ethnic diversity, support or hinder the formation of this sort of neighbourhood social organization.

3. *Contagion.* Child outcomes are influenced by the power of neighbourhood relations, especially with peers, to spread problem behaviour.

4. *Competition.* Child outcomes reflect competition between neighbours for scare resources.

5. *Relative deprivation.* Child outcomes are influenced by how children and their families evaluate their own circum-stances relative to those of neighbours and peers.

Contagion and collective socialization models suggest that affluent and/or family-oriented neighbourhoods convey benefits to children, especially from low-income families. By contrast, the competition and relative deprivation models imply that children from less privileged homes will struggle in affluent community contexts because they may not be able to keep up with class-mates or they may suffer lower self-esteem if they compare them-selves to others.

Starting with roughly 100 census variables, we produced "best fit" models for the five EDI scales, as well as "one or more vulnerability" models that depict the relationship between SES and vulnerability rates across the 469 B.C. neighbourhoods (as well as the school districts). In each case, seven or fewer Census variables entered the model. The following fractions of neigh-bourhood variation in EDI vulnerability were accounted for by these "best fit" models:

EDI Scale	Proportion of Variance Explained
Physical health and well-being	33.8%
Social competence	20.9%
Emotional maturity	23.4%
Language and cognitive development	27.2%
Communication skills and general knowledge	46.9%
One or more EDI vulnerabilities	42.7%

Readers should recall that this explanatory power is considerably higher than that attributed to the combined influence of neighbourhood and family SES effects in traditional analytic studies, because the focus here is on ecological correlations for which neighbourhood rates of vulnerability are the unit of analysis — not on individual children. The six "best fit" models collectively identify 19 *neighbourhood* SES indicators to be significant predictors of the share of children at risk of developmental delays in British Columbia as measured by EDI scores. These cover a range of constructs, such as:

- neighbourhood income characteristics,
- immigration and ethnic mix,
- level of childcare provided by men,
- occupational characteristics of men and women,
- residential transiency, and
- proportion of Aboriginal population.

Despite access to roughly one thousand variables from the 2001 Census, we expect that the explanatory power of the SES-EDI models would have been higher had we had access to additional information, including the following:

• a child's period of residence in the neighbourhood, since some studies report that children are significantly influenced by neighbourhood income only if they have lived there for at least three years (e.g., Turley & Lopez, 2003),

• crime rates,

• the concentration of persistent poverty and/or unemployment, say over five to six years, in contrast to LICO and employment measures in the Census, which only allow us to consider these issues at one point in time,

• depth of poverty,

• concentration of household high income,

• the general physical and social surroundings of the neighbourhood, including such things as traffic,

• garbage/litter,

• people loitering or congregating,

• persons arguing, shouting, or otherwise behaving in a threatening manner,

• frequency of intoxicated people visible on the street,

• the general condition of most nearby buildings, and

• the level of neighbourhood cohesion as indicated by the extent to which neighbours get together to deal with problems collectively; there are adults to whom children can look up; neighbours demonstrate a willingness to help one another; and neighbours are available who can be counted on to watch that children are safe.

In order to examine the resilience of communities, we take advantage of the relationship between each neighbourhood (or school district) and the Census characteristics that best explain variations in vulnerability, to determine which neighbourhoods (school districts) are doing "as predicted" in terms of ECD, which ones are doing better than expected, and which ones are doing worse than expected. This idea is depicted graphically in the Atlas.

Readers of the Atlas should notice the addition of three-slice pie charts. These are assigned to school districts and neighbourhoods to summarize how communities compare to others in the province in terms of the three socioeconomic characteristics that correlate most strongly with the EDI scale under consideration. The pie slices are colour coded individually to illustrate whether the community is more or less advantaged in terms of the socioeconomic variable at issue. In keeping with the colour coding employed throughout the Atlas, green slices depict when the community is relatively advantaged in terms of the socioeconomic characteristic; yellow shows that the district is mid-range; and red draws attention to districts that face the greatest obstacles in terms of the socioeconomic condition under consideration. Second, each school district retains its approximate original shape but is sized according to the numbers of children who live there. Although there is some abstraction of shape, the resulting display corrects for British Columbia's uneven population distribution while still retaining the visual cues of shape and proximity that are often crucial to map interpretation. Readers should note that the size of school districts indicates the size of the population under age 6. *The size does* not *reflect their actual geographic size.*

The relationship between SES and child development can be read directly from maps with SES pie charts. *Chameleon communities* (those that take on the colour of their SES variables) show the relationship most directly. A green pie on green background shows communities that are relatively privileged in terms of the selected socioeconomic characteristics and are also enjoying less childhood vulnerability. This pattern is what we would expect to find. Red-on-red patterns illustrate a similar story about the relationship between SES and vulnerability, although it moves in the opposite direction. Communities that struggle with more disadvantaged social and economic circumstances typically suffer higher rates of vulnerability.

For policy and community development purposes, some of the most interesting communities are those that do the opposite of the chameleon: they stand out because their EDI vulnerability colours are distinctly different from their SES pie charts. In such communities, children's development is less influenced by socioeconomic characteristics than we would predict. The colour contrast can be good news or bad news. For example, some school districts have a pie chart that is entirely red; yet their physical vulnerability is relatively low and portrayed as dark green. These areas on the map are good news stories because they represent communities that are overcoming socioeconomic circumstances that would generally result in higher rates of vulnerability among kindergarten children. Policymakers will want to pay particular attention to these kinds of communities to learn what is allowing citizens in these districts to protect children from the negative SES influences. Does it have something to do with the community resources and assets that citizens enjoy; the level of trust in the community; the level of collective socialization or cohesion; or something else entirely? It is vitally important for us to understand the factors that allow some neighbourhoods and school districts to do better than predicted because it will likely be easier to transfer these factors to other regions than it will be to change socioeconomic conditions.

Colour-contrasting communities can also have EDI outcomes that are particularly worrisome. Communities that enjoy relatively favourable green SES pie charts may report mid-range yellow or low-range red vulnerability rates. This colour combination paints the picture of a community with vulnerability rates falling below expectations that are based solely on social and economic conditions in the community.

Evaluating Change in ECD over Time

Vancouver is one of the first communities in the province for which two rounds of the EDI have been conducted: in February 2000 and in February 2004. This means that Vancouver is among the first places in British Columbia where change in the status of early child development can be assessed over time. The period 2000–2004 saw the introduction of federal-provincial transfer payments for early child development, followed later by funding for early learning and care, under the rubric of the Canadian Children's Agenda. These arrangements, together with several other federal and provincial initiatives, may mark the beginning of a period of public commitment to a "structural advance" for young children in Canada. The 2000–2004 comparison is thus a good one because there was a high level of public discourse and activity in relation to young children during this period. At the same time, policy initiatives and socioeconomic pressures were changing in the city of Vancouver. Although these factors were indifferent to early child development, they undoubtedly influenced family composition and neighbourhood character, as well as EDI results. *Thus, the comparison of EDI from 2000 to 2004 reflects all the changes in Vancouver as an ecosystem for early child development, not just those changes that have been consciously made to improve ECD.*

Data from Vancouver and all other districts will soon participate in Round 2 of EDI data collection. In order to make reliable inferences about child development over time, these data will be examined in several ways, using the scores that individual children receive for each scale, average neighbourhood scores, and neighbourhood vulnerability rates. Clear evidence of positive change over time will be indicated by:

- an upward shift in the distribution of individual scores across the entire district,

- increasing average scores across neighbourhoods,

- decreasing inequality in average scores across neighbourhoods,

- decreasing proportions of vulnerable children across neighbourhoods, and

- decreasing inequality in the proportion of vulnerable children across neighbourhoods.

- Conversely, the reverse will signal clear evidence of negative change.

The Atlas displays the proportion of individuals living in households below "LICO," the low-income cutoff for Vancouver. This is our principal indicator of neighbourhood income status because, unlike direct income measures, it is sensitive to local food and housing costs. With respect to LICO and any other Census variable, two aspects are worthy of mention: their level and the range of neighbourhood differences seen. The level of each variable indicates the degree to which each neighbourhood is challenged or privileged with respect to that variable. The range of difference indicates the level of "social distance" between neighbourhoods. In general, the greater the difference, the more difficult it is to build social solidarity around children and the more likely it will be to find a "gated community" mentality with regard to children. In the case of LICO, the typical neighbourhood in Vancouver has a high proportion (25%–30%) living below the cutoff, largely because of the high cost of housing. The range for Vancouver as a whole is very wide — nearly sixfold, at 11.7%–65.1%. Of note is the great difference between the highest LICO neighbourhood (Strathcona, at 65.1%) and the next highest (Grandview-Woodlands, at 37.7%). Also of note is the fact that, despite the affluence of many Vancouver neighbourhoods, none falls below 10% on LICO. This finding is likely explained by the presence of basement-suite dwellers and property-rich but income-poor seniors in wealthy neighbourhoods. In the case of this and most other Census variables, the neighbourhood pattern for Vancouver is broadly similar, with the greatest privilege on the west side of town, the least in the north-central areas, with the northeast, southeast, and northwest somewhere in between.

In other words, Vancouver emerges as a place where multiple socioeconomic challenges and multiple privileges concentrate in the same neighbourhoods, driving relatively large cumulative social distances. Taken together, the Census variables show that Vancouver neighbourhoods differ sharply from one another in a series of characteristics that will likely influence early child development by kindergarten age. Although these differences are large compared to those in smaller centres in British Columbia, they are comparable to the differences in other large cities in Canada and smaller than those in most American cities. Moreover, Vancouver is one of the few major centres in Canada where the socioeconomic differences between neighbourhoods have *not* been increasing over the past 10 to 20 years.

Understanding the State of ECD in Special Populations

Many different special populations could be identified for particular analysis using the population-based EDI from British Columbia — for example, recent immigrants, those with English as a second language, and those living in highly transient or poor neighbourhoods. Here, we explore the development of Aboriginal children as a special population. Aboriginals have traditionally been at developmental and educational disadvantage in Canada. Between 1890 and 1960, Aboriginal children were routinely taken from their parents and put in residential schools, where they were meant to be assimilated into the majority culture. In British Columbia, these facilities were gradually

175

phased out, and the last one closed in 1984. Aboriginal children now make up approximately 8% of B.C. children aged 0 to 5, and due to high Aboriginal fertility rates, they are growing as a proportion of the total. In 7 of 59 school districts, they already form a majority of the students.

Despite the history of forced assimilation, there are reasons to be optimistic about the fate of Aboriginal children. Just 15 years ago, status Aboriginal children were twice as likely to die in their first year of life as children in the B.C. population as a whole. The Atlas shows that this gap in infant mortality in the province had disappeared by the end of the 1990s. Such progress is remarkable — unmatched in the rest of Canada or in Australia. Infant mortality can be taken as a leading indicator of child well-being. That is, if there is an improvement in infant mortality rates, one would expect that the broader aspects of child development would follow the same trend in the not too distant future. Thus, current EDI outcomes for Aboriginal children should be interpreted as a single point on a trajectory of catching up that has gradually been taking place within the Aboriginal community since the last residential school was closed in 1984. In contrast, B.C. Aboriginal children are eight times more likely to be in state care than non-Aboriginal children, and close to half the provincial care caseload consists of Aboriginal children (Chrisjohn et al., 1997). In other words, at present there appears to be a large disjunction in the conditions for child survival and child development for Aboriginal children in British Columbia. Why should this be so?

Insights into this question may come from the work of Chandler and Lalonde (1998) on Aboriginal teenage suicide. Their work has shown that, although Aboriginal teenagers in British Columbia are, on average, more likely to commit suicide than non-Aboriginal teenagers, these figures conceal huge variations among different "bands" of Aboriginals. More than half of the province's

Aboriginal bands reported no youth suicides during the six-year period covered by the study (1987–1992), while more than 90% of the suicide occurred among less than 10% of the bands. Chandler and Lalonde concluded that youth suicide is not an Aboriginal problem, but a problem confined to select Aboriginal bands. They demonstrated that the rate of Aboriginal teen suicide varied dramatically in relation to half a dozen markers of "cultural continuity." The markers are community-level variables that are intended to document the extent to which each of B.C.'s almost 200 Aboriginal bands have taken steps to preserve their cultural past and secure future control over their community's life. Teenagers coming from bands with low levels of control of land, health, education, and cultural and municipal services, for example, have high rates of suicide, while those coming from bands with high levels of control have low rates of suicide (regardless of whether the teenager actually lived on the reserve lands or elsewhere). Every band that had control of all six cultural continuity markers measured in the study experienced low youth suicides during the six-year reporting period, while those bands in which none of these factors were present suffered suicide rates that were well above the national average. Although these data are about teenagers and not young children, they are important because they show that thinking about Aboriginal children *on average* and in comparison to non-Aboriginal children may frame the issue the wrong way. A more accurate framework may be derived from the question Why are some contexts better for Aboriginal children to grow up in than others?

As of February 2005, the Human Early Learning Partnership had completed EDI evaluations on more than 3,500 Aboriginal children around the province. These represent a complete sample of those in public kindergarten but lower coverage of those in kindergarten in exclusively Aboriginal schools. Nonetheless, our sample represents at least 80% of Aboriginal kindergarten children in British Columbia. The following analyses are based upon the 51 geographic school districts where there were sufficient numbers of Aboriginal children to report average EDI scores and vulnerability rates without compromising confidentiality. The level of vulnerability on any EDI-scale category for the entire population ranges across B.C. school districts from a low of 13.4% to a high of 54.1%. Among Aboriginal school district neighbourhoods, the range is 19.2% to 80.0%. Thus, for Aboriginal children, the range of vulnerability is very wide, stretching from better-than-average vulnerability (less than 24% is better than average) to high vulnerability. Rather than emphasizing how Aboriginal children are doing on average compared to the broader population, the Atlas directs attention to the range of vulnerability between the Aboriginal children in each district. It shows that the range of vulnerability for Aboriginal children across communities is huge, and largely overlaps the range for the population as a whole. This, in turn, emphasizes the relevance of the question Why are some communities better places for Aboriginal children to grow up in than others?

Looking across the 5 scales of the EDI, the ranges of vulnerability for physical and language/cognitive development across school districts are shifted "upwards" compared with the population as a whole, while the ranges for social and emotional vulnerability overlap the overall population range quite closely. Thus, physical health and well-being and language and cognitive development pose the greatest challenges for Aboriginal ECD at present, followed by communication skills and general knowledge, particularly in rural and remote areas. Social and emotional development pose the lowest level of challenge overall for children in this special population. The Atlas reinforces this point by showing that, for Emotional Maturity, there are several school districts where the Aboriginal children, as a group, are less vulnerable than the children of that school district as a whole.

Informing Community Development and Policy for ECD

The Atlas illustrates the geographic reach of two key programs in British Columbia that are building local coalitions around the theme of early childhood development: *Children First* and *Success by Six®*. The former have been established in conjunction with the B.C. Ministry of Children and Family Development. *Children First* programs target families in which children are at risk of poor social, emotional, cognitive and/or physical outcomes, with the intention of integrating and enriching the province's community-based service delivery system for early child development. *Success By 6®* is an initiative of the United Way that is building ECD coalitions in a number of local B.C. communities to bring together community leaders from the business, labour, government, and social services sectors. Coalitions help decision makers identify local needs and decide upon interventions that will help parents and communities create healthy, nurturing environments for young children. In this way, by age 6, children are physically, socially, and emotionally ready to succeed in school. The United Way uses its fundraising prowess to finance interventions and ensures that funds raised in local communities will stay in those communities to support identified early childhood development priorities.

Considering the Barriers to Access

With the right mix of interventions, the entire population of young children can have access to improved conditions for healthy development. In light of this ideal, it is necessary to engage directly with the notion of timely access to programming and the barriers that may impede this access. In response, the Human Early Learning Partnership, in conjunction with community service providers, has compiled a list of barriers that we categorize under two headings: (1) barriers that families confront when trying to access services and (2) barriers that agencies encounter when trying to provide services.

Barriers for families include:

1. *Program or service not available.* Potential clients are unable to access services because the services simply do not exist within their community.

2. *Cost.* Potential clients are unable to access services due to financial constraints.

3. *Transportation.* Lack of transportation to and from services prevents potential clients from accessing the program.

4. *Time program is offered.* The times of the day or week that the program or service is offered present a barrier to access for potential clients.

5. *Time poverty.* Parents may struggle to balance multiple roles, including paid work and caregiving, and thus do not have sufficient time to access resources. Time poverty is likely an especially significant barrier among lone-parent families.

6. *Language.* The language in which the service is offered prevents potential clients from accessing the program/service.

7. *Fragmentation.* Families have children of various ages and are unable to access the desired programs for each child due to conflicting schedules or locations of programs.

8. *Lack of information.* Due to lack of available information about programs, potential clients do not access services.

9. *Conflicting expectations.* Parents of children who could benefit from services do not use them because they disagree with agencies providing the service about what the program should look like and how it should be delivered.

10. *Social distance.* Parents of children who could potentially access services are from different class, social, or cultural circles than those who provide the service. Lack of trust or embarrassment, for instance, may result in unwillingness to access available services.

11. *Parental consciousness.* Parents are unaware of the benefits to their children of the available programs and services. For example, many parents may not be aware that it is important to read to their children and therefore do not access the available literacy programs.

Barriers for agencies include:

1. *Agency mandate.* The mandate of the agency does not encompass supporting such a service.

2. *Skill base.* Agency personnel do not have the appropriate skill base to adequately provide the service.

3. *Resources.* The agency does not have sufficient resources to adequately provide the service.

4. *Absence of intersectoral group.* Agencies may be unable to innovate or offer a service without the support of a broader coalition or intersectoral group.

5. *Planning cycle.* Planning cycles are longer than local cycles of mobility and economic security. For example, many resource communities measure economic security in months, not years.

6. *Taxation authority.* Federal and provincial agencies provide funding incentives to entice local governments and other stakeholders to assume responsibility for providing ECD services without transferring sufficient taxation authority.

Levels of Intervention: Civil-Society, Universal, Targeted and Clinical Programs

A second consideration in developing a strategic approach to early child development is understanding and defining the levels of intervention that are available across communities, including civil-society, universal, targeted, and clinical interventions. Communities are well served when they explore the relationships between each of these levels of intervention to determine their implications for program and policy development.

Civil Society

Civil-society interventions are designed to make communities "friendlier" to families and children. Examples of civil-society interventions include socioeconomically diverse neighbourhoods that reduce class, race, and gender inequalities; access to parks and play spaces; strong intersectoral support for early child development; and neighbourhood safety. Many of these interventions relate to town planning and access issues, as well as to provincial and federal policy. Civil-society interventions can have dramatic effects on healthy child development.

Universal Programs

In theory, universal programs are available for everyone to use (e.g., library storytimes, Family Resource Programs, quality childcare). However, a universally *available* program is not the same as a universally *accessible* one, since barriers can limit access to these programs for some groups of people.

Targeted Programs

Targeted programs are interventions designed for a subset of families and young children that are defined by a characteristic such as income, geographic location, ethnicity, family risk (e.g., child protection issues), and biological risk (e.g., identified health problems). The success of targeted programs can also be limited by barriers to access.

Clinical Programs

Clinical programs are designed for treatment of a child and usually involve one-to-one treatment by a caregiver (e.g., speech and language services, physical therapy).

Determining the Best Intervention Mix for a Community

The Atlas provides a starting point for discussions about how EDI results can help communities consider strategies for overcoming access barriers to programs. Specifically, Figure 5.1.4 in the Atlas is designed as a *planning tool* to assist communities in determining the mix of interventions that might be useful for strategic ECD planning. It is *not* designed as the definitive answer to a community's needs. The bell curve in Figure 5.1.4 represents the distribution of EDI scores in a given neighbourhood or community. The curve may represent any one of the five EDI scales or vulnerability on at least one scale. The vertical axis shows the percentage of children within a community, while the horizontal axis displays the range of EDI scores across the community. In this distribution, one can see that the highest percentage of children fall in the middle range of EDI scores (at the peak). The dark vertical line shows the (hypothetical) vulnerability threshold. The percentages of children who fall to the left of this line and under the lower left of the developmental curve would be considered "vulnerable,." The arrows on the figure indicate how different levels of intervention can influence the developmental distribution in different ways. Following are examples of how these interventions can influence developmental distribution.

Civil-society interventions tend to influence the entire distribution of the developmental curve, so that if these programs are successful, the entire curve will shift to the right. If these interventions really "bring a community together" to create family-friendly environments across class and ethnic divides, they should have a larger influence at the vulnerable end of the distribution than at the other end. In other words, the distribution will both move to the right and be compressed. As a result, the range, or inequality in distribution, will be reduced.

Universal interventions have the capacity to influence a large number of children and shift the entire distribution to the right, *if* barriers to access can be addressed for children who fall below the vulnerability threshold. If barriers are not addressed, universal interventions will have a larger effect at the nonvulnerable end of the distribution. In other words, distribution will improve, but the range will *expand*, not compress. Developmentally speaking, this would mean that the "the rich will get richer." Thus, in order for these interventions to have the most positive effect across the entire EDI vulnerability continuum, access issues must be addressed proactively, especially among the most vulnerable children and families.

Targeted interventions, in principle, are meant to pick up a group of children who are likely to be vulnerable, and thus they can shift the left end of the distribution to the right. If these programs are successful, a percentage of at-risk children will become less vulnerable and cross the vulnerability threshold. The development of the remainder of children under the curve is generally not influenced. The success of these kinds of programs rests in part in correctly identifying vulnerable children so that interventions can have the greatest effect.

Clinical interventions affect only a small percentage of children, who are identified individually as vulnerable. They are meant to shift the left side of the distribution to the right.

Conclusion

In our hands, the Early Development Instrument has been used to transform the issue of early child development, taking it from the purely private and informal, and putting it in the public realm. In the era of the information society, the public realm is where early child development certainly belongs. No society can allow large numbers of children to miss out on the opportunity to thrive during the early years and still expect to end up with a population that can cope in the modern world. Using the EDI as a population-based tool is a necessary step in defining the scope of this challenge, which is the first step in addressing it.

NOTES

The British Columbia Atlas of Child Development can be downloaded at: **http://ecdportal.help.ubc.ca/bc-atlas-child-development.htm**. The file size is 31.5 MB and will take about five minutes to download. Adobe Acrobat 7.0 and Windows XP or better are required.

1   A distribution that has been divided into fifths. **www.google.ca** (accessed May 17, 2006).

REFERENCES

Boyle, M.H., & Lipman, E.L. (2002). Do places matter? Socioeconomic disadvantage and behavioural problems of children in Canada. *Journal of Consulting and Clinical Psychology 70*(2), 378–389.

Brooks-Gunn, J., Duncan, G.J., Klebanov, P.K., & Sealand, N. (1993). Do neighborhoods influence child and adolescent development. *American Journal of Sociology 99*(2), 353–395.

Burton, L.M., & Jarrett, R.L. (2000). In the mix, yet on the margins: The place of families in urban neighborhood and child development research. *Journal of Marriage and the Family 62*, 1114–1135).

Chandler, M.J., & Lalonde, C. (1998). Cultural community as a hedge against suicide in Canada's First Nations. *Transcultural Psychiatry 35*(2), 191–219.

Chrisjohn, R.D., Young, S.L., & Maraun, M. (1997). *The circle game: Shadows and substance in the Indian residential school experience in Canada*. Penticton: Theytus Books.

Curtis, L.J., Dooley, M.D., & Phipps, S. (2004). Child well-being and neighbourhood quality: Evidence from the Canadian National Longitudinal Survey of Children and Youth. *Social Science and Medicine 58*, 1917–1927.

Hertzman, C. (2000). The case for an early childhood development strategy. *Isuma: Canadian Journal of Policy Research 1*(2), 11–18.

Hertzman, C., McLean, S.A., Kohen, D., Dunn, J., & Evans, T. (2002). *Early development in Vancouver: Report of the Community Asset Mapping Project (CAMP)*. Human Early Learning Partnership 2002. http://www.earlylearning.ubc.ca/vancouvermaps.pdf.

Hertzman, C., Power, C., Matthews, S., & Manor, O. (2001). Using an interactive framework of society and lifecourse to explain self-rated health in early adulthood. *Social Science and Medicine 53*, 1575–1585.

Jencks, C., & Mayer, S. (1990). The social consequences of growing up in a poor neighborhood. In L. Lynn & M.M. McGeary (Eds.), *Inner-city poverty in the United States*. Washington, DC: National Academy Press.

Keating, P., & Hertzman, C. (1999). *Developmental health and the wealth of nations: Social, biological, and educational dynamics*. New York: Guildford Press.

Kohen, D., Brooks-Gunn, J., Leventhal, T., & Hertzman, C. (2002). Neighborhood income and physical and social disorder in Canada: Associations with young children's competencies. *Child Development 73*(6), 1844–1860.

Turley, R., & Lopez, N. (2003). When do neighborhoods matter? The role of race and neighborhood peers. *Social Science Research 32*, 61–79.

Wadsworth, M.E.J. (1997). Health inequalities in the life course perspective. *Social Science and Medicine 44*, 859–869.

Willms, J.D. (Ed.). (2002). *Vulnerable children*. Edmonton: University of Alberta Press.

APPENDIX: DEFINITIONS

National Children's Agenda[1]

The National Children's Agenda reflects the commitment of the Government of Canada and provincial and territorial governments to work together to ensure the health and well-being of Canada's children. A key component of the NCA vision is a focus on the importance of early childhood development — a firm belief that a healthy start in the first years of childhood is a strong foundation for a better life.

Early Development Instrument (EDI)[2]

The Early Development Instrument: A Population-based Measure for Communities (EDI) is a research tool to gauge school readiness of children at the junior and senior kindergarten levels, that is, just before entering Grade 1.

The EDI serves a number of purposes:

1. It can evaluate the effectiveness of community environments and resources for groups of children and help communities decide how best to support their young children.

2. It can be employed as a predictor of later school performance for groups of children.

3. When it is widely administered, comparisons can be made of the patterns of school readiness for groups of children and the effectiveness of different communities in Canada.

4. It can be used as a first-stage screen to identify children who may require special assessments and interventions

The EDI is completed by the teacher, and it is estimated that it takes about twenty minutes of the teacher's time per child. The questions measure child characteristics in five domains that have been identified as important in evaluating a child's readiness to learn:

• Physical health and well-being

• Social competence

• Emotional maturity

• Language and cognitive development

• Communication skills and general knowledge

Human Early Learning Partnership (HELP)[3]

The Human Early Learning Partnership (HELP) is a pioneering, interdisciplinary research partnership that is directing a world-leading contribution to new understandings of, and approaches to, early child development.

187

Directed by Dr. Clyde Hertzman, HELP is a network of faculty, researchers, and graduate students from British Columbia's six major universities. HELP facilitates the creation of new knowledge and helps apply this knowledge in the community by working directly with government and communities.

HELP works in partnership with the British Columbia Ministry of Children and Family Development (MCFD) and the British Columbia Minister of State for Child Care. HELP is partially funded by MCFD and maintains a close liaison with other provincial government ministries.

National Longitudinal Survey of Children and Youth[4]

The National Longitudinal Survey of Children and Youth (NLSCY) is a long-term study of Canadian children that follows their development and well-being from birth to early adulthood. The NLSCY began in 1994 and is jointly conducted by Statistics Canada and Social Development Canada (SDC), formerly Human Resources Development Canada (HRDC).

The study is designed to collect information about factors influencing a child's social, emotional, and behavioural development and to monitor the impact of these factors on the child's development over time.

The survey covers a comprehensive range of topics, including the health of children and information on their physical development, learning, and behaviour, as well as data about their social environment (family, friends, schools, and communities).

Information from the NLSCY is being used by a variety of people at all levels of government, in universities, and in policy-making organizations.

APPENDIX NOTES

1   http://www.hc-sc.gc.ca/ahc-asc/performance/budget/children-enfants_e.html (accessed May 17, 2006).

2   http://www.founders.net/ (accessed May 17, 2006).

3   http://www.earlylearning.ubc.ca/ (accessed May 17, 2006).

4   http://www.statcan.ca/start.html (accessed May 17, 2006).

Cognitive Assimilation, Culturalism, and Diversity: Evolving Educational Discourses for First Nations Students

Marie Battiste

The education of First Nations[1] students was the prime concern of their ancestors in the treaties. It was also central to the shared vision of their future and an enriched livelihood of First Nations (Henderson, 1995). These treaties create specific educational rights in First Nations families and a corresponding duty and obligation for the Crown to finance educational facilities and opportunities. However, Canadian educators have not been able to implement this vision. The legacy of federal residential schools and provincial schools has failed to fulfill the educational promises of the treaties. Despite the many changes that have been made to Canada's educational system over the years, it will take First Nations students more than twenty years of accelerated and restorative education to catch up to the national average for high school graduation (Auditor General of Canada, 2000). These statistics represent a significant educational challenge, and the need to improve them presents a crucial test of the resolve of many educators, policymakers, and First Nations people.

Understanding and remedying this failure of education have been issues for many agencies, federal and provincial. Discovering ways to enable educators to generate a nourishing and learning experience for First Nations youth has been my own personal quest as a teacher of teachers in the College of

189

Education at the University of Saskatchewan. This has led to many insights over the years. At different times, I have felt close to understanding what is needed to help bring about equitable outcomes for all peoples in schools and universities, and I have explored, researched, experimented with, and written in many publications about numerous features of language, cultural education, and pedagogy. In these writings, I have used anticolonial, antiracist, and antisexist principles and frameworks, as well as decolonizing and postcolonial discourses in order to present solutions to these problems. But most importantly, I have drawn on my own insights from being a Mi'kmaq First Nations woman, who has lived and worked within a reserve community, having to generate educational achievement.

As an advocate of Aboriginal knowledge, language, and scholarship, my own scholarship might be seen as embroiled in revisionist postcolonial politics of knowledge. However, my approach is different than this. In my analyses, the term "postcolonial" is not a reference to temporal time, a time after colonialism; instead, it is about criticisms of the existing academic canons based on the universal norms of Western Europe and of the knowledge and cognitive frameworks diffused throughout the Americas by Western European settlers. Postcolonial, then, for me, is about the need to reject the "Centre" as the source of norms for everyone and to seek an education that responds to diversity from various locations, freely, openly, and with no requirement of Western authority to legitimate one's experience. "Postcolonial" is a term that has emerged in literature to help raise consciousness about the imagined and privileged Centre and its exclusions, which formalize privilege and authority of knowledge. Postcolonialism is also about the recovering and reclaiming of knowledge and voices made silent by Eurocentric privileges.

In this essay, I attempt to understand the failure of First Nations education and the nature of needed transformations from the perspective of a Mi'kmaq woman and educator, a former education director and principal of a First Nations school, and now a professor of education in a Canadian university. Having lived and worked under the federal Indian policy and worked with and for First Nations and elders, I have sought to address and critique the foundation of assumptions, theories, and discourses that inform First Nations education policy and practice, in an attempt to bring different perspectives and, hopefully, help effect different outcomes for First Nations peoples. I consider these critiques and changes to be vital to the future of education and to the future of all Canadians, not just those who are First Nations.

The rate of population growth among Aboriginal peoples is nearly three times greater than that among the non-Aboriginal population in Canada (Statistics Canada, 2001), and with a multifaceted, growing demographic for Aboriginal populations, tragedy will loom if educational systems do not correct the failures affecting Aboriginal students. Educational planners and administrators often remind the profession of the related costs of a continued high failure rate among Aboriginal people in terms of their social and economic systems. I do not suggest that Canadian educators have not pursued this agenda academically or attempted to solve these problems adequately; rather, I suggest that they have tried to address these educational issues with a focus on integration and assimilation based on Canadian values. These long-time and ongoing assimilation strategies have been repeatedly critiqued for adversely affecting Aboriginal people's lives — causing multiple other costs to their lives and particularly to their diverse knowledge and heritages, which can survive only if their Aboriginal languages, identities, and cultures remain intact. Assimilative strategies affect the social and cultural lives of First Nations people, and these disruptions do not build the needed capacity but cause related problems, many of which have been found in the policy repercussions surrounding the residential schools. It is from this context and awareness that this essay is written.

I take this essay through four parts: the first will offer a brief introduction concerning the policy formations of First Nations education in order to give a basic, core understanding of federal and provincial/territorial education responsibilities; the second will consist of a discussion of the indicators of failure that have been revealed in a number of reports and an analysis of the foundations of culturalism (a construct drawing on a complex mix of ideologies, discourses, and practices that serve to legitimate Eurocentrism in its many forms of scholarship, law, and social practices so as to make them invisible to those who benefit from them [McConaghy, 2000] and cognitive imperialism (the normalization of hegemony that establishes the dominant group's knowledge, experience, culture, and language as the universal norm for scholarship, education, language policy, and disciplinary knowledge, among other things [Battiste, 1986]; the third will present an analysis of postcolonial mandates in educational transformation, and in the fifth, concluding section, I will propose a notion about how Canadian society and schools can integrate Indigenous peoples' knowledge and heritage into their systems.

Policy Framework for Aboriginal Education

The education of First Nations people is a federal responsibility under treaties settled with First Nations that preceded Confederation of the provinces. The *British North America Act* (BNA) of 1867 establishes the authority of the federal government and articulates the diverse roles of the provinces. Under Section 91(24) of the BNA of 1867, the federal government assumed responsibility for "Indians and lands reserved for Indians," and implementation of the obligations of these treaties was assigned to Canada. Education, or schooling, is specifically named in the treaties, creating a unique fiduciary responsibility for the education of First Nations students in Canada. Canada has narrowly interpreted this obligation as applying only to First Nations people living on reserves. Under S.93 of the BNA of 1867, each province has constitutional authority to make laws and in them provide health and education for its citizens. Section 93 provides the constitutional base for the establishment of administration of schools and universities as a provincial responsibility.

Canada implements treaty obligations to First Nations through the *Indian Act*. This federal legislation has empowered federal agents and/or civil servants to carry out their administrative duties and obligations on Indian lands. The *Indian Act* was initially intended to empower federal agents to operate on First Nations reserves and to enable them to secure funds from the federal government to undertake school construction, operate schools, hire teachers, and offer other services. In the early treaties, First Nations could choose schools when they wanted them or when they were ready for them. Regardless of schools, however, First Nations parents retain the right to knowledge transmission in the continuing traditions of the people and in their languages as Aboriginal rights. The federal obligation provided monies taken from the sale of Indian lands — an authority that the federal government authorized for itself (Henderson, 1995) — to fund schools and education for First Nations youth. In the early negotiations, chiefs and councils were empowered to oversee the operations of schools in their communities, including acting as advisors for the construction of school buildings and for their maintenance and repair. Gradually, however, Canada used its delegated treaty authority of implementation of the treaties to create a policy of assimilation — to position its own cultural system of beliefs and values over that of the First Nations and to establish its own privileges as norms. In addition,

Canada began to broaden the scope of its performance of treaty obligations to oversee all aspects of First Nations people's lives and families and chose churches to provide educational personnel to implement those services.

Ways of life that First Nations peoples saw as normal and that were built on their relationships with their land and environment and with each other gradually became viewed as the "Indian problem" — to be eliminated along with their treaty economy. In the residential schools and purchased educational services of the day, biases and prejudices toward First Nations people were the norm. The educational obligations envisioned by chiefs and parents of achieving parity with European economic prosperity in the treaties were ignored in the search for solutions to the "Indian problem." In 1920, Canada removed the authority of the chiefs and parents; mandated English-only instruction; instituted compulsory, British-modelled schooling for youth up to eighteen years of age; and removed many day schools, replacing them with residential schools. Educational practices left a wake of tragic outcomes for First Nations people that continue to reverberate in First Nations communities today — blocking or impeding access to an enriched livelihood.

In 1951, Canada recognized its failure in First Nations education, but rather than building First Nations capacity, it decided to rely on provincial educational systems to rectify the evident failures of the federal system. As a consequence, it entered into financial agreements with the provinces and territories for the education of First Nations children. Thus, in return for their enrolling First Nations children in public schools, the provinces were supplied with federal funding in the form of tuition subsidies that, in effect, helped to build the infrastructure that allowed provincial schools to increase their capacity without having to account for the low levels of school achievement among First Nations youth. In addition, the Minister of Indian Affairs agreed to pay tuition for First Nations students living on reserves to the local school boards, a per-head fee that has grown considerably. In New Brunswick, for example, in 2004 that tuition rate was $5,894 per capita (Canadian Press, 2004). However, Indian and Northern Affairs Canada (INAC) has not been accountable to either First Nations parents or the federal government with regard to these tuition payments (Auditor General of Canada, 2000).

The transfer of educational authority was another failure. Despite high tuition-subsidy rates, few First Nations students graduated from high school or attended universities. Seventy-three percent of First Nations students do not graduate from high school, only 9 percent of those who do graduate attend postsecondary institutions, and only 3 percent of these students graduate from institutions of higher learning (Royal Commission on Aboriginal Peoples, 1996).

In 1966, *A Survey of the Contemporary Indians of Canada: A Report on Economic, Political, Educational Needs and Policies*, which later became known as the Hawthorn Report, after the name of its principal editor, first raised awareness of the failures of the educational initiatives at the federal level and made extensive recommendations for their improvement. The survey affirmed First Nations' view of education in the treaties, noting that education was a prerequisite to meaningful choices and to the social well-being and economic prosperity of First Nations and Inuit youth. It also rejected the previous policy context that had focused on assimilating First Nations and Inuit children by removing them from the influence of their parents and communities. Finally, the survey emphasized the importance of greater parental involvement and improved communication between schools and First Nations and Inuit communities (Hawthorn, 1966, p. 130).

However, the survey, created from a Eurocentric point of view, offered as its key solution the "integration" of First Nations children into provincial systems "with the retention of some of their cultural characteristics such as pride of origin, knowledge of their history, passing on of their tradition and preservation of their language" (p. 28). Recognizing that provincial systems were not well equipped to take on these initiatives, the study acknowledged that compromises were needed in order for provincial school systems to accommodate the needs of First Nations students in their policies and practices. Finally, it urged that "remedial" programs be offered for First Nations students. Since then, the provinces and territories have worked on developing multiple initiatives of integration, remediation, and accommodation, which followed similar paths, such as "increasing aboriginal content in the curriculum, improving heritage language studies, creating employment equity programs for aboriginals and re-structuring the workplace and post-secondary institutions to make them more accessible to aboriginals" (Owens, 2006, p. 1). (See also Alberta Education, 1987; Owens, 2006; Saskatchewan Learning, 1985, 1995.

Recognizing the lack of capacity in the federal government and, in particular, in Indian Affairs, Prime Minister Pierre Trudeau tried to resolve the problem in 1969 by transferring the failed federal efforts in relation to First Nations education entirely to the provinces. The plan was to transfer federal treaty obligations for education to the provinces, but the move was firmly rejected by First Nations parents across Canada. Furthermore, the provinces were unwilling to take on these extraordinary new responsibilities, leaving Canada with few alternatives but to accept a solution being offered by First Nations people themselves. The National Indian Brotherhood (NIB) called for First Nations self-determination in their policy proposal entitled *Indian Control of Indian Education* (National Indian Brotherhood (NIB), 1972). The NIB proposed a First Nations remedy to this educational failure, offering, with the resources of the federal government, to develop their own schools founded on First Nations culture and languages. The education of Aboriginal people was conceptualized as a way of revitalizing First Nations cultures and economies, rather than being based on the assumption that assimilation was the only alternative for First Nations people. The NIB articulated this vision of linking education with cultural preservation and cultural promotion as follows:

> We want education to provide the setting in which our children can develop the fundamental attitudes and values which have an honoured place in Indian tradition and culture ... We want the behaviour of our children to be shaped by those values which are most esteemed in our culture ... it is important that Indian children have a chance to develop a value system which is compatible with Indian culture. (NIB, 1972, p. 2)

The National Indian Brotherhood also stressed that in the past, First Nations students were asked to integrate, "to give up their identity, to adopt new values and a new way of life." They argued that this approach would have to be altered radically if Aboriginal children were to benefit from future education programs (NIB, 1972, p. 25).

In 1973, Canada accepted this policy transformation, which started the devolution of authority to First Nations communities to administer their own education programs. Since then, First Nations communities have been developing their own educational capacity to undo the forced assimilation policies enacted in federal boarding schools and day schools, albeit with far fewer personnel and resources and lower levels of funding than the provinces have had (Battiste, 2005). As a result, those initiatives have met with varied success. In 2000, the Report of the Auditor General of Canada noted:

Although some progress has been noted in recent years, the record of educational achievement for Indian students living on reserves continues to be much worse than that of other Canadians (2000, at **http://www.oag-bvg.gc.ca/domino/ reports.nsf/html/0004ce.html**).

Some schools are still emerging as their capacity in terms of infrastructures, teachers and administrators, and curricula continues to grow. Reserve schools and communities have also had to engage with conditions characterized by fewer Aboriginal administrators and teachers, as well as dealing with generations of people traumatized under the prior federal systems of assimilation and boarding schools. Today, racism and discrimination remain key deterrents in Aboriginal students' experiences with schools and workplaces, and Aboriginal and non-Aboriginal people continue to require healing and transformative initiatives before education can have any real measured effect (Saskatchewan Human Rights Commission, 2004).

The Canadian initiatives concerning First Nations control also had effects on provincial institutions. Given that over 68 percent of First Nations students are involved in provincial schooling at some point in their education — mostly at the secondary and postsecondary levels — the provinces have had to consider providing programming and capacity to achieve success with First Nations youth. The Prairie provinces, where Aboriginal population is significantly large, have been among the first provinces to address First Nations educational issues, and Alberta's experience represents how most of these provinces have grown to address education for Aboriginal people.

In its 1972 *Report of the Task Force on Intercultural Education: Native Education in the Province of Alberta*, an Alberta Department of Education task force summarized data for policies and practices that would serve the educational needs of cultural minorities. Assuming that First Nations capacity was a problem, the task force did not consult directly with First Nations people on their educational needs and desires, relying instead on the existing literature review by the Canadian professorate. The task force set out its operating educational philosophy as follows:

> Cultural understanding can develop only when diverse people see others not as imperfect reflections of themselves but as these people really are; when social behaviour is observed not to reinforce one's own biases but to promote objective analysis; when different cultural patterns are viewed not as evidence of backwardness but as manifestations of a belief system that is worthy of respect.... [T]he report which follows attempts to help the reader see and believe in Alberta's Native peoples. (p. iv)

The Alberta Department of Education refined this policy discourse in 1985 after seeking Aboriginal people's input regarding their education. This publication, entitled *Native Education in Alberta: Native People's Views on Native Education*, helped to clarify some of the needed changes that led to the 1987 policy document entitled *Native Education in Alberta's Schools: Policy Statement on Native Education in Alberta*. The newly refined policy was described as one that would provide the knowledge, skills, and attitudes necessary for First Nations students to survive in modern society, as well as reflecting the contribution First Nations cultures have made to Canadian society. Both the dialogues held with Aboriginal people and the subsequent policy directives aimed to develop positive self-esteem and pride in their First Nations heritage. With the Minister of Education's 1987 policy to encourage the "continued development of a culture that respects and cherishes individuality and individual initiative" (Alberta Department of Education, 1987, p. i), the ministry committed itself to working with First Nations people and provincial school boards in order to develop curriculum materials and programs that included and highlighted Aboriginal culture and to encourage more representation of Aboriginal people as administrators, teachers, and language instructors.

The Alberta Department of Education's policy framework, like many other provincial initiatives, created a discourse of cultural diversity with a set of undefined policies and practices that have since been championed as inclusive and transformative but that have actually fallen short of their objectives. These policies were contextualized within an educational system contaminated by cognitive imperialism and racism based on Eurocentric norms and assumptions. It has not been the solution to the problem of lack of capacity and cultural support in First Nations education.

The next section will begin to expose, question, and critique these Eurocentric norms and assumptions, which can be viewed as constituting the foundation that failed First Nations education. By reviewing the current systems of education and how they have defined educational "discourses of diversity" within systems of racism and cognitive imperialism, I assert that these discourses of diversity have not been successful because educators have assumed that the problem lies with First Nations students and their apparent lack of capacity in language and other literacy skills, rather than with the operating assumptions and structures of the education system. From my perspective, First Nations students in Canada continue to suffer the ideological effects of cognitive imperialism in education, including the belief in the inferiority of First Nations students and their need to be transformed into another self through education based on assimilation. For First Nations students, the terror inherent in an educational process based on culturalism (McConaghy, 2000) and cognitive imperialism (Battiste, 1986) is often politely called integration, inclusion and diversity. Educators need to unpack and understand the assumptions underlying these concepts in order to begin to remedy the intractable educational failures they have caused.

Culturalism, Cognitive Imperialism, and Education

Education has never been a neutral enterprise. It is always imbued with meanings constructed from the economic, political, social, and cultural ideologies related to race, class, and gender (Calliste & Dei, 2000; Dei, James, Karumancherry, James-Wilson, & Zine, 2000; St. Denis, 2002). Developed within a colonial system of Anglo-Christian patriarchy, Canadian education has systematically excluded the rich diversity of peoples of Canada, and in particular, women, minorities, and First Nations perspectives, experiences, beliefs, and diverse knowledge (Minnich, 1990). Socially constructed for an imagined Canadian society, education has not served all peoples equally, nor have certain sectors of Canadian society gained or benefited from Canada's de facto culturally exclusive educational systems.

Contemporary Canadian education is rooted in the Eurocentric foundations of scholarly study. Privileging ancient Greco-Roman culture, philosophy, language, and thought, it has not strayed far from those early foundations even as British and European philosophy and thought have evolved. These origins have been maintained and reinvented as core ideals for contemporary education (Axelrod, 2002). In the past, practical education served as a liberating mechanism for the poor and the underprivileged, while formal education was reserved for the privileged. While Canadian educational content has gone through multiple refinements and additions, it has always been based on Eurocentrism in the sciences, philosophy, literature, poetry, history, music, ethics, and logic. These foundations, when applied to First Nations students, have been based on what I continue to call "cognitive imperialism."

Cognitive imperialism is a form of cognitive manipulation used in Eurocentric educational systems. Built on damaging assumptions and imperialist knowledge, educational curricula and pedagogy have been built on a monocultural foundation of knowledge and privileges that have developed through public education (Battiste, 1986). Cognitive imperialism relies on colonial dominance as a foundation of thought, language, values, and frames of reference, as reflected in curricula, language of instruction, discourses, texts, and methods (Farmer, 2004; St. Denis, 2002). As a result of cognitive imperialism in education, cultural minorities in Canada have been led to believe that their poverty and powerlessness are the result of their cultural and racial origins and their inability to draw from those origins, rather than on the power relations that create inequality in a capitalistic global economy.

Many Aboriginal people have been led to believe that learning English to the exclusion of their Aboriginal languages and other assimilative practices will be their only path to success. This belief has contributed to the multiple and intergenerational losses of cultural and linguistic diversity (Skutnabb-Kangas, 2000), although such opportunities for education and employment have not emerged as promised (Fleras & Elliott, 1992). Despite the disconnections from their own knowledge, voices, and understandings, First Nations students' prospects for being hired in urban and rural Canada have not improved. Rather, they have ushered in other problems, evidenced in discontinuities between the youth and their elders and in their loss of sense of identity, connections, and responsibilities to themselves and their communities (Battiste & Semeganis, 2002). Urbanization, increasing poverty, and social maladjustments all contribute erroneously to the view that their "difference," their being First Nations, Métis or Inuit, are the source and cause of their impoverished state.

Similarly, the provinces are failing Aboriginal peoples. In a special report on the academic achievement of Aboriginal students, the Fraser Institute (Cowley & Easton, 2004) attempted to raise public awareness of First Nations students' achievement in British Columbia and Alberta. Based on the results of educational testing within British Columbia and Alberta, it concluded: "The available evidence shows that this student group [First Nations students] has, on average, substantially and chronically under-performed relative to the total student population" (p. 4). In British Columbia, the failure rates for First Nations students on reading tests are over 40 percent in Grades 4, 7, and 10. In the last thirty-five years, literature dealing with Aboriginal pedagogical studies and learning styles has focused on how to reduce these gaps and improve educational outcomes for these diverse groups, but largely, these reports and initiatives share similar problems in that reducing "gaps" is viewed as raising Aboriginal people's performance on achievement tests and increasing their literacy or math skills rather than reassessing public school curriculum and teacher education. Bringing Elders to the classrooms and increasing the number of Aboriginal teachers have not led to needed transformations in provincial educational institutions. Since 1985 the Saskatchewan Human Rights Commission has been monitoring the province's public schools for equity activity and results, and while many activities have occurred, the schools have not been able to uniformly arrest the dropout rates, recidivism, student mobility, and low graduation rates among First Nations students in the public schools (Saskatchewan Human Rights Commission, 2004).

At the same time, First Nations people have continued to articulate their high aspirations for their children. They still believe that education is a liberating process. The few successes in First Nations education have created a remarkable belief in the capacity of education. They have generated a new constitutional framework and new visions and context for First Nations education. According to the *Report of the Royal Commission on*

Aboriginal Peoples (RCAP), "education is seen [by First Nations people] as the vehicle for both enhancing the life of the individual and reaching collective goals" (pp. 3, 5, 433). Yet as of 1991, only 11 percent of First Nations students had completed high school, and over 37 percent had less than a Grade 9 education, compared with 18.9 percent of the non-Aboriginal population completing high school (Royal Commission on Aboriginal Peoples, 1996, vol. 3, p. 440). The commission's findings were confirmed again in the Auditor General of Canada's audit of the elementary and secondary education program of the Department of Indian Affairs in the year 2000. The Auditor General found that 37 percent of First Nations students completed high school, compared with 65 percent of the general population, adding that it will take approximately twenty-three years before First Nations students reach parity with the current Canadian rate for high school completion (Auditor General of Canada, 2000, para. 4.44).

These statistics represent a significant educational failure, and the need for improvement presents a significant challenge to, and a crucial test of, the resolve of many educators, policymakers, and First Nations people. While many recommendations from the Royal Commission on Aboriginal Peoples and from the Auditor General and others have been issued with regard to needed transformations in education, the solutions coming from the first generation of First Nations scholars and educators have created the context for the Minister of Indian Affairs Educational Renewal Initiatives at Indian and Northern Affairs Canada (INAC, 2002). Most importantly, however, First Nations educators have offered their understanding and their receptivity to fashioning First Nations education that relies on First Nations heritage and knowledge, in order to facilitate educational achievements for First Nations students.

Many other educators have recognized the damage done to Aboriginal students, and many are committed to the idea of a transformed education in some form. The literature on this issue is extensive, as it is passionate and pedagogical. But culturalism has clouded the issues for educational reform, building in resistances to change through cultural connections that do not change the core foundations of knowledge and values toward others. Diversity and multiculturalism discourses in education have become a complex façade of converging ideologies and discursive and programmatic practices that have served to unreflectively legitimate culturalism and to make power and agency invisible to those who benefit from them (St. Denis & Hampton, 2002). They have not resulted in educational success for First Nations students and have, in fact, contributed to damaging First Nations students. Anthropology and ethnography have combined to offer scientific research methods and diverse discourses of culture and education that have offered exotic views of Indigenous cultures. Such research has generated normative narratives that homogenously and anonymously pathologize Aboriginal youth — of their being trapped between two worlds with little capacity or agency (McConaghy, 2000). Inclusion, then, is perceived as a means of motivating and inspiring First Nations students through cultural thematic and additive First Nations content to help bridge their two worldviews. This additive content, then, is intended primarily for the Aboriginal students, not for non-Aboriginal students, and as a result, Native Studies is not viewed as a necessary foundation for Canadian studies for all Canadians.

Drawing on culturalistic assumptions, educational literature dealing with equity has suggested that the process for achieving benefits for diverse groups of people requires a foundation not only for improving access to education but also for ensuring that students benefit from education. Since 1972, when multiculturalism was instituted in Canada, and since 1988, when the *Multiculturalism Act* was legislated, much thought, research, and practice have gone into educational considerations of cultural difference and special needs. Great effort has also been expended in trying to understand when these are significant and when they are not, as well as when they lead to greater justice or greater equity (McConaghy, 2000, p. 15).

The literature on culture-based education is extensive. Since the 1970s multiculturalism has been tossed into every education policy corner from managing population diversity to its therapeutic use to induce a new consciousness in teachers and educators and thus in their student populations. While multiculturalism has been widely critiqued, it has not entirely lost its flavour in Canada, and the notion of diversity continues to mark multiple discourses. However, without clear policy foundations or definitions, diversity discourses resolve little. In some instances, diversity is understood as an equity policy measure for including a diverse population of students or teachers. In other instances, it is meant to imply an additive curriculum or is synonymous with an employment strategy. In each instance, as a notion of cultural inclusion, the conceptualization of diversity needed a foundation from which it could discuss the "other." A theory of difference was then created as a base that offered an "othering" strategy embodied in culturalism.

Culturalism is a strong and influential tradition in Indigenous education. Intimately related to cognitive imperialism, it is a complex mix of ideologies, discourses, and practices that serve to legitimate Eurocentrism in its many forms of scholarship, law, and social practices so as to make it invisible to those who benefit from such a worldview. Culturalism, like "cultural racism," is based on strategies developed to mask its Eurocentric foundations and educational purposes and its privileged consciousness and perspectives. For example, adding Native Studies to the core content of a high school may appear to be progressive until one examines the curriculum. Native Studies does little to affect attitudes toward Aboriginal peoples or to influence their situation. As legitimated in high school, Native Studies is a narrative of Aboriginal and white relations and the events that created those relationships. It offers sequential events as interpreted from diverse perspectives, but not from First Nations perspectives. Indigenous people do not tell the story; instead, typically non–First Nations historians tell the tale from their perspectives and their selected facts. Native Studies then becomes a colonialist explanation of events and their impact on Indigenous peoples. This culturalistic form of knowing acts as an analytic lens that offers evidence of, and explanations for, deficits among "other" cultural groups. It also acts as a filter to sort out "solutions" for education, such that the practice and discourses of seeking answers to solutions in cultural education and multiculturalism become fraught with contradictions and confusion for those attempting to understand and implement these strategies. Eurocentrism and culturalism, then, function together, one as the substance and the standard; the other as the justification and method for its maintenance.

Postcolonial Mandates in Educational Transformation

Section 35 of the *Constitution Act*, 1982, affirmed Aboriginal and treaty rights as constitutional rights in Canada, thus generating a postcolonial policy context in education. The courts have affirmed rights to Aboriginal knowledge and their validity in the modern context. Canada has further affirmed the validity of traditional First Nations ecological knowledge in the Convention on Biodiversity, a multilateral treaty that applies to First Nations as part of the exclusive federal jurisdiction (s.91 (24) *Constitution Act*, 1867) and as constitutional holders of Aboriginal and treaty rights (ss. 35 and 52 *Constitution Act*, 1982). It complements the existing human rights and Aboriginal and treaty rights.

Combined with antiracism, decolonization, and reconstruction of First Nations education, this constitutional provision offers INAC and the provincial and territorial education system a framework for renewing First Nations education and also establishes a respectful education reform. Article 1 of the 1966 UNESCO Declaration of the Principles of International Cultural Co-operation offers an inspirational principle: "each culture has a dignity and value which must be respected and preserved." This prime postcolonial principle harmonizes with the assertion of Aboriginal and treaty rights in education and forms a basis for constitutional rebuilding and reclaiming of First Nations heritage and languages in Canada. Aboriginal and treaty rights, in turn, offer a practical and theoretical foundation for postcolonial First Nations education.

In practical terms, this means that in the postcolonial framework, First Nations people must be involved at all stages and in all phases of planning and future governing in educational contexts. Each First Nations treaty area can offer an opportunity to Canadians to rededicate themselves to protecting First Nations knowledge and heritage and to redressing the damage and losses that First Nations peoples have experienced in relation to their languages, cultures, and properties. In these treaty areas, Canada and the provinces also have the opportunity to enable First Nations heritage and knowledge and to create an authentic educational system based on an inclusive view of humanity. Many educators have recognized the assumptions and sources of the damage done to First Nations students by culturally oppressive curricula, and many remain committed to the idea of culture-based education.

Postcolonial education emanating from the *Constitution Act, 1982*, offers some hope to Indigenous people that solutions to cognitive imperialism will soon be addressed and implemented. It creates a constitutional place to address educators' complicity in the devaluation of First Nations peoples and to take an active constitutional role in repairing the existing damage. Unfortunately, much of the current thinking about treaty First Nations peoples and their communities has been affected by a media focus on social problems, partly derived from the vast educational failures. While these cannot be minimized or disregarded, each educator and prospective teacher has a role in changing conceptions about First Nations students, their heritage, and their contributions to society. Constitutional reforms have given Canadians the responsibility to understand the harm done through past educational practices, and conversely, they have given Canadians the mandate to reshape the order of the world and to break the chains of oppression that still bind First Nations peoples in this country.

Although the decolonization of Eurocentric thought is already underway in the works of many scholars, Indigenous people engage in decolonization in a distinct manner. Maori educator and scholar Linda Tuhiwai Smith, one of the leading theorists of decolonization in New Zealand, clarifies the nature of the task: "Decolonization is about centring our concerns and world views and then coming to know and understand theory and research from our own perspectives and for our own purposes" (Smith, 1999, p. 39). The interrelated strands of scholarship and experience intersect to weave solutions not only to decolonize education, but also to sustain the Indigenous renaissance and to empower intercultural diplomacy. The decolonizing frame is constructed in relation to First Nations language, knowledge, and heritage — based on the constitutional foundation of Aboriginal and treaty rights to education. This requires the deconstructing of curricular knowledge and reframing First Nations humanities and scientific knowledge to the contemporary contexts of peoples' aspirations and lives.

Renaissance and empowerment are two essential features of the postcolonial movement. Postcolonialism is not about rejecting all theory or research connected with Western knowledge. It is about creating a new space where Indigenous peoples' knowledge, identity, and future are inserted into the global and contemporary equation. Decolonization has both a negative movement and a positive, proactive one. As E. Daes noted at the UNESCO Conference on Education in July 1999:

> Displacing systemic discrimination against Indigenous peoples created and legitimized by the cognitive frameworks of imperialism and colonialism remains the subtle most crucial cultural challenge facing humanity. Meeting this responsibility is not just a problem for the colonized and the oppressed, but also rather the defining challenge for all peoples. It is the path to a shared and sustainable future for all peoples. (Daes, 1999, p. 1)

Those who are researching Indigenous knowledge must understand both the historical development of Eurocentric thought and the Indigenous contexts. A body of knowledge differs when viewed from different perspectives. Interpretations or validations of Indigenous knowledge will depend not only on the researcher's attitudes, capabilities, and experiences, but also on his or her understanding of Indigenous consciousness, language, and order. Depending on the Eurocentric reductionist analysis used, Indigenous knowledge may be seen as segmented or partial, utilitarian or nonutilitarian. However, Indigenous knowledge needs to be interpreted based on form and manifestations, as Indigenous peoples themselves understand them.

The positive proactive movement is a complex and daunting task. Educators must reject colonial curricula that offer students a fragmented and distorted picture of Indigenous peoples. Instead, they must provide students with a critical and enlarged perspective that resists historical fragmentation and engages Indigenous knowledge and humanities as part of a more informed curriculum. In order to effect change, educators must help students to understand the Eurocentric assumptions of superiority within the context of history and to recognize the continued dominance of these assumptions in all forms of contemporary knowledge.

According to historian Lise Noël (1994), domination and oppression are grounded in intolerance. The fact that modern intolerance is implicit in Eurocentric consciousness itself has profound implications for the liberation of Indigenous knowledge. For educating, finding knowledge, doing research, and constructing research ethics, where are Indigenous people to find experts who can rise above the value contamination of their own consciousness? Where are these people being trained? By what faculty are they being taught? Because of the pervasiveness of Eurocentric knowledge, few universities, colleges, or educational institutions have the personnel with the requisite knowledge and methods for seeking different kinds of knowledge and truth. This is why a postcolonial framework cannot be constructed unless Indigenous people renew and reconstruct the principles underlying their own worldviews, environments, languages, and forms of communication, and re-examine how all these elements combine to construct their humanity.

Newly empowered Indigenous people and their non-Indigenous allies are providing critical frameworks for addressing these issues while acknowledging excellence through the proper valuing and respectful circulation of Indigenous knowledge across and beyond Eurocentric disciplines (Battiste, 2000; Findlay, 2000; Findlay, 2003; McConaghy, 2000). Indigenous people are seeking to heal themselves, to reshape their contexts, and to effect reforms based on a complex arrangement of conscientization, resistance, and transformative action. Through collaborative work with scholars in Canada and in Australia, New Zealand, and the United States, Indigenous scholars and leaders are demonstrating the strength of the postcolonial movement by constructing the multidisciplinary foundations essential to remedying the acknowledged failure of the current system. They are achieving this transformation in multiple sites, where diverse problems engage multiple strategies, strategic goals, and broad political agendas.

What is understood is that Indigenous peoples' struggles cannot be reduced to single solutions in singular locations. They need to be carried out in many sites using multiple strategies. Among these important sites and strategies is the work being done by Indigenous peoples at the United Nations, where lobbying bodies have raised awareness of the plight of many oppressed peoples around the world. The United Nations has produced a number of declarations and covenants embracing or urging the adoption of standards to protect women, children, and cultural minorities. Until 2007, Indigenous peoples could not secure their rights; however on September 17, 2007, 143 nation states ratified the Declaration of the Rights of Indigenous Peoples. Canada was one of four countries that did not sign the Declaration.

Decolonization of the Humanities

Every conception of humanity and education begins from a consciousness in which a specific place takes prominence. This locale initially shapes an understanding of being and by experiencing that place, people are shaped and sustained and provided with an understanding of themselves and an awareness of their being at home in the world. Each child represents a micro–ethnic group of schemata that reflects their worldview, and teachers need to become aware of these. In the Eurocentric versions of humanity, this concept is sometimes referred to as cultural diversity; yet to

First Nations peoples, the concept is the Indigenous humanities. Indigenous humanities seeks to resist the discursive Eurocentric categories and regimes of "othering" embodied in the concept of "culture," which has been built on the oppositional binary of race. Indigenous humanities speak instead to the core of humanity, to the similarities and diversities of all peoples, who develop from their ecological and spiritual origins, rather than from their cultural differences.

Humanities represent ecological teachings and practices of what constitutes being human. Ecology is the animating force that teaches us how to be human; it does not derive from theological, moral, or political ideology. Ecology privileges no particular people or way of life. Like ecologies, heritages or cultures have a respectful place in education. They honour and nourish a respect for diversity, rather than narrow preferences and needless authoritarian hierarchy. First Nations concepts of humanity relate to a certain style of being human, of doing wonderful tasks, and of overcoming the forces of doubt and inertia. This concept is best illustrated by action, rather than reflection, definitions, or categories. One of the best examples of the Indigenous humanities in action is the work of many writers, poets, singers, and dramatists. Among these are Buffy Sainte-Marie, Linda Hogan, Maria Campbell, Thomas King, Dale Auger, and many others who offer voices that expand Indigenous artistry, creativity, imagination, and dreams. They understand concepts of the humanities and creativity as performance or doing or living. Action brings humanity and creativity to life, and doing and being turn life into knowledge and wisdom.

Indigenous Humanities, as a broad concept, bring together core capacities of all societies and cultures, including First Nations ones. They operate locally and distinctively but confirm tendencies of constructs that characterize all human beings. These include the ability to communicate through language and art, to mark our place and progress across time and space, and to locate ourselves reflectively and spiritually in relation to each other, to the world we all share, and to the forces that lie beyond our understanding or control. They could be represented in all the disciplines of secondary and postsecondary education.

The First Nations Humanities, however, have been systematically excluded in the Eurocentric narratives. Since they did not originate from ancient Greece and were not created and monopolized by Europe, these disciplines have never been linked to the First Nations peoples, and thus First Nations humanities seem implausible. First Nations humanities are not synonymous with ethnic and class elitism. Instead, they have long been associated with versions of the "barbarian" or savage, in order to authenticate and privilege Eurocentrism. Within this characterization — and its pseudo-civilizing mission — the First Nations Humanities seem a contradiction in terms. This categorization also made it impossible for the socially contrived primitive or uncivilized Indigene to credibly lay claim to such knowledge in earlier centuries. Indigenous peoples may only do so now via imitation and assimilation, because of the continuing misguided perception that there is no such thing as Indigenous knowledge and nothing to be learned from Indigenous peoples.

As a postcolonial strategy for better education, First Nations Humanities function as critique and creativity, resistance and celebration. It is a force of reconceptualization of Canadian humanity. As critique, it works against the grain of "white" pretensions to racial supremacy, using the master's tools to dismantle the master's house (Findlay, 2003). Eurocentric education originated with the Greek classical philosophers and evolved through modern scientific inquiry, having its roots in misperception — a politics of knowledge and knowing that has not been thoroughly debunked as a culturally influenced system that has taught slavery, sexism, racism, and xenophobia. Educators must recognize the

Eurocentric ideologies that have shaped educational curricula and their students, and they also need to recognize very different and legitimate ways of knowing and doing that are not currently part of the educational process. A postmodern analysis suggests that all uniform and grand narratives about education or about how the world is reflected to students must take into consideration all peoples, the diversities of culture and knowledge, and solutions that are not universally owned, socialized, and acknowledged. Critical theorist Henry Giroux (2000) notes that we need

> [t]o develop definitions of pedagogy that admit new knowledge from subordinated groups, address the "production of knowledge, social identities, and social relations [that] challenge racist assumptions and practices that inform a variety of cultural sites, including but not limited to the public and private spheres of schooling." (Giroux, 2000, p.196, as cited in Klug & Whitfield, 2003, p. 155)

The great forgetting or disinformation replayed in educational pedagogy and curricula has dealt unjustly and/or inadequately with First Nations peoples, their rights, interests, accomplishments, and potential contributions. For example, the golden age of the Eurocentric humanities was the Renaissance in early modern Europe: the rediscovery of the ancient languages, disciplines, and texts occurred virtually simultaneously with voyages of "discovery" that were the prelude to modern colonialism. The golden age of Renaissance humanism was, and not at all coincidentally, the first heyday of modern Euro-colonialism.

The postcolonial First Nations renaissance and the related Indigenous Renaissance, by contrast, is about being respectful of ecologies, not about mastery or conquest. It is about replacing elite and popular misunderstandings of Indigenous peoples and celebrating the generous and respectful teachings of First Nations heritage and thought. It is about Canadian scholars and educators working together with First Nations scholars and about the transdisciplinary, multimediated, transcultural imagination of a better educational system. It is about reclaiming First Nations heritage and knowledge for vision and creativity, and perhaps even peace. But the work requires a certain process, a deconstructing of the socially constructed canons and dialogues among and between various communities. The First Nations Humanities gesture toward a place for education to prosper, but we will arrive there only if Canadians agree to work within an authentic version of humanity that includes First Nations. This postcolonial educational strategy invites us back to sustainable teaching. An inclusive Canadian educational system is well placed to nourish and export the protocols of respect, collaboration, and creativity that achieve justice in education and lead to the international revaluing and protection of Indigenous knowledge and heritage.

Conclusion: Generating Postcolonial Remedies

Many educational institutions in Canadian federalism state in their mission statements or in their institutional goals that the education of First Nations people is a priority. However, to date, these priorities have been neocolonial. In other words, First Nations people can access available content and resources, but they cannot change the existing knowledge base of the educational system. In order for educational institutions to live up to their constitutional priorities, they must introduce postcolonial frameworks for their curricula and pedagogy. To do this, educators must confront and explain the colonial history of education, the Eurocentric content of current curricula, and the attitudes of superiority that continue to demean First Nations knowledge and people. This sense of superiority is especially evident in the public perception that First Nations stewardship, responsibilities, and management of their territory and resources, indeed of their knowledge and education, is conflict prone and incompatible with progress and prosperity.

In Canada, educational institutions have a pivotal responsibility in transforming relations between Aboriginal peoples and Canadian society. The Royal Commission on Aboriginal Peoples has firmly held that all institutions should consider respect for Aboriginal knowledge and heritage to be a core responsibility, rather than a special project to be undertaken after other obligations have been met (Royal Commission on Aboriginal Peoples, 1996, *3*, p. 515). Multidisciplinary work is beginning to offer transcultural coalitions across education, the humanities, the social sciences, and law. Physical scientists are coming onstream as issues of biodiversity and globalization are pressuring institutions to seek innovative and holistic solutions to ecological and global problems.

While it is gratifying to see these bridges being built by non-Indigenous scholars, respect for First Nations heritage and knowledge must begin with First Nations people themselves. It is First Nations people who must provide the standards and protections that accompany the centring of First Nations cognitive heritage and humanity. Many educators have taken up this challenge in a variety of forms and forums (Battiste & Henderson, 2000). Particularly exemplary are the works of Maori scholars and educators Graham Smith (1997) and Linda Smith (1999) of New Zealand, both of whom have influenced, mentored, and supported Indigenous scholars here and abroad.

In the constitutional context of education rights, it is time for educators to rethink the assumptive values on which contemporary society has built its knowledge base and institutions, the mythical portraits of First Nations peoples that have been assumed from this biased knowledge base, and our nations' neglected traditions of knowledge and humanity. These neglected knowledge bases can be sources of inspiration, creativity, and opportunity within a postcolonial educational system. They can also contribute to humanity, equality, solidarity, tolerance, and respect.

The significance and justification for respectful dialogue among educators as a basis for arriving at a postcolonial educational agenda cannot be overemphasized. This dialogue should take us beyond the processes of cross-cultural awareness, inclusion, and bridging programs to a new perspective that supports Indigenous knowledge, communities, languages, and self-determination in a new, decolonized way. Despite the painful experiences of First Nations students over the last century or more, education is still understood as the hope for their future, and First Nations people are determined to see education fulfill its promise (Royal Commission on Aboriginal Peoples, 1996, 3, pp. 433–34). Postcolonial strategies for both Indigenous peoples and non-Indigenous educators offer appropriate protocols and respectful methodologies that will help educators to enter into educational transformation. To achieve the Canada everyone desires, its institutions will need to view First Nations peoples not as disadvantaged racial minorities, but as distinct, historical, and sociopolitical communities with collective rights (Chartrand, 1999). Canada has a responsibility to live up to its reputation as a compassionate and innovative nation that is on the way to becoming a truly just society. We can arrive at this position only by recognizing our First Nations heritage, knowledge, languages, and humanities, and by renewing our investment in holistic and sustainable ways of educating, thinking, communicating, and acting together.

NOTE

1 "First Nations" is a respectful term for "Indians." The term "Aboriginal" is also inclusive of Inuit and Métis. Federal policy has historically dealt with Indians and Inuit and more recently with the Métis. I use "First Nations" to refer to those who have historical relationships embedded in treaties. When referencing all Indigenous peoples of Canada, I use the term "Aboriginal."

REFERENCES

Alberta Department of Education. Task Force on Intercultural Education. (1972, June). Report of the task force on intercultural education: Native education in the province of Alberta. Edmonton: Alberta Department of Education.

(1987). *Native education in Alberta: Native people's views on Native education.* Edmonton: Alberta Department of Education.

(1987). *Native education in Alberta's schools: Policy statement on Native education in Alberta.* Edmonton: Alberta Department of Education.

Auditor General of Canada. (2000). Indian and Northern Affairs Canada: Elementary and secondary education. *Report to the House of Commons,* Ch. 4. Ottawa: Minister of Public Works and Government Services Canada. **http://www.oagbvg.gc.ca/domino/reports.nsf/html/0004ce.html/$file/0004ce.pdf.**

Axelrod, P. (2002). Roots and branches of liberal education. In *Values in conflict: The university, the marketplace, and the trials of liberal education* (pp. 8–33). Montreal, and Kingston: McGill–Queen's University Press.

Battiste, M. (1986). Micmac literacy and cognitive assimilation. In J. Barman, Y. Hébert, & D. McCaskill (Eds.), *Indian education in Canada: The legacy* (pp. 23–44). Vancouver: University of British Columbia Press.

(Ed.). (2000). *Reclaiming Indigenous voice and vision.* Vancouver: University of British Columbia Press.

(2005). State of Aboriginal learning. Background paper for the national dialogue on Aboriginal learning. Ottawa: Canadian Council on Learning. **http://www.ccl-cca.ca/NR/rdonlyres/210AC17C-A357-4E8D-ACD4B1FF498E6067/0/StateOfAboriginalLearning.pdf.**

Battiste, M., & Henderson, J.Y. (2000). *Protecting Indigenous knowledge and heritage: A global challenge.* Saskatoon: Purich Publishing.

Battiste, M., & Semeganis, H. (2002). First thoughts on First Nations citizenship: Issues in education. In Y. Hébert (Ed.), *Citizenship in transformation in Canada* (pp. 93–111). University of Toronto Press.

Calliste, A., & Dei, G.J.S. (Eds.). (2000). *Anti-racist feminism: Critical race and gender studies.* Halifax: Fernwood Press.

Canadian Press (CP). (2004, August 23). N.B. First Nations won't pay off-reserve tuition. *Halifax Herald.*

Chartrand, P. (1999). Aboriginal peoples in Canada: Aspirations for distributive justice as distinct peoples. In P. Havemann (Ed.), *Indigenous peoples rights in Australia, Canada, & New Zealand* (pp. 88–107). Auckland, NZ: Oxford University Press.

Convention on Biological Diversity. **http://www.biodiv.org/**.

Cowley, P., & Easton, S. (2004). Report card on Alberta's elementary schools. *Studies in education policy* (A Fraser Institute Occasional Paper.) Vancouver: The Fraser Institute.

Daes, E. (1993). *Study on the protection of the cultural and intellectual property rights of Indigenous peoples.* E/CN.4/Sub. 2/1993/28. Sub-Commission on Prevention of Discrimination and Protection of Minorities, Commission on Human Rights, United Nations Economic and Social Council.

(1999, July). *Cultural challenges in the decade of Indigenous peoples.* Unpublished paper presented at the UNESCO Conference on Education, Paris, France.

Dei, G.J.S., James, I.M., Karumancherry, L.L., James-Wilson, S. & Zine, J. (2000). *Removing the margins: The challenges and possibilities of inclusive schooling.* Toronto: Canadian Scholars' Press.

Farmer, T.S. (2004). *Grade 12 Canadian history: A postcolonial analysis.* M.Ed. thesis, University of Saskatchewan, Department of Educational Foundations, Saskatoon.

Findlay, I. (2003). Working for postcolonial legal studies: Working for the Indigenous humanities. Law, Social Justice and Legal Development (LGD) 1. **http://elj.warwick.ac.uk/global/03-1/findlay.html**.

Fleras, A., & Elliott, J.L. (1992). Multiculturalism in Canada: The challenge of diversity. Scarborough, ON: Nelson Canada.

Haveman, P. (Ed.) (1999). *Indigenous rights in Australia, Canada, and New Zealand.* New York: Oxford.

Hawthorn, H.B. (Ed.). (1966). A survey of the contemporary Indians of Canada: A report on economic, political, educational needs and policies. (Vols. 1 & 2). Ottawa: Indian & Northern Affairs Canada. http://www.ainc-inac.gc.ca/pr/pub/srvy/sci1_e.pdf.

Henderson, J.Y. (1995). Indian education and treaties. In M. Battiste & J. Barman (Eds.), *First Nations education in Canada: The circle unfolds.* (pp. 246-260). Vancouver: University of British Columbia Press.

Indian and Northern Affairs Canada (INAC). (2002). Literature reviews commissioned by the Minister's National Working Group on Education in support of their work. http://www.ainc-inac.gc.ca/pr/pub/krw/wal_e.html.

Klug, B.J., & Whitfield, P. (2003). *Widening the circle: Culturally responsive pedagogy for American Indian children.* New York: Routledge Falmer Press.

McConaghy, C. (2000). *Rethinking Indigenous education: Culturalism, colonialism and the politics of knowing.* Flaxton, Queensland, Australia: Post Pressed.

Minnich, E. (1990). *Transforming knowledge.* Philadelphia: Temple University Press.

National Indian Brotherhood (NIB). (1972). *Indian control of Indian education.* Policy Paper presented to the Minister of Indian Affairs and Northern Development. Ottawa: National Indian Brotherhood.

Noël, L. (1993). *Intolerance: A general survey.* Kingston and Montreal: McGill–Queen's University Press.

Owens, D. (2006). *Aboriginal education in Manitoba.* Winnipeg: Frontier Centre for Public Policy.

Royal Commission on Aboriginal Peoples (RCAP). (1996). *Report of the Royal Commission on Aboriginal Peoples.* 5 vols. Ottawa: Canada Communication Group.

St. Denis, V. (2002). Exploring the socio-cultural production of Aboriginal identities: Implications for education. Ph.D. dissertation, School of Education, Stanford University, Stanford, CA.

St. Denis, V., & Hampton, E. (2002). *Literature review on racism and the effects on Aboriginal education.* Prepared for Minister's National Working Group on Education, Indian and Northern Affairs Canada, Ottawa, Ontario. http://www.ainc-inac.gc.ca/pr/pub/krw/rac_e.pdf.

Saskatchewan. Department of Education. (1984). *A five year action plan for native curriculum development.* Regina: Saskatchewan Department of Education.

(1991). *Indian and Métis education policy from kindergarten to grade 12*. Regina: Saskatchewan Department of Education.

Saskatchewan Human Rights Commission. (2004). Aboriginal educators consultation: Equity program review. April 8, 2003. Saskatoon: Saskatchewan Human Rights Commission. **http://www.gov.sk.ca/ shrc/equity/pdf/Abor-Educators2.pdf.**

Skutnabb-Kangas, T. (2000*)*. *Linguistic genocide in education or worldwide diversity and human rights?* Mahwah, NJ: Lawrence Erlbaum Associates.

Smith, G. (1997). Kaupapa Maori theory and praxis. Ph.D. dissertation, University of Auckland, New Zealand.

(2000). Protecting and respecting Indigenous knowledge. In M. Battiste (Ed.) *Reclaiming Indigenous voice and vision* (pp.209–224). Vancouver: University of British Columbia Press.

Smith, L. (1999). *Decolonizing methodologies: Indigenous peoples and research*. London: Zed Books.

Statistics Canada. (2001). Aboriginal peoples in Canada. (Catalogue No. 85F0033MIE). Ottawa: Canadian Centre for Justice Statistics. Catalogue No. 85F0033MIE. ISSN 1496-4562. ISBN 0-662-29821-7.

UNESCO. (1966). Declaration of the Principles of International Cultural Co-operation. **http://www.unesco.org/culture/laws/cooperation/ html_eng/page1.shtml.**

United Nations. (1989). *Report of the United Nations seminar on the effects of racism and racial discrimination on the social and economic relations between Indigenous peoples and states*. UN Commission on Human Rights, 45th Sess., UN Doc. E/CN.4/1989/22.

From Literacy to Multiliteracies: Designing Learning Environments for Knowledge Generation in Culturally and Linguistically Diverse Schools

Jim Cummins

The term "multiliteracies" was introduced in the mid-1990s by a group of Australian, North American, and European academics who met originally in New London, in the U.S. state of New Hampshire. The group self-titled themselves The New London Group. Their article, "A Pedagogy of Multiliteracies: Designing Social Futures," published in the *Harvard Educational Review* in spring 1996, aimed to articulate an orientation to literacy education that took into account the rapidly increasing cultural and linguistic diversity within Western education systems and the many new forms of technology that are transforming literacy practices in our global societies. According to the New London Group, if literacy pedagogy is to be effective, it must take into account and build on the various forms of vernacular literacy that are manifested in ethnocultural communities and also expand the traditional definitions of literacy beyond the linear, text-based reading and writing of Western schooling.

My goal in this essay is to build on the theoretical insights of the New London Group and explore further our options for literacy pedagogy within Canadian schools. What pedagogical frameworks are available to guide policy makers and educators in designing curricula and instruction that respond to the realities of an Information Age global society? This question implies that current conceptions of literacy, and ways of teaching it, are rooted in Industrial Age assumptions that do not respond to current social, economic, and technological realities. Literacy as it is taught and tested in our schools is conceived as linear, text-based reading and writing skills. In most parts of the country, the dominant language, English or French, is the default language of instruction, and languages spoken by students and their communities are ignored as largely irrelevant to education.

Pedagogical gaps are also evident in the ways in which technology is employed in schools. In Ontario, for example, according to the Education Quality and Accountability Office (EQAO) (2005), 96 percent of Grade 10 students have a computer at home, and they are involved in a wide variety of literacy practices related to technology, from sharing music files to instant messaging on cell phones to MSN chat groups. However, only a relatively small fraction of these students use computers at school for meaningful or substantive academic work. Despite significant investment by governments in educational technology in recent years, students typically still have only sporadic access to computers and other forms of new technologies (e.g., digital cameras or video players) within schools. Furthermore, when they do gain access, it is often not clear either to them or their teachers what they should be doing with these technologies (Cuban, 2001).

A central theme in this essay is that the major challenge with respect to integrating technology into our school systems in a rational and socially responsible way does not reside primarily in the technology itself. Rather the incoherent use of technology derives from the fact that our schools are lost in a pedagogical twilight zone with no clear focus on the instructional goals that technology can and should address. Another way of expressing this is to say that educational technology currently represents a solution in search of a problem. In the sections below, I propose some directions for developing a pedagogical framework that tries to respond to the twin realities of cultural and linguistic diversity in our schools and the profound transformations of our societies that technology is in the process of bringing about. These twin realities are powerfully captured in the term "multi-literacies," particularly in view of the fact that technology and diversity have hitherto remained largely isolated from each other in educational and scholarly debate.

Initially, I review some of the research relating to core concepts that must be considered in developing a pedagogical framework for literacy education. Then I present a framework that might serve as a starting point for discussion of literacy policies and practices within the school. Finally, I discuss some examples of how multiliteracies pedagogy is being put into practice in Canadian schools. The emerging pedagogical framework highlights the importance of maximizing students' cognitive engagement and identity investment in learning. Technology represents a powerful amplifier for pedagogical practices that enable students to generate new knowledge, create literature and art, and act on social realities.

Key Constructs in Literacy Policies and Practice

Literacy

Fuelled by concerns that we are in the midst of a "literacy crisis," policy makers in many Western countries have implemented changes in curriculum and assessment designed to raise standards and monitor attainment of these standards. However, as noted above, there has been minimal analysis of the extent to which the forms of literacy traditionally promoted in schools are, in fact, those that are most relevant to the new economic and social realities we now face as a nation. Few would dispute the continued relevance of linear, text-based literacy, but it is also clear that multiple forms of literacy associated with information, communication, and multimedia technologies are becoming increasingly salient to the Canadian economic and social fabric. Similarly, to ignore diversity issues risks increasing dropout rates among New Canadian students (Roessingh, 2004; Watt & Roessingh, 2001) as well as squandering cultural and linguistic resources increasingly relevant within a globalized economy.

Traditional literacy clearly involves more than just the ability to decode text. We all have varying degrees of literacy according to our knowledge and interest in the domain (e.g., books on gardening versus books on nuclear physics), context (e.g., school versus out-of-school), and purpose for reading. In the context of school, the development of academic language proficiency includes knowledge of the less frequent vocabulary of English, as well as the ability to interpret and produce increasingly complex written text. As students progress through the grades, they encounter far more low-frequency words (primarily from Greek and Latin sources), complex syntax (e.g., passives), and abstract expressions that are virtually never heard in everyday conversation. Students are required to understand linguistically and conceptually demanding texts in the content areas (e.g., literature, social studies, science, mathematics) and to use this language in an accurate and coherent way in their own writing.

The nature of academic text and its distance from conversational language is clearly expressed by Corson:

> Academic Graeco-Latin words are mainly literary in their
> use. Most native speakers of English begin to encounter
> these words in quantity in their upper primary school reading
> and in the formal secondary school setting. So the
> words' introduction in literature or textbooks, rather than

in conversation, restricts people's access to them. Certainly,
exposure to specialist Graeco-Latin words happens much
more often while reading than while talking or watching
television ... Printed texts provided much more exposure to
[Graeco-Latin] words than oral ones. For example, even
children's books contained 50% more rare words than
either adult prime-time television or the conversations of
university graduates; popular magazines had three times as
many rare words as television and informal conversation.
(1997, p. 677)

Commenting on the relationship between vocabulary and
reading, Nation and Coady (1988) point out that vocabulary
difficulty has consistently been found to be the most significant
predictor of overall readability. Once the effect of vocabulary
difficulty (usually estimated by word frequency and/or familiarity and word length) is taken into account, other linguistic
variables, such as sentence structure, account for little incre-
mental variance in the readability of a text. They summarize
their review as follows: "In general the research leaves us in little doubt about the importance of vocabulary knowledge for
reading, and the value of reading as a means of increasing
vocabulary" (p. 108).

In short, there is extensive research evidence that from about
Grade 4 on, vocabulary knowledge and reading comprehension
are so strongly related that they are virtually inseparable psycho-
metrically. It is therefore not surprising that the research evidence
also suggests that reading extensively in a wide variety of genres
is essential for developing high levels of both vocabulary knowledge and reading comprehension (Krashen, 2004).

A significant challenge for educators is how to motivate students to engage in extensive reading both inside and outside the
school. Expressed differently, how can we create an affective bond

between students and literacy such that students will want to read and write rather than seeing reading and writing as simply one more school task? In the Academic Expertise framework outlined below, identity investment plays a central role for the simple reason that students will engage cognitively in literacy and other academic endeavours much more intensely when they invest their identities in the learning process. The development of both traditional literacy and multiliteracies expertise will be enhanced by pedagogical approaches that build on the cultural and linguistic funds of knowledge (Moll, Amanti, Neff, & González, 1992) that exist in students' communities and that use technology to amplify the impact of students' intellectual and imaginative work.

Diversity

Cultural and linguistic diversity has become the norm in major urban school systems across both North America and Europe. More than 50% of the school population in Toronto and Vancouver, for example, come from non-English-speaking backgrounds, and in other large Canadian cities, there are also substantial numbers of culturally and linguistically diverse student populations. Across Ontario, 22% of the Grade 10 student populations in English-language schools speak a language other than English most frequently at home (Education Quality and Accountability Office, 2005).

The same trends are evident in Europe, giving rise in some cases to highly controversial social policies (e.g., France's recent legislation to prohibit prominent religious symbols or clothing in schools). The likelihood of escalating tensions around issues of diversity in many contexts highlights the importance of including critical literacy prominently within our conceptions of the forms of "literacy" we emphasize in schools. If students do not recognize how to "read" societal power relations and their expression in the media, then the line between democratic and totalitarian societies becomes blurred. Money buys media and media manu-facture consent (Chomsky, 2000).

The new global economy is similarly characterized by a plethora of languages and cultures, despite the current domi-nance of English in many cultural, scientific, and economic spheres. Thus, any pedagogical framework that aspires to pro-mote literacy and prepare students for a globalized Information Age economy must assign a central role to linguistic and cul-tural diversity. Currently, in the vast majority of European and North American school systems, diversity occupies only a mar-ginal place in policy discussions despite occasional rhetoric about multicultural and antiracist education.

The increase of cultural and linguistic diversity in schools has created both challenges and opportunities for education. Specifically, is it feasible or reasonable to expect a one-size-fits-all, homogenized curriculum to meet the needs of an increas-ingly diverse student body? To what extent should the educa-tion system attempt to acknowledge and promote the linguistic and cultural resources that students bring to school? If we see it as educationally desirable to promote students' multilingual and multicultural potential in schools, then what kinds of cur-ricula and pedagogy are likely to achieve this goal? How do we evaluate a differentiated approach to curriculum and pedagogy as opposed to a homogenized, centrally imposed model? Are current models of both large-scale assessment and diagnostic assessment of individual students valid for students who are in the process of learning English? Currently, these measures do not assess individual student progress across grade levels, and thus they provide a relatively crude indicator of accountability. For example, if average scores rise from one year to the next, does this reflect real improvement in student achievement or, alternatively, change in test content, marking criteria, or more efficient teaching to the test?

Technology

Computer access has expanded dramatically in North American and European schools. Within Canadian schools, a Statistics Canada survey (Plante & Beattie, 2004) conducted in 2003/2004 reported that:

> With more than one million computers for 5.3 million students, the median number of students per computer in elementary and secondary schools in Canada was estimated at 5. The median student-to-Internet-connected computer ratio was only slightly higher with 5.5 students per computer. The typical number of students per computer was lower in small schools than in larger schools and in secondary schools than in elementary schools. (2004, p. 29)

The report noted that the growth in Information and Communications Technology (ICT) infrastructure in schools has increased the complexity and cost of managing these facilities:

> Nearly 67% of principals reported that "having sufficient funding for technology"was an extensive challenge to using ICT in their school. Related to this, "ensuring that computers and peripherals are up to date", "obtaining sufficient copies/licences of software for instructional purposes", "having enough training opportunities for teachers", and "obtaining sufficient number of computers" also placed high among the challenges.
>
> Despite the perceived financial challenges, more than nine principals out of ten (92%) either slightly agree or strongly agree, "ICT is worth the investment." (2004, p. 30)

In the United States, surveys suggest a similar student-to-computer ratio and a reduction of the gap in technology access between schools in affluent and poverty areas and between schools with low and high minority populations. There remains, however, a very significant gap in how computers are used in affluent and less affluent schools. Students in less affluent schools are much more likely than those in affluent schools to engage in technology-supported drill and practice activities at school. By the same token, they are less likely to engage in technology-supported collaborative inquiry activities. Thus, a significant pedagogical divide exists despite the fact that some aspects of the digital divide at school have been reduced.

With respect to out-of-school access to technology, low-income students in the United States are significantly less likely than affluent students to have access at home to computers and to the Internet (Kleiner & Farris, 2002). This gap appears to be greater than in the Canadian context, as reflected in the Ontario data that 96% of Grade 10 students have home access to computers (EQAO, 2005). The difference may be attributable to the greater social stratification in the U.S. as compared to Canada. The gap in home access in the United States is exacerbated by the fact that even when students of low socioeconomic status (SES) do have access, they benefit less academically from home computer access than do high-SES students (Attewell & Battle, 1999). Warschauer, Knobel & Stone (2004) suggest that this phenomenon may reflect the fact that teachers assume that most low-SES students do not have access to computers at home and so do not assign homework or projects that require technology access.

The recent massive investment in ICT has been undertaken on faith rather than evidence. Critics in the United States have pointed to the absence of any overall impact on national reading achievement levels despite more than a decade of increasing access to IT in U.S. schools (Bennett, 2002). Canadian critics have berated the disinformation highway (Barlow & Robertson, 1994) and the diversion of scarce resources from other areas of the curriculum (Armstrong & Casement, 1998).

Some of the causes of this lack of demonstrated impact of computers on achievement relate to problems such as shortage of computers, lack of computer maintenance, the rapid dating of operating systems and memory capabilities, and the increasing cost of keeping up with the range of software and hardware available (Cuban, 2001). However, beyond these "technical" impediments, a major reason for the lack of demonstrable impact of IT on academic achievement is that there has been minimal focus on the kinds of pedagogy that are required to exploit the potential of new technologies (Cuban, 2001; Cummins & Sayers, 1995) and the forms of assessment required to evaluate these potential impacts. Tyner (1998) has forcefully expressed this point: "The scholarship on the uses of electronic and digital communication forms for literacy purposes is abysmally weak" (p. 41). This situation is beginning to change. For example, a recent volume (Feldman, Konold, & Coulter, 2000) analyzing ten years of data on the use of computer net-working to support the learning of Science (e.g., the National Geographic Kids Network) highlighted the naïveté underlying aspects of the initial pedagogical vision. They articulated the importance of a social constructivist approach to pedagogy if IT projects are to yield academic gains.

Curriculum/Pedagogy

Clark (2001) points to the polarized debate in many countries between "traditionalists" and "progressivists," the former being portrayed as "representing order in the classroom with a defined sense of what was right and wrong, whilst 'progressivists' were represented as child-centered, relativist and presiding over chaotic classrooms" (p. 149). The pedagogical framework articulated below attempts to avoid these caricatured extremes by highlighting the centrality of knowledge generation in an Information Age economy and the need for rigorous guided student inquiry as a foundation for learning. The framework also emphasizes (a) the centrality of language to all areas of the school curriculum, (b) the role of imagination as one of the "most powerful and energetic intellectual tools children bring to school" (Egan, 1986, p. 18), and (c) the importance of collaborative critical inquiry that builds on and validates students' experience and culture (Cope & Kalantzis, 2000; Cummins, 2001). The framework does not discard the utility of transmitting information and skills but highlights the importance of collaborative knowledge building and experiential learning designed to promote critical literacy and higher-order thinking. A central component of critical literacy is that it focuses on problem solving in relation to social realities, in addition to cognitive realities.

Assessment

Standardized assessment has become a major tool in the drive to increase literacy attainments in schools. There is considerable concern, however, that an overemphasis on tests has narrowed the curriculum and is causing teachers to "teach to the test," consigning broader educational goals such as the development of imagination, critical literacy, and higher-order thinking to the status of "off-task" activities. Most centrally mandated, large-scale assessment programs in countries around the world focus narrowly on traditional school-based literacy and ignore the multiple literacies (linguistic and technological) that may be equally relevant to students' future economic advancement and civic participation. These large-scale assessment efforts also run into major logistical and ethical dilemmas in a linguistically diverse school system. There is extensive data showing that second-language learners typically require at least five years to catch up academically to native-speaker norms (see Cummins, 2001, for a review). Thus, it is hardly surprising that 50% of Grade 10 students in Ontario designated as ESL failed the Grade 10 literacy test (EQAO, 2005). What structural and pedagogical changes are required to ensure that bright and motivated students are not denied a high school diploma simply because they have had insufficient time to catch up academically in English?

An additional consideration in reconceptualizing high-stakes assessment procedures is that the design of innovative virtual learning environments will be severely constricted if students' accomplishments within these environments are ignored for assessment purposes. If traditional reading, writing, and numeracy skills are the primary (or exclusive) focus of assessment, then students who spend time pursuing multiliteracies endeavours and/or critical literacy activities are likely to be penalized, rather than rewarded, for their achievements.

From the perspective of multiliteracies pedagogy, assessment should reflect and reinforce the range of pedagogical orientations and goals that are being implemented in the classroom. Unfortunately, in many contexts, assessment succeeds in reinforcing only transmission-oriented pedagogy and effectively eliminates broader pedagogical orientations from the classroom. Thus, different forms of assessment are appropriate according to the specific learning activities being pursued. For example, traditional paper-and-pencil tests may be appropriate for a vocabulary-learning activity, but this form of assessment is incapable of capturing the learning objectives of group-based, multimedia project work (e.g., creating a video). The latter forms of activity might be better assessed through portfolio assessment that tracks students' academic accomplishments over time. Thus, just as an applicant for Art College would submit his or her portfolio of work for assessment, students' accomplishments in multiple spheres of literacy endeavour (e.g., web-page design or writing of bilingual stories for younger students), both in school and outside school, could be gathered in portfolios, assessed, and given academic credit. Implementation of portfolio assessment was a major factor in the outstanding academic outcomes obtained during the 1990s by recently arrived, low-income ESL students attending the International High School in LaGuardia Community College in New York City (Cummins, 2001; DeFazio, 1997).

A Framework for Academic Language Learning and Multiliteracies Pedagogy

The central sphere in Figure 1 represents the interpersonal space created in the interactions that take place within the learning community. Teachers have the power to orchestrate patterns of teacher-student, student-student, and school-community inter-actions that result in very different forms of cognitive engage-ment and identity investment on the part of students. Within this interpersonal space, knowledge is constructed and identities are negotiated. In other words, teacher-student interactions can

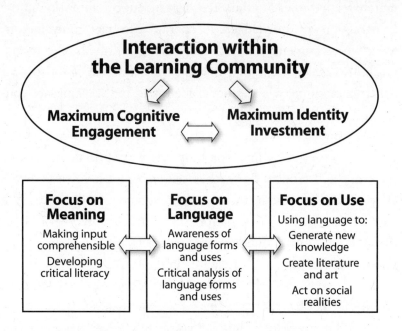

A Framework for Academic Language Learning and Multiliteracies Pedagogy.
Adapted from Cummins, J. (2001), p. 125.

be viewed through two lenses: (a) the lens of the teaching-learning relationship in a narrow sense, represented by the strategies and techniques that teachers use to promote literacy, numeracy, content knowledge, and cognitive growth and (b) the lens of identity negotiation reflected in the messages communicated to students regarding their identities — who they are in the teacher's eyes and who they are capable of becoming. The framework proposes that an optimal learning environment, whether virtual or real, requires that both cognitive engagement and identity investment be maximized.

The interpersonal space represented in Figure 1 extends Vygotsky's (1978) notion of the zone of proximal development beyond the cognitive sphere into the realms of affective development and power relationships. The two related processes of reciprocal negotiation of identity and collaborative generation of knowledge take place within this construction zone and are seen as being intimately related to each other. Teacher-student collaboration in the construction of knowledge will operate effectively only in contexts where students' identities are being affirmed. The framework also makes clear that the construction zone can also be a constriction zone, where student identities and learning are constricted rather than extended.

Teachers have the power to structure the classroom community in a variety of ways. For example, a traditional classroom structure will tend to be teacher centered and involve one-way transmission of content from teachers to students. By contrast, a social constructivist orientation will tend to involve a more dynamic, two-way dialogue and a focus on co-constructing knowledge among the participants in the learning community. A transformative orientation will promote a collaborative, critical-inquiry focus on social as well as academic issues.

The relevance of identity investment derives from the fact that affect is a major determinant of the extent to which students

236

are likely to engage cognitively and academically. Students will be reluctant to invest their identities in the learning process if they feel their teachers do not like them, respect them, and appreciate their experiences and talents. In the past, students from marginalized social groups have seldom felt this sense of affirmation and respect for language and culture from their teachers, and consequently their intellectual and personal talents rarely found expression in the classroom. This perspective implies that in considering the potential of ICT projects or programs to increase academic engagement among students from marginalized communities, two significant factors are likely to be (a) the extent to which students are encouraged to explore and appreciate aspects of their own cultural and linguistic heritage and (b) the extent to which they come to see themselves as intelligent and capable human beings in the process of carrying out these projects.

There is a reciprocal relationship between cognitive engagement and identity investment. The more affirmed and respected students feel in the learning environment, the more they are likely to engage cognitively; similarly, cognitive engagement results in learning, and the more students learn, the more their academic self-concept grows, which, in turn, results in more cognitive and academic engagement.

Although the construct of identity investment has not received much attention in the cognitive psychology or educational-reform research literature, it has emerged as a significant explanatory construct in the educational anthropology and second-language learning literature (e.g., Fordham, 1990; Norton, 2000).

With specific reference to academic language learning, the framework proposes that instruction should focus on meaning, language, and use. Each of these foci is sketched below.

Focus on Meaning

The framework shown in Figure 1 highlights the fact that effective instruction in a first or second language must focus initially on meaning. Virtually all applied linguists agree that access to sufficient comprehensible input in the target language is a necessary condition for language acquisition. With respect to academic language learning in both first and second languages (L1 and L2), there is a vast amount of research showing a strong positive relationship between extensive reading and the development of reading comprehension.

In the Focus on Meaning component, the interpretation of the construct of comprehensible input must go beyond just literal comprehension. Depth of understanding of concepts and vocabulary, as well as critical literacy, are intrinsic to the notion of comprehensible input when we are talking about the development of academic language proficiency. This implies a process whereby students relate textual and instructional meanings to their own experience and prior knowledge (i.e., activate their cognitive schemata), critically analyze the information in the text (e.g., evaluate the validity of various arguments or propositions), and use the results of their discussions and analyses in some concrete, intrinsically motivating activity or project (e.g., making a video or writing a poem or essay on a particular topic).

Focus on Language

The Focus on Language component in Figure 1 attempts to put controversial issues such as the appropriate time and ways to teach grammar, the role of phonics in reading instruction under the "umbrella" of Language Awareness. The development of language awareness includes not only an explicit focus on formal aspects of the language, but also the development of critical language awareness that encompasses exploration of the relationships between language and power. Students, for example, might carry out research on the status of different varieties of language (e.g., colloquial language versus formal, "standard" language) and explore critically why one form is considered by many educators and the general public to be "better" than the other. They might also research issues such as linguistic code switching and the functions it plays within their own lives and their bilingual communities. Or they might analyze letters to the editor on controversial issues such as immigration and examine how the language used in these letters positions and potentially stereotypes minority group learners such as themselves and their parents.

In short, the framework proposes that a focus on formal features of the target language should be integrated with critical inquiry into issues of language and power. Also, to be effective, a focus on language must be linked to extensive input in the target language (e.g., through reading) and extensive opportunities for written and oral use of the language (e.g., oral or written discussion of controversial issues).

Focus on Use

The Focus on Use component is based on the notion that L1 and L2 acquisition will remain abstract and classroom-bound unless students have the opportunity to express themselves — their identities and their intelligence — through language. In order to motivate language use, there should ideally be an authentic audience that encourages two-way communication in both oral and written modes. Clearly, computer-mediated, sister-class projects provide such an audience. The three examples of language use presented in Figure 1 (generate new knowledge, create literature and art, act on social realities) are intended to illustrate important components of critical literacy. Language must be used to amplify students' intellectual, aesthetic, and social identities if it is to contribute to student empowerment, understood as the collaborative creation of power (Cummins, 2001). Unless active and authentic language use for these purposes is promoted in the classroom, students' grasp of academic (and conversational) aspects of their second language is likely to remain shallow and passive.

There is little question that technology can provide many of the essential components required to stimulate active written language use. Collaborative sister-class projects, publication of student work on classroom or school web pages, or simply the use of computers to lay out and print newsletters or other forms of publication all facilitate access to wider audiences than would otherwise be possible. Technology can dramatically expand the communities of inquiry to which students have access and provide immediate outlets for communicating the results of students' intellectual and artistic work (e.g., through school or class web pages).

In short, the Academic Expertise framework articulates the conditions for cognitive and personal engagement in the learning process. Furthermore, it integrates research on language and literacy development in such a way that critical engagement with interpreting and producing text (broadly defined) for authentic purposes is prioritized. These dimensions of the learning process are consistent with the pedagogical framework for multiliteracies pedagogy proposed by the New London Group (1996). The New London Group (1996) highlighted the importance of situated practice, overt instruction, critical framing, and transformed practice. The essence of this framework is that students should be given opportunities to engage in meaningful experience and practice within a learning community, and the development of concepts and understanding should be supported by explicit instruction as required. Students should also have opportunities to step back from what they have learned and examine concepts and ideas critically in relation to their social relevance. Finally, they should be given opportunities to take the knowledge they have gained further — to put it into play in the world of ideas and to come to understand how their insights can exert an impact on people and issues in the real world. In the sections that follow, some concrete directions for putting the Academic Expertise and Multiliteracies Pedagogy frameworks into classroom practice are discussed. The notion of identity texts has emerged as a central construct in thinking about how teacher-student interactions can create conditions for identity investment in school-based literacy practices.

Identity Texts

The relevance of what we are calling identity texts can be appreciated by visiting the Dual Language Showcase site created by educators at Thornwood Elementary School in the Peel District School Board (**http://thornwood.peelschools.org/Dual/**). Grades 1 and 2 students from culturally and linguistically diverse backgrounds created stories initially in English (the language of school instruction); they illustrated their stories and then worked with various resource people (parents, older students literate in L1, and some teachers who spoke a variety of students' languages) to translate the stories into their home languages. The stories and illustrations were then entered into the computer through word processing and scanning. The Dual Language website was created to enable students' bilingual stories to be shared with parents, relatives, or friends in both Canada and the students' countries of origin who had Internet access (Chow & Cummins, 2003). The Academic Expertise framework proposes that optimal academic development within the interpersonal space of the learning community occurs only when there is both maximum cognitive engagement and maximum identity investment on the part of students. The products of students' creative work or performances carried out within this pedagogical space are termed "identity texts," insofar as students invest their identities in these texts (written, spoken, visual, musical, dramatic, or combinations in multimodal form). These texts then act like mirrors to students, reflecting back their identities in a positive light. When students share identity texts with multiple audiences (peers, teachers, parents, grandparents, sister classes, the media, etc.), they are likely to receive positive feedback and affirmation of self in interaction with these audiences. Although not always an essential component, technology acts as an amplifier to enhance the process of identity investment and affirmation. It facilitates the production of these texts, makes them look more accomplished, and expands the audiences and potential for affirmative feedback.

In our work in various highly diverse classrooms where students have worked collaboratively to write and publish bilingual/multilingual identity texts, we have found evidence for the following claims:

1. Students' home language (L1) knowledge is an educationally significant component of their cultural capital.

2. Even in an English-medium instructional context, teachers can create an environment that acknowledges, communicates respect for, and promotes students' linguistic and cultural capital.

3. Newly arrived students whose knowledge of English is minimal are enabled to express their artistic and linguistic talents, intelligence, and imagination through the creation of identity texts written initially in their L1. (In this way, they quickly join the classroom and school learning community as valued members, rather than remaining at the periphery for an extended period.)

4. Students' attitude toward and use of L1 changes positively in L1-supportive classroom contexts.

5. Parent-student communication and collaboration increase when dual-language literacy projects such as book authoring are initiated.

6. Technology can increase the audience for students' books and provide reinforcement for students' literacy practices.

7. Dual language initiatives can serve to normalize linguistic diversity within the school and result in more coherent and effective school policies with respect to (a) affirming students' linguistic and cultural identities, (b) parental involvement, and (c) technology use within the school.

These claims become relevant for policy and pedagogy in the context of the fact that the normalized "default options" in most schools are very different. Specifically, the following assumptions and practices have become normalized in ways that constrict both the identity options for culturally diverse students and their cognitive and academic engagement:

- literacy is assumed to equal English literacy;

- there is minimal acknowledgement or promotion of students' cultural/linguistic/imaginative capital;

- the involvement of culturally and linguistically diverse parents is limited and passive; and

- technology use is sporadic and unconnected to coherent pedagogical philosophies and practices.

A radically different image of the child is implied in the classrooms we have observed than in more typical transmission-oriented classrooms. Within the framework of multiliteracies pedagogy, broadly defined, educators expand the opportunities for children to express themselves — their intelligence, imagination, and linguistic and artistic talents. When this kind of expression is enabled, children come to see themselves as intelligent, imaginative, and talented. In some cases, identity texts will involve children's home languages; in other cases, English may be the medium. Similarly, technology has the power to amplify and enhance the "peak experience" (Maslow, 1968, 1999) that the identity text represents, but it is not always an essential component.

On the basis of the collaboration with educators in the project schools, we can articulate in a very concrete way five central components of a multiliteracies pedagogy that prioritize the role of identity investment in learning for deep understanding.

• multiliteracies pedagogy constructs an image of the child as intelligent, imaginative, and linguistically talented; individual differences in these traits do not diminish the potential of each child to shine in specific ways;

• multiliteracies pedagogy acknowledges and builds on the cultural and linguistic capital (prior knowledge) of students and communities;

• multiliteracies pedagogy aims explicitly to promote cognitive engagement and identity investment on the part of students;

• multiliteracies pedagogy enables students to construct knowledge, create literature and art, and act on social realities through dialogue and critical inquiry; and

• multiliteracies pedagogy employs a variety of technological tools to support students' construction of knowledge, literature, and art and their presentation of this intellectual work to multiple audiences through the creation of identity texts.

These components are also identifiable in the descriptions of "New Literacy Studies" classroom pedagogy discussed by Pahl & Rowsell (2005). They are also much more closely aligned than traditional forms of transmission pedagogy with the consensus from the cognitive psychology literature regarding how people learn. In their National Research Council volume with that title,

Bransford, Brown, & Cocking (2000) highlighted the centrality of learning for deep understanding, building on students' pre-existing knowledge, active learning, and support from within the learning community. In the section below, concrete classroom applications of the framework outlined above are discussed.

Options for Pedagogically Powerful Applications of Technology among Culturally and Linguistically Diverse Students

The following list is intended to illustrate the range of powerful applications of technology in schools with large numbers of culturally and linguistically diverse students.

- From kindergarten on, students bring words (in L1, L2, or L3) to class to explore with peers and teacher, and they incorporate these words into technology-supported bilingual/multilingual dictionaries. These words can be discussed in the class and entered into Google image searches to find images that depict the meanings. Students can also look up the words in electronic dictionaries and create their own multimedia glossaries (print, image, audio) to reflect their "language detective" work.

- Students write creatively in L1 and L2 and amplify these identity texts through technology (as in the Dual Language Showcase). Audio can also be integrated into the texts that appear on the web. For example, students can read their stories (in L1 and/or L2) and enable the sound to be turned on or off by those who visit the web page. If the student is not fully literate in his or her L1 (or L2), a parent, teacher, or peer might read the story in that language.

- Students create movies, audio CDs, and/or web pages to communicate the outcomes of their projects aimed at generating new knowledge, creating literature and art, and acting on social realities. Durán and Durán (2001) and Hull and Schultz (2001, 2002) have described how low-SES minority students in the United States created various kinds of multimedia resources on substantive topics of relevance to their lives in the context of after-school, technology-mediated initiatives.

• New arrivals (immigrant students) write in L1 and work with peers, teachers, older students, community volunteers, and technology (e.g., Google or Babel Fish translations) to create bilingual identity texts. For example, a newly arrived student in Grade 5 might write a story or a personal account of some aspect of his or her experience in L1. Students and/or the teacher can then cut and paste this text into Google or Babel Fish for automatic translation into English. The resulting translation will likely be somewhat garbled and inaccurate but sufficiently comprehensible to give the teacher (and other students) the gist of what the new arrival is trying to communicate. A group of students can then be assigned to work with the newly arrived student to edit the English version of the text and to "teach the computer proper English." Then the dual language text can be entered into the class or school website as a bilingual identity text. Thus, the newly arrived student very quickly attains the status of a published bilingual author.

• Students engage in technology-mediated sister-class exchanges using L1 and L2 to create literature and art and/or to explore issues of social relevance to them and their communities (e.g., Social History of Our Community, Voices of our Elders, Working Conditions of Farm Workers). These sister-class exchanges can provide powerful motivation for students to engage in language learning and/or language-maintenance activities. In one project that linked students in Greece and Canada (Kourtis-Kazoullis, 2002; Skourtou, Kourtis-Kazoullis, & Cummins, in press), students completed a story begun by a popular Greek children's writer and generated more than eighty versions of the story in Greek and English on the project website.

All of these different genres of technology-mediated projects can take place in school or in out-of-school contexts and be aligned with content standards across the curriculum.

Conclusion

Canadian school systems, like those in most other developed countries are in the process of reframing their mission and pedagogical approaches to take into account the realities of a globalized Information Age society. This reframing involves consideration of the nature of literacy and the ways in which traditional school-based literacy relates to the literacy practices that students engage in outside of school. The imperatives of a globalized, knowledge-based society suggest that education systems should orient themselves in the following directions:

• the cultural and linguistic diversity represented in school populations should be viewed as a resource to be developed, rather than as a problem to be solved;

• pedagogy should shift from a predominant reliance on transmission of information and skills (particularly among low-income students) to the promotion of active learning for deep understanding, involving the collaborative construction of knowledge and the development of critical literacy; and

• technology should be harnessed to enable students to generate new knowledge, create literature and art, and act on social realities that affect their societies.

The term "multiliteracies pedagogy" serves as a convenient label to capture these directions for change. The five components of multiliteracies pedagogy that were articulated above have emerged from classroom-based action research and are highly consistent with fundamental principles of learning identified in the cognitive psychology literature (Bransford, Brown, & Cocking, 2000). The multiliteracies pedagogy that has been described stands in stark contrast to the "default option" pedagogy that has been the norm in Canadian schools for generations but which is no longer functional in light of changing global and local realities. Hopefully, this contrast will serve as a stimulus for intense discussion of policy and pedagogical options in Canadian schools in the immediate future.

NOTE

The analysis in this essay reflects some of the ideas emerging from a three-year, SSHRC-funded project entitled "From Literacy to Multiliteracies: Designing Learning Environments for Knowledge Generation within the New Economy" (Early et al., 2002). The research team aims to bring theoretical work that is ongoing in many parts of the world related to the concept of multiliteracies into dialogue with actual multiliteracies practice in Canadian schools. Our ultimate goal is to develop a pedagogical framework that can guide policy makers and educators in designing curricula and forms of instruction that respond to the realities of a global Information Age society (for more information see **www.multiliteracies.ca**).

REFERENCES

Armstrong, A., & Casement, C. (1998). *The child and the machine: Why computers may put our children's education at risk.* Toronto: Key Porter.

Attewell, P., & Battle, J. (1999). Home computers and school performance. *The Information Society, 15*(1), 1-10.

Barlow, M., & Robertson, H.-J. (1994). *Class warfare: The assault on Canada's schools.* Toronto: Key Porter.

Bennett, F. (2002). The future of computer technology in K-12 education. *Phi Delta Kappan, 83*(8), 621-625.

Bransford, J.D., Brown, A.L., & Cocking, R.R. (2000). *How people learn: Brain, mind, experience, and school.* Washington, DC: National Academy Press.

Chomsky, N. (2000). *Chomsky on miseducation*. Edited and introduced by Donaldo Macedo. New York: Rowman & Littlefield.

Chow, P., & Cummins, J. (2003). Valuing multilingual and multicultural approaches to learning. In S.R. Schecter and J. Cummins (Eds.), *Multilingual education in practice: Using diversity as a resource* (pp. 32–61). Portsmouth, NH: Heinemann.

Clark, U. (2001). *War words: Language, history and the disciplining of English*. Oxford: Elsevier.

Cope, B., & Kalantzis, M. (2000). Multiliteracies: The beginnings of an idea. In B. Cope and M. Kalantzis (Eds.), *Multiliteracies: Literacy, learning and the design of social futures* (pp. 3–8). New York: Routledge.

Corson, D. (1997). The learning and use of academic English words. *Language Learning, 47,* 671–718.

Cuban, L. (2001). *Oversold and underused: Computers in the classroom.* Cambridge, MA: Harvard University Press.

Cummins, J. (2001). *Negotiating identities: Education for empowerment in a diverse society* (2nd ed.). Los Angeles: California Association for Bilingual Education.

Cummins, J., & Sayers, D. (1995). *Brave new schools: Challenging cultural illiteracy through global learning networks.* New York: St. Martin's Press.

DeFazio, A.J. (1997). Language awareness at The International High School. In L. Van Lier & D. Corson (Eds.), *Knowledge about language* (Vol. 6, pp. 99–107). Dordrecht: Kluwer Academic Publishers.

Durán , R., & Durán, J. (2001). Latino immigrant parents and children learning and publishing together in an after-school setting. *Journal of Education for Students Placed at Risk, 6*(1/2), 95–113.

Early, M., et al. (2002). From literacy to multiliteracies: Designing learning environments for knowledge generation within the new economy. Proposal funded by the Social Sciences and Humanities Research Council of Canada.

Education Quality and Accountability Office (EQAO). (2005). *Ontario secondary school literacy test: Report of provincial results — English-language schools.* Toronto: EQAO.

Egan, K. (1986). *Teaching as story telling: An alternative approach to teaching and curriculum in the elementary school.* Chicago: University of Chicago Press.

Feldman, A., Konold, C., & Coulter, B. (2000). *Network science a decade later: The Internet and classroom learning.* Mahwah, NJ: Lawrence Erlbaum Associates.

Fordham, S. (1990). Racelessness as a factor in Black students' school success: Pragmatic strategy or Pyrrhic victory? In N. M. Hidalgo, C. L. McDowell, & E. V. Siddle (Eds.), *Facing racism in education* (Reprint series No. 21, pp.232–262). Cambridge, MA: Harvard Educational Review.

Hull, G., & Schultz, K. (2001). Literacy and learning out of school: A review of theory and research. *Review of Educational Research, 71*(4), 575–612.

Hull, G., & Schultz, K. (Eds.). (2002). *School's out! Bridging out-of-school literacies with classroom practice.* New York: Teachers College Press.

Kleiner, A., & Farris, E. (2002). *Internet access in U.S. public schools and classrooms: 1994–2001.* Washington, DC: National Center for Educational Statistics.

Kourtis-Kazoullis, V. (2002). DiaLogos: Bilingualism and the teaching of second language learning on the Internet. Unpublished doctoral dissertation, University of the Aegean, Primary Education Department, Rhodes, Greece.

Krashen, S. (2004). *The power of reading* (2nd ed.). Portsmouth, NH: Heinemann.

Maslow, A. (1968, 1999). *Towards a psychology of being* (3rd ed.). New York: John Wiley & Sons.

Moll, L.C., Amanti, C., Neff, D., & González, N. (1992). Funds of knowledge for teaching: Using a qualitative approach to connect homes and classrooms. *Theory into Practice, 31*(2), 132–141.

Nation, P., & Coady, J. (1988). Vocabulary and reading. In R. Carter & M. McCarthy (Eds.). *Vocabulary and language teaching* (pp. 97–110). London: Longman.

New London Group. (1996). A pedagogy of multiliteracies: Designing social futures. *Harvard Educational Review, 66*, 60–92.

Norton, B. (2000). *Identity and language learning: Gender, ethnicity and educational change.* London: Longman.

Pahl, K., & Rowsell, J. (2005). *Understanding literacy education: Using new literacy studies in the classroom.* San Francisco: Sage.

Plante, J., & Beattie, D. (2004). Connectivity and ICT integration in Canadian elementary and secondary schools: First results from the Information and Communications Technologies in Schools Survey,

2003–2004 (Catalogue No. 81-595-MIE — No. 017). Ottawa: Statistics Canada.

Skourtou, E., Kourtis-Kazoullis, V., & Cummins, J. (in press). Designing virtual learningenvironments for academic language development. In J. Weiss, J. Nolan, & V. Nincic (Eds), *Handbook of virtual learning*. Dordrecht: Kluwer Academic Publishers.

Roessingh, H. (2004). Effective high school ESL programs: A synthesis and meta-analysis. *Canadian Modern Language Review, 60*, 611–636.

Tyner, K. (1998). *Literacy in a digital world: Teaching and learning in the Age of Information*. Mahwah, NJ: Lawrence Erlbaum Associates.

Vygotsky, L.S. (1978). *Mind in society: The development of higher psychological processes*. Cambridge, MA: Harvard University Press.

Warschauer, M., Knobel, M., & Stone, L. (2004). Technology and equity in schooling: Deconstructing the digital divide. *Educational Policy, 18*(4), 562–588.

Watt, D.L.E., & Roessingh, H. (2001). The dynamics of ESL drop-out: Plus ca change. *Canadian Modern Language Review, 58*, 203–22.

Genders, Sexualities, and Schooling: Taking Difference into Account

Paula S. Cameron and Blye Frank

O ver the past decade, fierce debates regarding sexual diversity have been unfolding in classrooms[1] and court-rooms — across Canada. Discrimination against lesbian, gay, bisexual, transgender, and intersexed (LGBTI)[2] individuals, arguably the "last respected prejudice of the century," has surfaced as a crucible for ethics and values within public institutions (Peter J. Gomes, as cited in Baker, 2002, p. 2). The debate spurs us to reconsider our firmly held assumptions regarding gender and sexuality and calls into question the role of social institutions in supporting sexually diverse youth.

In this essay, we suggest that supporting sexually diverse students in Canadian high schools requires moving beyond simplistic prescriptions and expressions of "tolerance" to a reconceptualization of gender and sexuality and how they play out in the many facets of school culture. Conceiving of gender and sexuality as plural, fluid, and consisting of complex power relations enables us to question a status quo that privileges "straight" over "LGBTI" and to take up homophobia and heterosexism as issues affecting all of us in diverse and changing ways. We will argue for the contributions of feminist poststructuralism to this new challenge and put forth suggestions for change in four general areas of school culture; these include pedagogy, language, curricula, and policy.

Lesbian, gay, bisexual, transgender, and intersexed youth often "learn their lack" (Smith, 2000) in Canadian schools. Although abuse and discrimination toward LGBTI individuals is often conceived as a "sexual minority" problem, its impact is also felt by heterosexuals targeted by peers for constant harassment and bullying (Kimmel & Mahler, 2003). In truth, *any* nongender-conforming behaviours might threaten narrow gender boundaries and inspire fear and rejection in others. In the end, then, we are all limited by the forced choice between "masculine" and "feminine" and "straight" and "LGBTI" and have a stake in ensuring that schools are supportive environments in which the integrity of all students is acknowledged.

Heterosexism, "the systematic, day-to-day, institutional mistreatment of gay, lesbian, and bisexual people by a heterosexually dominated culture" (Creighton, 1992, p. 45) is a subtle form of discrimination, permeating the culture in which schools and other social institutions operate. As it is often enacted by individuals who do not appear to be overtly homophobic or to hold negative views toward sexual minorities (Berkman & Zinberg, 1997), it is both difficult and important to identify and address. Homophobia can be considered "one of heterosexism's major expressions, a way each of us — whether heterosexual or lesbian, gay or bisexual — carries the oppression in ourselves" (Creighton, 1992, p. 45). Homophobia is institutional discrimination distilled and embodied in emotional form: it is fear, rage, shame, guilt, and horror directed at those who dare transcend conventional gender boundaries — and these emotions may be directed at ourselves.

Discrimination can be manifested not only in overt homophobic statements, but also in subtle absences and silences that prevent LGBTI students from being acknowledged and represented in pedagogy, language, curriculum, and policy. Within the complex ecosystem of school communities, persistently framing heterosexuality as the norm, from official policies to everyday jokes and gossip, creates a context in which particular students perceive themselves as being "less than normal" (Warwick, Aggleton, & Douglas, 2001, p. 131). As Bernstein points out, "The question is: who recognizes themselves as of value [in schools]? What other images are excluded by the dominant image of value so that some students are unable to recognize themselves?" (Bernstein, 1996, p. 7).

Theoretical Background

Our current approach to gender and sexual diversity is informed by feminist poststructuralist theories.[3] Both feminism and poststructualism are highly contested terms, and like all knowledge claims, are saturated with the power dynamics of competing worldviews. In this context, any claims to mastery over language and knowledge could be considered fallacious or even suspect. As such, our use of the term "feminist poststructuralism" is not intended to "capture" the totality of a theoretical field but to highlight three commonly cited aspects and to consider the possible implications of taking sexual diversity into account in schools.

"Feminist poststructuralism" is intended to refer loosely to theoretical trends over the past few decades that have developed out of a merging between (1) a structuralist awareness of language as a predetermined system of meaning and (2) a feminist emphasis on action and social change (Weedon, 1997). Feminist poststructuralist theories have commonly emphasized the subtle ways in which power plays out in the social interactions of day-to-day life. In the sections below, we will briefly discuss three relevant and frequently cited contributions of feminist poststructuralism and articulate an alternative conception of gender and sexuality.

1. Our day-to-day relations in schools are saturated by power.

Chris Weedon describes power as "a relation [which] inheres in difference and is a dynamic of control, compliance and lack of control between discourses[4] and the subjects constituted by discourses, who are their agents" (1997, p. 110). The traditional notion of power as a stable, independent entity with discernable boundaries is therefore disrupted; power becomes simultaneously social (via discourse) and individual (via subjectivity) and subject to ever-changing contexts. It is constituted by constant struggle and made and un-made within the interactions of real people and institutions; simultaneously, we as "subjects constituted by discourses" are similarly made and un-made in intricate dances of control, compliance, and lack of control. In the school context, then, poststructuralism brings the focus on power from "out there" to "in here." This shift reveals that power struggles occur not only in overt or official, externally located sites (e.g., courtrooms, Parliaments, and school boards), but also in the daily social interactions of all members of school communities.

2. Language is the primary means by which power "plays out" in our daily lives.

Many postmodernists assert that language is the site of social and political struggle for differently privileged discourses (Lather, 1991; Weedon, 1997); "yet it is also the place where our sense of ourselves, our subjectivity, is constructed" (Weedon, 1997, p. 21). As such, language is saturated with power relations and must be scrutinized for oppositions that privilege one group over another (e.g., male/female, straight/LGBTI). Within the language we use are assumptions that perpetuate heterosexual bias in schooling; in the classroom, this may be as simple as using heterosexual examples when discussing relationships or families.

Patti Lather points out that when we speak language, language also speaks *us* (1991). Language reflects our assumptions about the world, yet it is also a predetermined and "ready-made" social system of meaning that we enter into at birth. It both reflects and creates our ways of seeing and being in the world. Thus, making an authentic attempt at gender and sexual equity in schools requires careful reconsideration of the language we use in our day-to-day lives.

3. Subjectivity is contradictory and constantly shifting.

Subjectivity, "the conscious and unconscious thoughts and emotions of the individual, her sense of herself and her ways of understanding her relation to the world" (Weedon, 1997, p. 32) is a common poststructuralist concern, and it is useful to take subjectivity into account when considering gender and sexuality. Poststructuralist feminists frame subjectivity as a social product, located in historical time; yet, as it is constantly shaped by competing worldviews, it is highly fluid and contradictory.

In fact, some poststructuralists posit that subjectivity constantly changes and shifts in our day-to-day lives — so much so that static, definitive boundaries are made impossible (and paradoxically, this applies to poststructuralism itself). It follows that we can no longer refer to a single, coherent identity, then, but must acknowledge that we are constituted by diverse and often conflicting identities. Nor can we consider these subjectivities to be "ours" or under our control: we are part of power relations beyond our control and often beyond our perception. Poststructuralists caution that as power relations saturate our subjectivities, the very means of comprehension, we are never fully able to step outside them — to be fully objective and in control. Thus, homophobia and heterosexism can be considered to be not simply results of individual "bad" people. They are the products of competing discourses that privilege certain groups and qualities over others (in this case, "straight" over "LGBTI") and that are manifested within individual subjectivities which determine (and are determined by) the language we use.

We have highlighted these three specific theoretical assumptions for the purposes of framing current challenges to conventional approaches to sexual diversity. These complex approaches to power, language, and subjectivity are vastly oversimplified here and constitute just three of many conflicting stances taken up by feminist poststructuralist theorists. Challenging popular notions of a fixed and unchanging identity, questioning the innocence of language, and reconsidering the ways in which power is manifested daily in schools all serve to unsettle conventional ideas that have fed discrimination against LGBTI students, staff, and parents. This discrimination, taking many forms, is commonly referred to as homophobia or heterosexism.

Homophobia and Heterosexism

Homophobia is part of an intricate web of gendered power relations in school and society. It may take the form of verbal abuse, including sexual slurs and epithets, or physical violence, including bodily harm and even murder (Amnesty International, 2001). A relatively modern phenomenon, it is a "highly culturally variable and by no means inevitable" (Plummer, 2001, p. 15). Homophobia is somewhat arbitrarily hinged upon a certain society's beliefs. It is not predestined or "natural" by virtue of its cultural specificity; consequently, the goal of changing homophobic attitudes and practices is realistic and worthwhile.

Homophobia is often justified by appeals to conventional values. For instance, it is commonly agreed that pedophilia, the sexual abuse of children by adults, is morally repugnant. In fact, pedophiles are arguably the most reviled members of North American society. On Family.org, a website of the right-wing American group Focus on the Family, James Dobson implicitly equates pedophilia with being LGBTI. Rejecting the claim that homosexuality is "natural," innate, and biologically determined, he asks, "What if a *pedophile* [italics added] could claim he inherited his lust for kids?" (Dobson, 2000). Allusions to traditional values, here the health and safety of children, infuse the sexual diversity debate with fear and panic. This obscures the matter at hand, shifting focus from the detractors' actual claim, to our collective horror regarding sexual abuse of children. Thus, homophobia can arise from our inability to identify and critique such weak arguments, a matter that illustrates the need for careful and critical thinking when approaching sexual diversity in schools and society.

The fear and rejection of nontraditional genders, regardless of the sexual identity of the person in question, exposes the gendered nature of homophobic beliefs. In many cases, homophobia is "misdirected" at heterosexual youth who do not conform to conventional gender roles. For instance, in a recent Australian study, teenagers reported applying sexual slurs such as "faggot" and "dyke" to peers exhibiting a wide range of nonsexual behaviors, including being artistic or studious (specifically for boys) or being a loner (Martino & Pallotta-Chiarolli, 2004).

From a feminist poststructuralist stance, we would add that homophobia often arises from the assumption that our gender roles and sexual orientations are stable and unchanging. According to North American convention, gender and sexuality consist of male/female and straight/LGBTI binary oppositions (Butler, 1990). They are rigidly polarized as opposites, with little or no overlap. As recently as the 1990s, for instance, young Canadian girls who resisted wearing dresses and preferred playing with trucks were labelled "gender non-conforming" and/or diagnosed with "Gender Identity Disorder" (Filax & Shogan, 2004). Implicit in this diagnosis is the unsubstantiated belief that clothing and play activities of boys and girls are naturally distinct and that transgressions of the masculine-feminine divide may indicate gender pathology, requiring intervention and possibly medical treatment.

Beyond more overt examples of homophobic attitudes and behaviours, heterosexism may permeate school climates in more subtle and therefore more elusive ways. Warwick, Aggleton, and Douglas (2001) note that

> too often schools work from the assumption that all their members are (or should be) heterosexual. This may be reflected in the issues that are talked about, the manner in which the curriculum is taught, and the issues that are seen as particularly problematic and therefore requiring of staff time. (p. 138)

For instance, we may inadvertently alienate LGBTI students by using heteronormative examples in the classroom. In a recent study, a lesbian youth commented that "teachers always talk about someone of the opposite sex. And so do the students ... It makes you really uncomfortable to talk about your same-sex interest. You just don't do it." (Lee, 2002, p. 20)

Often compounding this inadvertent silencing are the ways in which sexualities are presented in curricula and texts. Nontraditional sexualities may be absent from the sex education curriculum or they may be medicalized or discussed solely in relation to AIDS (Monahan, 1997). Subtle heterosexist assumptions may also pervade other aspects of school culture, such as language and pedagogy, which interact in complex and contradictory ways within a school community. We will explore these issues later in this essay as we provide suggestions for change. First, however, we will consider the ways in which sexual diversity within schools is being negotiated in Canadian courtrooms.

Legal Context

Despite a lack of governmental and policy support for sexual inclusiveness in North American schools (DeCrescenzo, 1994), sexual diversity is being renegotiated in high-profile court cases across Canada (e.g., *British Columbia College of Teachers v. Trinity Western University*, 2001; *Chamberlain v. Surrey School District No. 36*, 2002). These cases have conveyed mixed messages regarding our national commitment to building capacity for sexual diversity in Canadian schools. In 2001, eight Supreme Court justices voted in favour of upholding Trinity Western University's right to require that their students sign a contract promising to refrain from "homosexual behavior" — as well as premarital sex, adultery, abortion, pornography, drunkenness, swearing, and lying. Madame Justice Claire L'Heureux-Dubé placed the sole dissenting vote; in the court decision, she commented:

> Evidence shows that there is an acute need for improvement in the experiences of homosexual and bisexual students in Canadian classrooms. Without the existence of supportive classroom environments, homosexual and bisexual students will remain invisible and reluctant to approach their teachers. They will be victims of identity erasure. (*British Columbia College of Teachers v. Trinity Western University*, 2001, para 12)

Central to her argument was the pressing need for LGBTI students to be represented in school policies and curricula, in order to be protected from the "identity erasure" resulting from homophobia and heterosexism in Canadian schools. The following year, Ontario teen Marc Hall won the right to take his boyfriend to his high school prom. In his decision, Superior Court Justice Robert MacKinnon cited the role of school as a "fundamental institution in the lives of young people" and noted

261

that exclusion from any aspects of school life constitutes a restriction to this institution (Egale Canada, 2002).

Later in 2002, the Supreme Court rejected an attempt by a British Columbia school board to ban elementary children's literature depicting same-sex-parented families. In the Supreme Court decision, Chief Justice Beverley McLaughlin noted,

> it is hard to see how the materials will raise questions which would not in any event be raised by the acknowledged existence of same-sex parented families in the K-1 parent population, or in the broader world in which these children live. The only *additional* message of the materials appears to be the message of tolerance. Tolerance is always age-appropriate. (*Chamberlain v. Surrey School District No. 36*, 2002, para 69)

These recent court cases reflect the growing debate among students, educators, lawmakers, parents, activists, and religious groups on the rights and representation of LGBTI students, parents, and teachers within the Canadian school system. The highly contested nature of such issues indicates that the conversation is critical if we are to collectively work toward inclusive education. We will not lay claim to any definitive answers; rather, this essay represents one piece of the dialogue as we explore, investigate, and analyze genders and sexualities as lived social practice in the ordinary, everyday routine of schooling and offer some examples and suggestions for change. We will outline recent mainstream research on LGBTI youth in schools and put forward suggestions for change in four areas of school culture.

Research

LGBTI-identified youth have been estimated to constitute between 1 and 10 percent of a school population. While this may seem low, research suggests that many LGBTI youth may not readily identify for several reasons. Social stigma and resulting feelings of guilt, confusion, and fear of rejection may lead them to attempt to "pass as straight." This strategy may be effective in avoiding immediate ostracization, but it comes at "significant, immeasurable cost to their developmental process, self-esteem, and sense of connection" (Uribe & Harbeck, 1992, p. 11). Same-sex-attracted youth may not identify as gay for other reasons as well, including not being out to themselves or to those close to them or embodying a sexuality that falls outside the rigid categories of "heterosexual," "homosexual," and "bisexual." Based on the results of a recent American survey, Savin-Williams (2001) suggests that if we altered the criteria for sexual minority status to reflect the amorphous nature of human sexuality (that is, including as criteria at least one occurrence of a same-sex fantasy), the official percentage would expand to six times its size.

Regardless of the exact proportions of LGBTI-identified youth in schools, quantitative justifications for taking sexual diversity into account are inherently problematic. A numerical focus requires approaching gender and sexuality as entities to be measured and categorized and often leads to framing sexual diversity as a "minority issue" largely irrelevant to the general population. These tendencies betray the complexity of gender and sexuality and create a false dichotomy between LGBTI individuals and their straight-identified peers.

While we question the underlying assumption that sexuality is a definitive "orientation" discovered or achieved, the social stigma attached to enactments of nontraditional genders and sexualities clearly *does* increase stresses on nonconforming students. Medical, educational, and sociological literature demonstrate that in addition to the challenges of adolescence alone, LGBTI youth are at-risk for suicide (LGBTI youth are estimated to be three to four times more likely to commit suicide than the general population) (Saewyc, Bearinger, Heinz, Blum, & Resnick,

1998). They also experience emotional difficulties, problems in school, verbal abuse from peers, physical assaults, sexual abuse, conflict with the law, substance abuse, and eating disorders (Saewyc et al., 1998). They are also more likely to face rejection, isolation, and physical violence in school and at home (Garofalo, Wolf, Kessel, Palfrey, & DuRant, 1998). Not surprisingly, these challenges can lead to dropping out of school (Remafedi, 1987) and lowered self-esteem (Savin-Williams, 1994).

Certain researchers, however, while acknowledging the accuracy and value of this alarming evidence, warn that such studies may inadvertently simplify the contradictions and tensions within the lives of LGBTI youth. Savin-Williams (2001) and Dobinson (2004), for instance, explain that because researchers may want to better the lives of sexual-minority youth, they often call attention to the difficulties these youth face — the specific cases of victimization and early death — rather than the strength, resiliency, and everyday strategies required to survive (and thrive) in homophobic and heterosexist environments. Researchers also run the risk of glossing over differences among LGBTI youth, with their layers of shifting identities by virtue of genders, sexualities, and factors such as age, race,[5] geography, ethnicity, class, and ablebodiedness. This may obscure the similarities between LGBTI-identified youth and their straight-identified peers, thus ghettoizing gender and sexuality studies and reinscribing the former as "outsider" or "other" (Savin-Williams, 2001). Finally, much of the literature on pressing educational issues such as bullying or violence lacks a gender critique that might expose the current of homophobia that runs through social interactions in schools (Kimmel & Mahler, 2003).

Interventions aimed at achieving sexual equity in schools are often informed by research that earnestly strives to address these issues, yet often fail to challenge the deeply embedded assumptions at the root of homophobia and heterosexism in our lives.

As we have shown, feminist poststructuralism provides alternative ways of conceiving gender and sexuality in schools. We will take a further step toward addressing this gap by complementing these possible contributions of feminist poststructuralism with practical suggestions for change within the overlapping areas of pedagogy, language, curriculum, and policy.

Four Potential Areas for Change

The complexity of the social context of schooling should not be underestimated. Challenging homophobia and heterosexism in schools requires more than isolated and superficial responses; as bias and prejudice are embedded in our daily lives both in and out of school and belong to much larger structures of social inequity, their eradication requires careful attention across disciplinary and organizational boundaries within day-to-day routines. Power and politics are played out not only in legislatures and court rooms, but in hallways and lunchrooms. Homophobia and heterosexism lie not only in what is explicitly taught, but in what is left out. They can manifest as assumptions behind pedagogical strategies and techniques or in the language spilling out into classrooms, locker rooms, and schoolyards.

Pedagogy

Meaningful challenges to homophobia and heterosexism often require examining our own complicity in heterosexual privilege. Michael Kimmel (2002) argues that challenging unevenly distributed power requires shifting focus from "the oppressed," and redirecting the critical gaze to "the oppressor." He uses the metaphor of the wind to describe the invisible force or power often accorded to us by virtue of our privileges:

> Being white, or male, or heterosexual in this culture is like running with the wind at your back. It feels like just plain running, and we rarely if ever get a chance to see how we

265

are sustained, supported, and even propelled by that wind. (Kimmel, 2002, p. 42)

Antisexist and antihomophobic pedagogies hold great promise for making the wind of privilege visible. As Kimmel suggests, when we locate isolated incidents and attitudes as part of a larger system of inequality, these emergent patterns challenge commonly held assumptions regarding the "level playing field" of schooling. In a celebrated essay, Peggy McIntosh (1990) uses the metaphor of a weightless "invisible knapsack": "an invisible package of unearned assets that [we] can count on cashing in each day, but about which [we were] 'meant' to remain oblivious. [It contains] special provisions, maps, passports, codebooks, visas, clothes, tools, and blank checks" (p. 31). McIntosh points out that identifying and naming privilege makes us newly accountable, leading us to the question "Having described it, what will I do to lessen or end it?" Similarly, those of us who identify as straight carry similar privilege throughout our lives. Educators and students who learn to identify and challenge such patterns will be better equipped to support sexually diverse students in school.

Antiheterosexist pedagogies provide unique challenges to educators. For instance, even popular, supposedly "liberating" pedagogical techniques such as "free writing" may be interrogated for heterosexist assumptions. As Barnard (2004) points out, "queer students are unlikely to include discussion of their sexuality or gender identity in such revelations, and in fact the revelations can reinscribe a painful process of marginalization and self-censorship for these students" (p. 2). Embedded in such exercises is the assumption that all students are equally "free" in sharing their uncensored thoughts with the teacher and/or the class, as well as the assumption that there is a single "true" self that can be "captured" in confessional genres. To address these pitfalls, Barnard suggests that teachers shape their pedagogical techniques to reflect the diversity and fluidity of subjectivities: for instance, students might adopt various narrative stances to explore "other" voices and engage with stories that may be undervalued in our society (2004).

Sexually inclusive pedagogical strategies require a carefully considered approach to addressing difference in the classroom. The specific methods you choose will depend on the grade level and unique needs of your students, your own teaching style, and your willingness to challenge your own deeply held assumptions regarding gender and sexuality. This may range from avoiding heterosexist examples when addressing the class (e.g., referring only to heterosexual couples or families) to inclusion of hetero-sexism when addressing racism and sexism. Creighton (1992) suggests that for those of us who identify as straight, challenging our assumptions will require learning more about LGBTI history and culture and making such knowledge available to our students. For those of us who are LGBTI, the decision to come out to students may be made, based upon careful consideration of our comfort and safety, as well as the comfort and safety of our students.[6] In both cases, taking up antihomophobic pedagogies involves planning, reflection, and sensitivity to the needs and safety of diverse class members. Specifically, it involves consider-ing the ways in which language perpetuates homophobia and heterosexism in school communities.

Language

The ways in which we as students and teachers speak and write the social text of our classrooms are critically important. Feminist poststructuralists suggest that historically specific words make up the medium through which we shape our lives. As such, we can put poststructuralism to work for us as we seek to identify and address the residue of homophobia and hetero-sexism in schools.

Use of sexual epithets, perhaps the most common form of homophobic harassment in schools, has been shown to begin in prepubescent years and to increase with age until the end of high school (Nayak & Kehily, 1996). In an American national school climate survey, the Gay, Lesbian and Straight Education Network (GLSEN) found that 91.5 percent of LGBTI youth respondents reported hearing "faggot," "dyke," or the expression "That's so gay" frequently or often (Kosciw, 2004). Despite the prevalence of such behaviour, a surprising lack of explicit attention is paid to the issue (Thurlow, 2001). As researchers in the burgeoning field of masculinities have pointed out, we need to consider the gendered nature of such homophobic abuse if we are to get at the heart of the issue (Frank, Kehler, Lovell, & Davison, 2003; Kimmel & Mahler, 2003; Martino & Pallotta-Chiarolli, 2004; Plummer, 2001). This might include, for instance, considering homophobic abuse as a response to everyday threats (perceived or otherwise) to dominant forms of masculinity and femininity, such as boys playing with dolls or girls playing with trucks.

Though "dyke" and "faggot" most clearly represent sexual slurs, they are generally directed at individuals at the margins of the school community, regardless of their sexuality. As one Albertan man writes,

> I first heard it in kindergarten. For the next thirteen years, I heard it daily. Most of those days, it was directed at me. That's because I'm a faggot. Or is that the only reason? All through my life, I've known young men who were driven through that route of humiliation over and over. Many of them weren't gay. Most of them were just ... not willing to resort to violence to prove themselves. (Hagen, 2004, p. 20)

Hagen's experience suggests that this rejection of violence, a stereotypically "male" pursuit, led to homophobic abuse directed at all boys and youth unwilling to play their peer-sanctioned masculine role.

Other research confirms this assessment. For instance, based on recent interviews with teenagers, Plummer (2001) compiled the following possible meanings for "faggot": being a baby; being soft, weak, and timid; being slow to mature physically; acting like a girl; being academic and studious; being artistic; appearing different; not integrating with peer culture; being an outcast or being a loner; not participating in prestigious team sports; conforming too closely to adult expectations at the expense of peer group loyalty; and sexual orientation (p. 18).

This miscellany suggests that more is at play than rejection on the basis of sexual identity or behaviour. It appears that in many of these cases, *sexual* difference is equated with *gender* differences. For boys, being gentle, studious, artistic, or unathletic means "acting like a girl" and therefore rejection for failing to enact a prescribed gender role. . In Kimmel and Mahler's (2003) study on random school shootings in the United States, almost all the shooters had been called "fag" or "queer" due to their studiousness, unique clothing, or social isolation. In an American survey of students from eighth to eleventh grade, 42 percent of boys and 29 percent of girls had been called gay or lesbian (Hostile Hallways, 2001). While girls are called "dyke" or "queer" by peers, these terms appear to be more commonly used by boys than girls (Thurlow, 2001). In spite of evidence of the gendered nature of homophobic taunts, however, much of research and media coverage of violence in North American schools lacks a gender analysis (Kimmel & Mahler, 2003).

There are several ways in which educators and administrators might address homophobic and heterosexist language in schools. While language policies prohibiting the use of homophobic slurs are important for positive sexual diversity climates, enforcing such policies may be difficult if school members underestimate the power of such epithets. For the classroom context, the Gay, Lesbian and Straight Education Network (GLSEN) provides lesson plans to educators seeking to introduce antiheterosexist activities into the curriculum.[7] One example is a lesson plan for middle and high school students entitled "What do 'Faggot' and 'Dyke' Mean?" (Goldstein, 2001).

By focusing attention on the historical, political, and social context of these words, this lesson plan encourages students to identify and examine the everyday language that shapes — and is shaped by — homophobic impulses in everyday life. The opening section of the lesson involves individual reflection upon these terms and how and why people use them. Written responses to questions such as "Who gets called 'faggot' in your school?" and "What does the term mean?" are then encouraged and later brought into a classroom discussion. Because of the gendered nature of such terms, a discussion of gender roles should also be introduced.

This lesson plan also encourages educators to connect these terms to current events and to demonstrate the far-reaching effects that such attitudes and language have on North American culture. Reattaching the weight of history to these popular epithets and linking them to the injustices committed against gays and lesbians in the Holocaust or to the 1998 hate-fuelled murder of Matthew Shepard, a young gay man can reframe verbal abuse as an everyday manifestation of violence. The lesson, however, moves beyond a critique of such homophobic practices into a consideration of *how* such practices occur and how they might be addressed by members of the school community. This final section of the plan consists of a fieldwork assignment in which students seek evidence of anti-LGBTI language in their school environment, as well as a discussion of tactics for eliminating such harassment in their school.

Of course, talking about sexual diversity in the classroom involves much more than following a lesson plan. Confronting and unlearning homophobia and heterosexism is a complex project that requires careful reflection for both students and teachers. In keeping with Kimmel's pedagogy of the oppressor, the Gay, Lesbian and Straight Education Network urges educators to focus on the behaviour of the harassers in these situations, rather than that of the targets. They caution, however, that students must not be forced to share their reflections on these issues. They may feel reticence due to fear of revealing their sexual orientation, traumatic memories of being the target of such harassment, or other reasons. It is important that students be provided with a safe space in which to explore these issues and time to reflect upon their personal experiences of, and perspectives on, heterosexism and homophobic language. Similarly, it would be helpful for the educator leading the discussion to provide herself with time to consider her own assumptions and beliefs regarding sexual diversity and to anticipate difficult questions or issues. This may help her feel more comfortable discussing the topic with students.

Merely implementing language guidelines in the school or classroom is not enough to ensure that homophobia beliefs are being challenged; it is also vital to facilitate in-depth discussions about the reasons why these guidelines are necessary and important. This will frame such guidelines not as rigid rules repressing dissenting opinions, but rather as a well-thought-out response to the everyday verbal harassment of LGBTI students. Feminist poststructuralism provides the theoretical vocabulary to explore how language is saturated with power relations, not only reflecting heterosexist assumptions but actively constituting them. The familiar refrain that "fag" and "dyke" are "only words" becomes problematic if we are to acknowledge the ways in which language shapes and is shaped by power relations that privilege dominant sexualities at the expense of others.

Curriculum

In the past two decades, several researchers have examined photographs, drawings, and verbal representations of members of minority groups in school and university texts, several of which have included representations of gender and homosexuality (e.g., Whatley, 1992). American sexuality textbooks, for instance, often portray LGBTI individuals in the same category as fetishism, prostitution, and sexual violence, and most often the subject of homosexuality and bisexuality is located in a separate section of the text, further emphasizing its separateness from "normal" sexuality (Whatley, 1992).

While critiques of homophobic and heterosexist textual representations can be powerful tools in identifying heterosexual privilege, a sexually diverse curriculum involves more than inclusion of sexual diversity in class texts. As educator and theorist Ian Barnard has pointed out, "Whether we teach queer texts or not, it is in the ways in which we read and teach all texts and the ways in which we organize our classrooms and construct our students that we must most relentlessly deploy anti-homophobic agendas" (Barnard, 1994, p. 26). For example, allotting one week to sexual diversity and failing to address it at other times sends the message that these issues are not of primary concern. With this in mind, we will put forward two examples of ways in which curricula can be shaped to take sexual diversity into account. These include inviting LGBTI class speakers and initiating school-wide diversity programming.

Inviting sexually diverse speakers to share their experiences with a class is another way of disrupting heterosexist privilege in mainstream curricula. This introduces often silenced voices into the learning environment and may encourage students (and teachers) to learn more about their own encounters with heterosexism. Listening to the embodied voices of those engaged in consciousness raising is more threatening to the current state of heterosexism than is engaging with a text.

At the same time, Ian Barnard (1994) reminds us that we should try to avoid "tokenizing" queer concerns in a syllabus or curriculum; one individual should not be expected to speak for all LGBTI people. Nor should LGBTI students or guest speakers be expected to speak for all queer people, but solely for themselves, based on their own experiences. Issues of sexual diversity can be available as possible essay topics, and students can be directed to further reading on these subjects in addition to the queer-authored texts in the curriculum.

Improving our schools' sexual diversity climate entails adopting sexually inclusive curricula throughout the school, not just in select classrooms. This also protects the future of sexually diverse curricula, ensuring that their implementation does not depend solely upon specific champions in a school, who may leave, throwing antihomophobic initiatives into jeopardy. Many curriculum packages and classroom guides can be adapted to a school-wide context. These might involve diversity displays, films, or activities, and murals and other art projects that address the contributions of LGBTI-identified individuals and groups and express the importance of a positive sexual diversity climate for all members of the school community.

Policy

Homophobia and heterosexism are enacted in personal contexts, which are simultaneously part of larger social patterns. As such, institution-wide initiatives are vital to fostering positive sexual diversity climates. Support from local, provincial, and national bodies is essential for the establishment of LGBTI-positive curriculum and school-level policies and programs (Griffin & Ouellett, 2002). Without administrative leadership and institutional support, underlying structures remain unchanged and LGBTI-positive efforts may fail to thrive over time. As Szalacha notes in her 2003 evaluation of the Massachusetts Safe Schools

Program, "Leadership of the principal ... is perhaps the most important feature that distinguishes effective from ineffective schools. The principal who establishes and enforces an official school policy sets the tone for acceptable behavior" (p. 82).

Like curriculum design, sexual diversity policies require addressing the issue both individually and as a part of the whole; this will likely mean introducing new policies that specifically address the unique needs of LGBTI community members while adjusting existing policies to include and protect sexual diversity as a form of difference that enriches the school community. Voluntarily self-identified LGBTI students and staff may be valuable sources of information and insight into the ways in which heterosexism permeates daily relations in schools. It is critical that these school members be active participants in the writing and revision of local, provincial, and national policies addressing sexual diversity in Canadian schools. LGBTI community groups are also highly valuable partners in devising sexually inclusive policies at all levels of schooling (Blumenfeld & Lindop, 2005; Griffin & Ouellett, 2002).

Such policies can take many directions. They can address language used in the school environment; support sexually diverse hiring policies for teachers, administrators, and other staff; address harassment of students by peers; and ensure mandatory education for staff on issues of gender and sexual diversity. In the following section, we will put forth several examples of such policies and describe how they might enhance the sexual diversity climate in Canadian schools.

1. Establishment of "safe contacts" and school-based support groups *(Burton, 1995; Griffin & Ouellett, 2002).*

In its "Lesbian, Gay, Bisexual, Transgender, Two-Spirit, Questioning Policy," the Vancouver School Board suggests the appointment of a staff person to be a safe contact for students on issues of sexual diversity and states that "where students request and where staff are willing to volunteer their time, Gay-Straight Alliance Clubs (GSAs) will be encouraged at secondary schools in the district" (p. 2). The establishment of such clubs "is one of the most visible and widely adopted strategies for calling attention to and addressing the needs of LGBTI students" (Griffin & Ouellett, 2002). This approach has also been linked with improvements in academic achievement and social relationships, comfort level with sexual identities, increased knowledge of coping strategies in heterosexist contexts, and an enhanced sense of belonging to a school community.

It is also vital that support be provided for students with LGBTI-identified parents or other family members and that Gay-Straight Alliance Clubs provide opportunities for straight-identified peers to learn about cultural and social issues relating to gender and sexuality (Lee, 2002). However effective, GSAs require external support; they are subjected to ever-changing membership as students and staff come and go, and they require larger institutional policies that do not rest on the presence of specific members and champions in the school community (Griffin & Ouellett, 2002).

2. Training in LGBTI issues for school teaching and administrative staff, counsellors, and healthcare professionals.

Szalacha (2003) notes the following:

> While a focus on schooling contexts reveals multiple inequalities that influence access to, treatment in, and outcomes of schooling, typically, neither teachers nor administrators are professionally prepared to examine the intersections between sexism, heterosexism, and sexual prejudice in the classroom. (p. 83)

Compulsory sexual diversity workshops often encourage staff to question their own assumptions regarding sexual diversity issues and may enable them to identify discrimination when they encounter it in the classroom or staff room. These workshops should move beyond surface considerations of "tolerance" and attempt to engage with the heterosexist assumptions underlying interactions in the school community. Both students and teachers should feel that their peers and colleagues are well informed regarding the pervasive and damaging effects of heterosexism in teaching and learning environments.

School counsellors will likely be sought for support and aid for LGBTI students and their friends and families. Similarly, school-based healthcare professionals require training to address the unique health needs of LGBTI teens; however, care should be taken to avoid addressing their health from the historical perspective of pathology. Instead, issues such as STDs should be approached with sensitivity and an awareness of the subtle differences in the ways such issues affect LGBTI youth (GLSEN, 1995). While it is critical that such students have access to educational resources, including pamphlets and a list of books and websites that will allow them to learn more about the history of LGBTI issues, these resources cannot replace approachability and support from teaching and administrative staff, counsellors, and healthcare professionals.

3. Development of sexual harassment, antibullying, and violence prevention programs, as well as crisis intervention strategies, including appropriate responses to expressions of sexual prejudice.

Existing school policies should be read for homophobia and/or heterosexism. Because heterosexism is often manifested as silence regarding LGBTI youth, it is often difficult to identify and address. Taking sexual diversity into account might involve revising current crisis/violence prevention policies to provide appropriate responses to expressions of sexual prejudice (Szalacha, 2003); reworking sexual harassment policies to include the unique needs of LGBTI youth (Epstein, 1997); and adjusting language and bullying policies to monitor the strong links between homophobia, gender identities, and harassment by peers (Kimmel & Mahler, 2003; Warwick, Aggleton, & Douglas, 2001).

4. Antihomophobic hiring policies.

School hiring policies should explicitly include sexual diversity as an area of difference to be protected. For example, the Vancouver School Board policy states that employees cannot be discriminated against on the basis of their sexual identification or gender identity and that "the confidentiality of the sexual orientation and gender identity of staff will be protected. Employees who are out as lesbian, gay, bisexual, transgender, or transitioning will be given the support they require to do their work in a safe and respectful environment" (Vancouver School Board, 2004, p. 3). Of course, such policies are effective only if they are being enforced, so members of school communities should be held accountable for discriminatory hiring practices.

Closing Thoughts

Taking sexual diversity into account is a complex process that requires reshaping the interrelated areas of pedagogy, language, curriculum, and policy in Canadian schools. Profoundly engaging with and taking up antihomophobic work in school communities requires starting with ourselves as we examine the heterosexist assumptions embedded in our cultures and everyday lives. Such work can be highly charged with emotion, as it often entails challenges to our commonly held beliefs. It involves taking responsibility for the ways in which our own language, actions, and assumptions perpetuate homophobia and heterosexism or coming to terms with painful memories of how we, too, learned our lack in school.

Feminist poststructuralism directs our attention to the restrictions placed on our identities by narrowly defined notions of gender and sexuality. It enables us to acknowledge the multiplicity of genders and sexualities and brings our conception of power from "out there" to "in here" — from the official decrees of courtrooms, school board offices, and legislatures to the subtle web of daily interactions between diverse school members. Such theoretical approaches to diversity encourage us to imagine pedagogical spaces in which sexual diversity is not a problem to be solved or tolerated but a quality belonging to all of us, constantly shifting and redefining our identities and what it means to know, learn, and love.

NOTES

Thanks to Anna MacLeod and Terrah Keener for generously providing feedback on this essay.

1   While many of the issues we have chosen to discuss are relevant to all grade levels, this essay may be most relevant to the junior and senior high school levels. For a discussion of how to tailor sexual diversity curricula to different age groups, see Reis (2004).

2   While we acknowledge that such labelling can be problematic and definitions remain in flux, "lesbian" tends to refer to women who are physically and emotionally attracted only to other women, while "gay" is often used for men who are exclusively attracted to other men. Bisexuality entails attraction to both same-sex and opposite-sex individuals. Transgender individuals diverge from traditional gender roles assigned to their sex at birth, whereas intersexed individuals are born with sex organs and/or secondary characteristics that are not distinctly male or female. Here we take up "LGBTI" first of all to refer to students who self-identify as such. This term is also meant to include those youth who self-identify as "Two-spirited." As we later note, due to the ever-changing nature of human sexuality, challenges and experiences faced by these students may affect "questioning" students, as well as *most* students in different times and contexts.

3   See Weedon (1997) for an in-depth treatment of feminist poststructural-
    ism.

4   The term "discourse" was devised by Michel Foucault as part of his
    explorations of relationships between language, institutions, identity, and
    power. Rooting her definition in Foucault's use of the word, Lather
    defines discourse as "a conceptual grid with its own exclusions and era-
    sures, its own rules and decisions, limits, inner logic, parameters and
    blind alleys" (1991, p. 166). Weedon (1997) adds that discourses are
    competing modes of meaning making, which offer a range of ways in
    which to organize social institutions such as schools, as well as a range
    of possible ways of being for school community members. An example
    would be child-centred educational discourses versus more teacher-cen-
    tred discourses, each of which would determine the curricula, policies,
    and pedagogies of the school, and the ways in which the educational
    process is carried out (and experienced) by teachers and students. These
    and several other discourses may be competing in a school environment
    at any time.

5   For thoughtful discussions of Canadian First Nations peoples' experi-
    ences of sexual diversity, see Cannon (2004) and Filax and Shogan
    (2004).

6   The issue of coming out to students may be fraught with difficulty; for
    more on this, see Khayatt (1997).

7 For a wealth of other lesson plans, policy suggestions, and other resources,
    see the website for the Gay, Lesbian and Straight Education Network
    (GLSEN) at glsen.org.

REFERENCES

Amnesty International. (2001). *Crimes of hate, conspiracy of silence: Torture
    and ill-treatment based on sexual identity.* http://web.amnesty.org/
    library/index/engact400162001 (accessed March 4, 2005).

Athanases, S.Z., & Larrabee, T.G. (2003). Toward a consistent stance in
    teaching for equity: Learning to advocate for lesbian- and gay-identified
    youth. *Teaching and Teacher Education, 19,* 237–261.

Baker, J.M. (2002). *How homophobia hurts children: Nurturing diversity at
    home, at school, and in the community.* New York: Harrington Park
    Press.

Barnard, I. (1994). Antihomophobic pedagogy: Some suggestions for teachers.
    Radical Teacher, 45, 26–28.

(2004). The pedagogy of diversity: The silence of sexuality. *Exchanges:
    The Online Journal of Teaching and Learning in the CSU.*

http://www.calstate.edu/itl/exchanges/viewpoints/1166_Barnard.html (accessed May 4, 2005).

Berkman, C.S., & Zinberg, G. (1997). Homophobia and heterosexism in social workers. *Social Work*, 42(4), 319–332.

Bernstein, B. (1996). *Pedagogy, symbolic control and identity: Theory, research and critique*. London: Taylor and Francis.

Blumenfeld, W.J., & Lindop, L. (2005). *Road blocks and responses in addressing lesbian, gay, bisexual and transgender (LGBT) issues: Responding to resistance from teachers, administrators, students and the community*. http://www.outproud.org/article_road_blocks.html (accessed April 4, 2005).

British Columbia College of Teachers v. Trinity Western University, No. 27168, 2001 SCC 31 (May 17, 2001). www.lexum.umontreal.ca/csc-scc/en/pub/2001/vol1/html/2001scr1_0772.html.

Burton, A. (1995). Things that could make a difference: Integrating lesbian and gay issues in secondary schools. *Health Education*, 5, 20–25.

Butler, J. (1990). *Gender trouble: Feminism and the subversion of identity*. London: Routledge.

Cannon, M. (2004). The Regulation of First Nations Sexuality. In J. McNinch & M. Cronin (Eds.), *I could not speak my heart: Education for social justice for gay and lesbian youth* (pp. 49–80). Regina: University of Regina, Canadian Plains Research Center.

Chamberlain v. Surrey School District No. 36, No. 28654, 2002 SCC 86 (December 20, 2002). http://www.lexum.umontreal.ca/cscscc/en/pub/2002/vol4/html/2002scr4_0710.html.

Creighton, A. (1992). Out proud: Unlearning heterosexism. In P. Kivel & A. Creighton (Eds.), *Helping teens stop violence: A practical guide for counselors, educators, and parents* (pp. 43–50). Alameda, CA: Hunter House.

DeCrescenzo, T. (Ed.). (1994). *Helping gay and lesbian youth: New policies, new programs, new practice*. New York: Harrington Park Press.

Dobinson, C. (2004). Everyday acts of survival and unorganized resistance: Gay, lesbian and bisexual youth respond to oppression. In J. McNinch & M. Cronin (Eds.), *I could not speak my heart: Education for social justice for gay and lesbian youth* (pp. 49–80). Regina: University of Regina, Canadian Plains Research Center.

Dobson, J. (2000). Do you think homosexuals should be granted special rights? Excerpt from the *Complete Marriage and Family Home Guide* [electronic version]. http://family-topics.custhelp.com/cgi-bin/ family_topics.cfg/php/enduser/std_adp.php?p_faqid=1216 (accessed May 13, 2005).

Egale Canada. (2002). *Excerpts from the judgment of MacKinnon J. in the Marc Hall case.* http://www.egale.ca/index.asp?lang= E&menu=72&item=290 (accessed February 12, 2005).

Epstein, D. (1997). Keeping them in their place: Hetero/sexist harassment, gender and the enforcement of heterosexuality. In A.M. Thomas (Ed.), *Sexual harassment: Contemporary feminist perspectives* (pp. 201–221). Philadelphia: Open University Press.

Filax, G., & Shogan, D. (2004). Gender ambiguity and heteronormativity: The case of two Alberta youth. In J. McNinch & M. Cronin (Eds.), *I could not speak my heart: Education for social justice for gay and lesbian youth* (pp. 81–92). Regina: University of Regina, Canadian Plains Research Center.

Frank, B., Kehler, M., Lovell, T., & Davison, K. (2003). A tangle of trouble: Boys, masculinity and schooling — Future directions. *Educational Review, 55*(2), 119–133.

Freiberg, H.J., & Stein, T.A. (1999). Measuring, improving, and sustaining learning environments. In H.J. Freiberg (Ed.), *School climate: Measuring, improving, and sustaining healthy learning environments.* Philadelphia: Falmer.

Garofalo, R., Wolf, R.C., Kessel, S., Palfrey, J., & DuRant, R.H. (1998). The association between health risk behaviors and sexual orientation among a school-based sample of adolescents. *Pediatrics, 101*, 895–902.

Gay, Lesbian and Straight Education Network. (1995). *What you can do: Ideas and resources for educators working to end homophobia in schools.* http://www.outproud.org/article_what_you_can_do.html (accessed May 4, 2005).

Griffin, P., & Ouellett, M.L. (2002). Going beyond gay-straight alliances to make schools safe for lesbian, gay, bisexual, and transgender students. *Angles, 6*(1), 1–26.

Hagen, D. (2004). Growing up outside the gender construct. In J. McNinch & M. Cronin (Eds.), *I could not speak my heart: Education and social justice for gay and lesbian youth* (pp. 19–27). Regina: University of Regina, Canadian Plains Research Center.

Hansman, G.P. (2005, February 14). Education and queer youth. *Gay and Lesbian Educators of British Columbia.*

Hostile hallways: The AAUW survey on bullying, teasing and sexual harassment in America's schools. (2001). Washington, DC: AAUW Educational Foundation.

Khayatt, D. (1997). Sex and the teacher: Should we come out in class? *Harvard Educational Review, 67*(1), 126–143.

Kimmel, M. (2002). Toward a pedagogy of the oppressor. *Tikkun, 17*(6), 42–48.

Kimmel, M.S., & Mahler, M. (2003). Adolescent masculinity, homophobia and violence: Random school shootings, 1982–2001. *The American Behavioral Scientist, 46*(10), 1439–1458.

Kosciw, J.G. (2004). *The 2003 national school climate survey: The school-related experiences of our nation's lesbian, gay, bisexual and transgender youth.* New York: GLSEN.

Lather, P. (1991). *Getting smart: Feminist research and pedagogy with/in the postmodern.* New York: Routledge.

Lee, C. (2002). The impact of belonging to a high school Gay/Straight Alliance. *The High School Journal, 85*(3), 13–26.

Martin, A. (1982). Some issues in the treatment of gay and lesbian patients. *Psychotherapy: Theory, Research, and Practice, 19*, 341–348.

Martino, W., & Pallotta-Chiarolli, M. (2004). "Men are tougher, bigger, and they don't act real girlie": Indigenous boys defining and interrogating masculinities. *Balayi: Culture, Law and Colonialism, 6*, 143–160.

McIntosh, P. (1990). White privilege: Unpacking the invisible knapsack. *Independent School, 49*(2), 31.

McNinch, J., & Cronin, M. (Eds.). (2004). *I could not speak my heart: Education and social justice for gay and lesbian youth.* Regina: University of Regina, Canadian Plains Research Center.

Monahan, N. (1997). Making the grade: Responding to lesbian, gay, and bisexual youth in schools. In M.S. Schneider (Ed.), *Pride and prejudice: Working with lesbian, gay, and bisexual youth* (pp. 203–22). Toronto: Central Toronto Youth Services.

Nayak, A., & Kehily, M.J. (1996). Playing it straight: Masculinities, homophobias and schooling. *Journal of Gender Studies, 5*(2), 211–30.

Plummer, D.C. (2001). The quest for modern manhood: Masculine stereotypes, peer culture and the social significance of homophobia. *Journal of Adolescence, 24*, 15–23.

Reis, B. (2004). *Learning about sexual diversity at school: What is age appropriate?* http://www.safeschoolscoalition.org/whatisageappropriate.pdf (accessed February 18, 2005).

Remafedi, G. (1987). Adolescent homosexuality: Psychosocial and medical implications. *Pediatrics, 79*(3), 331–337.

Rich, A. (1980). Compulsory sexuality and lesbian existence. *Signs, 41*(5), 631–60.

Russell, S.T. (2003). Sexual minority youth and suicide risk. *The American Behavioral Scientist, 46*(9), 1241–1257.

Saewyc, E.M., Bearinger, L.H., Heinz, P.A., Blum, R.W., & Resnick, M.D. (1998). Gender differences in health and risk behaviors among bisexual and homosexual adolescents. *Journal of Adolescent Health, 23*, 181–188.

Savin-Williams, R.C. (2001). A critique of research on sexual-minority youth. *Journal of Adolescence, 24*, 5–13.

Smith, D.E. (2000). Schooling for inequality. *Signs, 25*(4), 1147–1151.

Szalacha, L.A. (2003). Safer sexual diversity climates: Lessons learned from an evaluation of the Massachusetts safe schools program for gay and lesbian students. *American Journal of Education, 110*, 58–88.

Thurlow, C. (2001). Naming the "outsider within": Homophobic pejoratives and the verbal abuse of lesbian, gay and bisexual high-school pupils. *Journal of Adolescence, 24*, 25–38.

Unks, G. (1995). Thinking about the gay teen. In G. Unks (Ed.), *The gay teen: Educational practice and theory for lesbian, gay, and bisexual adolescents* (pp. 3–12). New York: Routledge.

Uribe, V. & Harbeck, K. (1992). Addressing the needs of lesbian, gay, and bisexual youth: The origins of PROJECT 10, and school-based intervention. *Journal of Homosexuality, 22*(3), 9–29.

Vancouver School Board. (2004, February). *Lesbian, gay, bisexual, transgender, two-spirit, questioning policy.* www.galebc.org/LGBTTQPOLICY FEB2004.pdf (accessed March 14, 2005).

Warwick, I., Aggleton, P., & Douglas, N. (2001). Playing it safe: Addressing the emotional and physical health of lesbian and gay pupils in the U.K. *Journal of Adolescence, 24*, 129–140.

Weedon, C. (1997). *Feminist practice and poststructuralist theory* (2nd ed.). Cambridge, MA: Blackwell.

Whatley, M.H. (1992). Images of gays and lesbians in sexuality and health textbooks. *Journal of Homosexuality, 3–4*, 197–211.

Peer Dynamics in Bullying: Considerations for Social Architecture in Schools

Debra Pepler and Wendy Craig

Around the world, there is an emerging awareness of the problems associated with bullying. With the burgeoning research in the field, there is a growing recognition that these problems are not "just a normal part of growing up" or something that "kids just grow out of". Bullying problems involve a substantial proportion of children and adolescents — as perpetrators, victims, or bystanders — and at some point, children may have been involved in each of the three roles. Recent data from 35 countries participating in the World Health Organization's (WHO's) survey of Health Behaviour in School-Aged Children (HBSC) confirm the ubiquity and magnitude of the problem of bullying. For adolescents aged 11 to 16 years old, the prevalence rates of bullying others more than two or three times in the last month range from 2%–37% for bullying and 2%–36% for being victimized (Craig & Yossi, 2003). Clearly bullying and victimization are problems for youth that transcend national boundaries. Once a problem such as bullying comes to the forefront of social consciousness, there is a logical call for strategies to address the problem.

Over the past 15 years of our research on bullying, we have come to understand bullying as a relationship problem — because it is a form of aggression that unfolds in the context of a relationship (Pepler, Craig, Yuile & Connolly, 2004). The children who bully[1] are in a position of power relative to the children who are being victimized. The power accrued by children who bully and the difficulties experienced by victimized children are frequently highlighted in our naturalistic observations of playground interactions (Atlas & Pepler, 1998; Craig & Pepler, 1997; O'Connell, Pepler & Craig, 1999). The power advantage of the children who bully can arise from many aspects of the relationship — a differential in size, strength, age, or social status — or through familiarity with the other child's vulnerabilities. As bullying unfolds over time, the power differential in the relationship becomes increasingly consolidated. Consequently, it is difficult for victimized children to extract themselves from a bullying relationship because they lack the power to shift the dynamics in the relationship and to put a stop to this form of abuse (Pepler, Craig & O'Connell, 1999). The problems of bullying, however, encompass more than the child who is being aggressive and the child who is being victimized. The observational research that we have conducted in the schoolyard and in the classroom confirms that bullying is a problem that unfolds in the context of the peer group. If peer dynamics are essential to the processes in bullying, then interventions for bullying will have to focus on and shift these dynamics to promote positive interactions. This essay highlights the peer dynamics of bullying uncovered in our observational research and draws implications for intervening with the peer group in the classroom and in the larger school community.

Our observational research on bullying in the classroom and on the playground is guided by a developmental-systemic perspective (Cairns, 1979; Ford & Lerner, 1992; Magnusson, 1988). Developmental theory directs us to focus generally on the changing behaviours, motivations, and challenges with development and specifically on the risks and protective processes in individual children's lives. Systemic theory focuses on the salient systems or contexts in which children are developing. During childhood and adolescence, the peer group emerges as a particularly important social context for development. Indeed, peers play a crucial role in maintaining, exacerbating, and intervening in bullying episodes (O'Connell, Pepler & Craig, 1999). Contrary to our initial expectations, bullying is not simply a dyadic interaction between a child who bullies and a child who is victimized. Bullying is a social event in the classroom and on the playground: In 85% of the episodes that we observed in these school settings, peers were present (Atlas & Pepler, 1998; Craig & Pepler, 1995; 1997). Peers assumed many roles during bullying episodes: as bystanders, co-bullies, and interveners. Therefore, to reduce bullying in schools, interventions that raise children's awareness of their roles in promoting the problems and supporting the solutions are necessary.

Developing an understanding of peer dynamics is the first step in determining appropriate intervention strategies for bullying problems. Using video cameras and remote microphones in two observational studies, we examined the central element of programs aimed at reducing primary school children's aggressive behaviour problems in classrooms and on the playground (Pepler & Craig, 1995; Pepler, Craig, O'Connell, Atlas & Charach, 2004; Pepler, Craig & Roberts, 1998). (The children were in Grades 1 to 6 and aged 6 to 11). We found that peers were consistently present in bullying episodes, serving as the audience for the theatre of bullying.

The dynamics of peer interactions during a bullying episode can be most clearly illustrated with an excerpt from our observational tapes. In this episode, we observed a focal girl in Grade 5 for a few minutes on the playground during lunchtime. This girl had been identified as both a bully and a victim by at least two of three respondents (i.e., the girl herself, her classmates, and/or her teacher). Alone on the playground, she was approached by a girl who initiated the interaction with a threat to kill her, which was spoken in a light-hearted tone: "If you are going to do that, can I kill you?" A second girl quickly joined the bullying and they walked the focal girl around the playground, with one girl holding her firmly around the neck. A crowd of other girls quickly gathered and the initial bully asked her to do a humiliating action: "Kiss the tree!" A bystander briefly joined and upped the ante by suggesting that she have sex with the tree. In the first few moments of the episode, the interactions of these girls appeared to unfold as rough-and-tumble play, which may be considered a form of play. The focal girl appeared to be relaxed, smiling, and calm. As the numbers of the group grew and other children were invited to join in "payback day," the level of excitement increased, as did the intensity of the aggression. As the bullying continued, the focal girl's facial expressions and tone of voice revealed her increasing distress. It was remarkable and disconcerting to observe the children's sense of entitlement to cause distress to a vulnerable child. A few moments into the interaction, the girl who initiated the episode with a threat, piped in with a request: "Can I pick on her too? It's my favourite thing." This comment leaves us bewildered and concerned that a child can find enjoyment in bullying; however, it is important to remember that an aggressive child may enjoy the increase in her or his power and status that occurs during bullying. What can we learn from this episode and similar events that unfold within the peer group?

Our observations indicate that:

• Bullying episodes are short.

• Adults may not recognize bullying.

• Peers quickly form an audience for bullying and contribute to the power imbalance.

• Peers contribute to the intensity of bullying.

- Peers' behaviours are influenced by children who bully.

- Victimized children are often isolated.

- Peers can effectively intervene to stop bullying.

Each of these features of bullying is discussed briefly below to provide a foundation for developing intervention strategies to support positive peer relationships and to reduce bullying.

The Peer Dynamics of Bullying

It Only Takes a Moment to Bully

The theatre of bullying on the school playground is fleeting. In our observational research, we found that bullying on the playground was most often brief, on average about 37 and 80 seconds in duration in our first and second studies, respectively (Craig & Pepler, 1997; O'Connell, Pepler & Craig, 1999). Our observational research indicates that it does not take very long to assert one's power by saying or doing something that causes distress to another child. Bullying is often described as a covert activity that is difficult for adults to detect. Part of the challenge may arise from the brevity of the interaction. The girls' episode described above lasted about two minutes, but in that time there were many aggressive behaviours directed at the victimized girl from at least five children. Given the short period of time that it takes children to exert power and cause distress to others, it is not surprising to learn that teachers seldom intervene to stop the bullying on the playground. Specifically, teachers intervene in 4% and 18% of the episodes on the playground and in the classroom, respectively (Atlas & Pepler, 1998; Craig & Pepler, 1997).

Adults Have Difficulty Recognizing Bullying

Through our research program, we have come to recognize that it is not always apparent to adults that bullying is taking place. Children are generally aware of teachers' disapproval of bullying and other forms of aggression; therefore, they seldom engage in bullying in clear view. In the classroom, bullying most often occurs when teachers ask students to work independently and when the teachers' attention is directed to one or two children who need help (Atlas & Pepler, 1998). We observed that much of children's bullying is effected through verbal barbs, rather than with overt physical actions, further contributing to the challenge of detecting bullying. Even if teachers are able to observe the interactions, the verbal and nonverbal signals that children send may not be readily identifiable. As indicated in the scenario above, children who are being victimized often mask their distress and pretend that the interactions are fun. When victimized, children's emotional expressions were coded from our classroom tapes. Interest, joy, and anger were the most common emotions, followed by surprise, sadness, contempt, and distress (Mahady-Wilton, Craig & Pepler, 2000). The mixed emotional signals may make it difficult for teachers to differentiate bullying episodes from rough-and-tumble episodes. Given that there is considerable shame in being victimized by peers, it is understandable that victimized children hide their distress and hesitate to tell teachers about their experiences of bullying at school.

Peers Form an Audience for Bullying and Contribute to the Power Imbalance

Bullying is a form of social power that is exhibited and consolidated in the presence of a relevant social group. With an understanding of the power dynamics in bullying, it is not surprising to learn that peers quickly form an audience for bullying and contribute to the imbalance of power. On average, there are 4.3 peers participating and watching a bullying episode, with a range up to 14 children watching at a time (O'Connell, Pepler & Craig, 1999). These children form the audience in the theatre of bullying. Also, the more peers that are present, the longer the duration of a bullying episode. Young boys (Grades 1 to 3; ages 6 to 8) are most frequently represented in the peer audience, and young girls are least frequently present. The attention of the peers clearly reflects the power differential in the bully-victim relationship. Peers comprising the "audience" in bullying episodes spend about half their time passively watching the child who is bullying and about a quarter of their time actively engaging in the aggression and joining the bullying. They spend only a quarter of their time attending to and intervening to support the victimized child.

Peers Contribute to the Intensity of Bullying

When peers actively engage and join in bullying, the intensity of the bullying behaviours tends to increase. In his dissertation research, O'Connell (1999) conducted sequential analyses and found that when a peer joins in bullying, there is an increase in both the level of excitement and the level of aggression on the part of the child who is perpetrating the bullying. This pattern of reinforcement for antisocial behaviour has been described as "deviancy training" by Dishion and his colleagues (Dishion, Andrews & Crosby, 1995; Dishion, McCord & Poulin, 1999). Therefore, the natural course of bullying interactions is shaped by the behaviours of other children, which appear to contribute to the aggression and power dynamics within bullying episodes.

Peers Are Influenced by Those Who Bully

There are bidirectional influences within the dynamics of bullying episodes. Not only do the peers influence the child who is bullying, but the peers who comprise the audience are also influenced by the child who is being aggressive. We observed that when children are bullying, they request the assistance of peer bystanders in approximately one-third of the episodes (O'Connell, Pepler & Craig, 1999). The requests take many forms: invitations, threats about standing by passively, and insults that were difficult to ignore. In the example cited above, the observers were invited to join in "payback day." Our observations indicated that the requests of the children who were bullying were effective: peers were significantly more likely to join in the aggressive attacks when the bully had requested or cajoled them in some way compared to situations where the joining in was not solicited. Consistent with gender differences in aggressive behaviour problems (Moffitt, Caspi, Rutter & Silva, 2001; Offord, Lipman & Duku, 2001), boys are more likely to join in bullying interactions than girls. Boys' interests in and concerns for dominance (Maccoby, 1998) may be influential in drawing them into bullying a more vulnerable child. By joining the powerful position of the bully against a vulnerable victim, peers may be able to align with higher-status children and gain some status from the power dynamics.

Victimized Children Are Often Isolated

Children who are victimized are often marginalized and isolated from a supportive peer group. This point can be most cogently illustrated with another scenario from our observations.

The videotape focuses on a Grade 1 boy who was identified as aggressive by his classroom teacher and received two three-month sessions of social skills training to address his undercontrolled behaviour problems. At the onset of the study, he was rated by his peers as highly aggressive and rejected (i.e., children disliked him). We had the privilege of observing a few moments of this little boy's life on the school playground after he had participated in six months of school-based social skills training (Pepler, Craig & Roberts, 1995; Pepler, King & Byrd, 1991). In spite of improved social skills and abilities to deal with provocation, this boy continued to be isolated and was bullied on the playground by four students over the course of three minutes.

These students apparently felt entitled to harass this boy and did not feel responsible to support him. The four students appeared to recognize this young boy's vulnerability and isolation and exerted power over him by taking his toy, crashing into him, and kicking sand at him. This young boy responded to these attacks by asking for the toy back and ignoring the physical aggression. Although we had been successful in bolstering this young boy's social skills, we had not shifted the behaviours and attitudes of other children on the school playground, nor had we provided this boy with a supportive peer context. This video observation was important to our understanding of the complexity of bullying because it revealed not only problems with this young boy, but also problems in his relationships with other students and in their relationships with him.

Peers Can Effectively Intervene to Stop Bullying

Finally, there is a positive side to the peer dynamics in bullying. Within bullying episodes, there is evidence that children are concerned about the victimized child, and some appear to sense their social responsibility for stopping this form of peer abuse. We found that a quarter of the time when peers are observing a bullying interaction, they are paying attention to the victimized child (O'Connell, Pepler & Craig, 1999). When children are asked about how they feel when they watch bullying, the vast majority admit that they feel uncomfortable (Charach, Pepler & Ziegler, 1995). The power of peers to intervene and shift the power dynamics in bullying is revealed in our playground observations. When a peer intervened, bullying stopped within 10 seconds in 57% of the episodes (Hawkins, Pepler & Craig, 2001). There is evidence, however, that peers need support in using positive strategies to intervene because peers' strategies were equally divided between prosocial and aggressive interventions (53% and 47%, respectively). Peers are more likely to use an aggressive intervention with the child who is bullying and to use a prosocial intervention with the victimized child. Although we found the two strategies to be equally effective in stopping bullying, we recommend educational efforts to promote prosocial interventions and a positive peer climate within the school context.

Interventions to Shift Peer Dynamics in Bullying

A consideration of the contexts for bullying must extend beyond peer group dynamics to include the contexts that adults create for children's daily interactions. Administrators and teachers influence the nature of bullying within the context of the school. They set the standards for behaviour and are responsible for supporting children who are having difficulties. The challenge for teachers and others who work with children and youth is to be alert to the complex social dynamics and to serve as "social architects." We have chosen the metaphor of "social architecture" to refer to the opportunity to structure children's peer groups to promote positive peer groupings and to deconstruct negative peer groupings. Within the framework of bullying interventions, social architecture can essentially function to reorganize children's group structures in two ways. First, it can be used to separate the child who is bullying from the victimized child and from the peers who reinforce the bullying behaviour through their attention and joining. Secondly, it can be used to embed isolated and victimized children within a positive peer context. In using the term "social architect," we do not mean to imply that adults responsible for children should be building rigid structures to constrain children's social experiences, but rather that adults have a role and responsibility to be aware of the positive and negative social dynamics in children's family, peer group, school, and community systems. With an understanding of these peer dynamics, we can move to promote positive social experiences and to dissipate negative social experiences for children and adolescents.

To provide direction for interventions, we return to the peer dynamics in bullying and consider strategies for moving these dynamics in a positive direction. The seven peer dynamics that we have highlighted include: bullying occurs over a short time, adults have difficulty recognizing bullying, peers quickly form an audience for bullying and contribute to the power imbalance, peers contribute to the intensity of bullying, peers are influenced by children who bully, victimized children are often isolated, and peers can effectively intervene to stop bullying.

It Only Takes a Moment to Bully

In a fleeting moment, children can assert power through aggression and cause distress to others. By educating them about the nature of bullying and by raising awareness and empathy for victimized children, we can discourage children from engaging in bullying and from becoming the audience for bullying. In addition to promoting empathic attitudes and intervention skills to support victimized peers, there are many strategies that teachers can employ to create a warm, supportive, and inclusive class climate. Peers are most often present and teachers are seldom present during these fleeting bullying episodes; therefore, it is important to encourage children to intervene to support victims or to relay their concerns about bullying situations to teachers, parents, or other responsible adults.

Adults Have Difficulty Recognizing Bullying

Bullying unfolds in a relationship characterized by a power imbalance and with prolonged bullying. It is difficult for victimized children to escape the torment. Therefore, it is essential that principals and teachers assume a central role in protecting victimized children at school and in reducing the use of negative power by children who bully. As discussed above, adults have a difficult time recognizing bullying because of the subtle and complex behaviours in the interactions. To overcome the challenge of detecting bullying, adults responsible for children (e.g., parents, educators, coaches, and recreation leaders) need training as part of a bullying-prevention initiative. Within a school context, training can promote an understanding of the nature of bullying with particular attention to the peer dynamics and power differentials in bullying, so that teachers can become increasingly sensitive to students' potential distress. Assessments of the degree of bullying problems within a school and identification of areas of the playground or school where bullying may be more likely to occur promote understanding and action. As school staff collaborate to develop strategies to address bullying problems, they may consider increasing supervision of the areas identified as "hot spots" for bullying. Teachers who are aware of the complexities of bullying in the peer group can also take preventive actions, such as encouraging children to discuss concerns about bullying and helping children to recognize the potential for bullying in groups that coalesce around children who assert their power negatively through bullying. Elements of these strategies have been included in interventions around the world that have been highlighted in a recent international volume entitled *Bullying in Schools: How Successful Can Interventions Be?* (Smith, Pepler & Rigby, 2004). Teachers can also respond to the positive and negative peer dynamics by using social architecture to structure children's groupings both in the classroom and on the playground. In taking the prerogative to create groupings, teachers can override the natural peer processes that consistently leave some children to be chosen last for group projects, team games, and other group activities. In this way, they can avoid a public display of humiliation for the most vulnerable children in their care.

Peers Form an Audience for Bullying and Contribute to the Power Imbalance

Children are most often present in bullying episodes and form the audience for the interactions. When asked about their roles in bullying, children seldom recognize that their watching behaviours affect the bullying interactions. They are generally not aware of providing differential reinforcement to the child who is bullying by attending to his or her behaviours. Neither are they aware that they are further isolating the victimized child through their lack of attention and supportive interventions. Peer support for bullying can be dissipated through education for all children about the nature and dynamics of bullying and about the multiple roles they can assume. For children who are specifically engaged as the proximal audience in a bullying episode, there are specific interventions to raise awareness and empathy and to discourage their participation in the future. If we recognize bullying to be a problem that arises not only from an individual child's propensity to be aggressive, but also from the dynamics in peer groups, then an approach that alters the behaviours of many children is indicated. The well-known Pikas Method of Common Concern (Pikas, 1989) and the Support Group Approach (formerly the No Blame Approach) (Robinson & Maines, 1997) are two examples of antibullying strategies that focus on shifting peer attitudes and behaviours.

Peers Contribute to the Intensity of Bullying

Those children who not only observe bullying, but also join in, require additional support to understand that their bullying behaviour exacerbates the problem, in addition to being unacceptable. In this situation, a social architecture strategy might be appropriate. Providing alternate recess or lunchtime activities for a specified time (e.g., a week) so that these children are separated from the child who has asserted power through bullying accomplishes two goals. First, the opportunities for 75% of the peer attention will be reduced for the child who bullies. Secondly, the joining which increases the arousal and aggression of the bullying child will also be reduced. We contend that students should be held responsible for their bullying behaviours and advocate that the consequences should be "formative." We call the consequences "formative" when they provide an opportunity for learning and development. The formative consequences should not only provide a clear message that bullying is unacceptable; they should also build awareness, empathy, and skills to promote the students' responsibility. The alternate recess or lunchtime activities might focus on promoting perspective-taking skills and empathy (e.g., novel study, story writing, drawing a picture of what it feels like to be a victim of aggression), and they may enhance the positive leadership capacity of the children involved in bullying (e.g., helping in the younger grades, reading to a younger child, planning an assembly to promote peer intervention in bullying).

Peers Are Influenced by Those Who Bully

As with many forms of deviant behaviours, there is pressure for children to join in bullying. By educating children as to the nature of bullying and working with them to develop empathy, moral understanding, and social responsibility, we can promote their attitudes and behaviours to withstand negative peer pressure. Children often need support in identifying when bullying is taking place and in developing the confidence and skills to intervene. Classroom discussions about what children can do when they are bullied or when they see another child being bullied are the first step in building a communal understanding and response to bullying problems.

Victimized Children Are Often Isolated

Recognition of the peer processes that differentially reinforce the child who is bullying, rather than supporting the victim, high-

lights the need for social architecture strategies to embed a victimized child within a supportive group context. In addition to monitoring the effectiveness of interventions to stop the bullying, there
is the possibility of social architecture to restructure the vulnerable child's peer group experiences in a way that will provide supportive peer contexts. One example of social architecture strategies is that of creating a "circle of friends." This involves identifying a designated group of same- or mixed-age students who will
provide a support team of peers to work with a vulnerable pupil
(Newton & Wilson, 1999). Another strategy is befriending or
"buddying," in which a pupil or pupils is/are assigned to "be
with" or "befriend" a peer (Cowie & Sharp, 1996).

Peers Can Effectively Intervene to Stop Bullying

The positive note in our research on bullying is that many children intervene to stop bullying. If a majority of children finds it
unpleasant to watch bullying, then there is considerable potential
to create a climate where social responsibility is expected and
valued. Following from Olweus' (1993) initial antibullying
work, most interventions within the classroom context involve
engaging the children to develop a set of rules that guide behavioural expectations. The goal is to engage students in addressing
problems of bullying when they see them and to encourage
prosocial action by the majority of students who do not like bullying. In working with children on developing a repertoire of
intervention strategies, it is important to steer them toward
prosocial strategies (e.g., taking the victim away from the situation) and to discourage strategies in which they "bully the bully."

Bullying: Canada's National Initiative

Over the past 15 years, there has been a growing awareness of
the problem of bullying and the need to address this issue within the school and broader community context. In our Canadian

context, we are concerned about bullying because it is a relationship problem that presents long-term risks for boys and girls who bully, as well as for the victims of their aggression. At this point, Canada lags behind many European countries in addressing problems of bullying (see Craig & Harel, 2004; Smith et al., 2004).

The opportunity for Canada to address bullying problems and to promote safe and healthy relationships is now before us. The authors of this essay were awarded a new initiative grant through the Networks of Centres of Excellence to develop PREVNet: Promoting Relationships and Eliminating Violence Network (www.prevnet.ca). The vision for PREVNet is to link 60 leading Canadian researchers with 40 national organizations involved with children and youth, to partner in disseminating understanding and effective practices related to bullying and in promoting healthy relationships to every community in Canada. We are building a diversity of partnerships to ensure that our education, assessment, intervention, and policy pillars respond to the experiences and needs of all Canadian children and youth regardless of diversity such as gender, disability, ethno-racial-cultural background, sexual orientation, and economic disadvantage.

We envision moving knowledge and effective practices and policies related to bullying to a hockey rink in Victoria, a kitchen table in Iqaluit, and a school playground in St. John's. Through PREVNet partnerships with organizations that reach into every Canadian community, we hope to transform the way children and youth are supported in their relationships. Through partnerships, PREVNet will provide a consistent, extensive, and organized platform for knowledge mobilization and exchange to promote safety and healthy relationships for Canadian children and youth wherever they live, work, and play.

NOTES

An earlier version of this essay was presented as part of the Building Capacity for Diversity in Canadian Schools lecture series. The research described in this essay has been supported by the Ontario Mental Health Foundation. We are indebted to the teachers and students who participated in the research and shared their understanding of the complex problem of bullying at school. We are also grateful to the many graduate and undergraduate students who assisted in bringing this research to fruition.

1   In writing and speaking about bullying problems, we try to avoid using labels such as: bully, victim, and bully/victim. Bullying unfolds within the context of relationships, in part, and as a function of group dynamics, rather than arising solely from individuals' personal characteristics.

REFERENCES

Atlas, R., & Pepler, D.J. (1998). Observations of bullying in the classroom. *American Journal of Educational Research, 92*, 86–99.

Cairns, R.B. (1979). *Social development: The origins and plasticity of social interchanges.* San Francisco: Freeman.

Charach, A., Pepler, D., & Ziegler, S. (1995). Bullying at school: A Canadian perspective. *Education Canada, 35*, 12–18.

Cowie, H., & Sharp, S. (1996). *Peer counselling in schools: A time to listen.* London: David Fulton.

Craig, W.M., & Harel, Y. (2004). Bullying, physical fighting and victimization. In C. Currie, C. Roberts, A. Morgan, R. Smith, W. Settertobulte, O. Samdal, & V. Barnekow Rasmussen (Eds.), Young people's health in context: International report from the HBSC 2001/02 survey. *WHO Policy Series: Health policy for children and adolescents* (Issue 4) (pp. 133–144). Copenhagen: WHO Regional Office for Europe.

Craig, W., & Pepler, D. (1995). Peer processes in bullying and victimization: An observational study. *Exceptionality Education Canada, 5*, 81–95.

(1997). Observations of bullying and victimization in the schoolyard. *Canadian Journal of School Psychology, 2*, 41–60.

Craig, W.M., Pepler, D.J., & Atlas, R. (2000). Observations of bullying on the playground and in the classroom. *International Journal of School Psychology, 21*, 22–36.

Craig, W.M., & Yossi, H. (2003). Bullying and fighting: Results from World Health Organization Health and Behavior Survey of school aged children. *International Report for World Health Organization.*

Dishion, T., McCord, J., & Poulin, F. (1999). When interventions harm: Peer groups and problem behavior. *American Psychologist, 54*, 755–765.

Dishion, T.J., Andrews, D.W., & Crosby, L. (1995). Antisocial boys and their friends in early adolescence: Relationship characteristics, quality, and interactional process. *Child Development, 66*, 139–151.

Ford, D.H., & Lerner, R.M. (1992). *Developmental systems theory: An integrative approach*. Newbury Park: Sage Publications.

Hawkins, D.L., Pepler, D., & Craig, W. (2001). Peer interventions in playground bullying. *Social Development, 10*, 512–527.

Maccoby, E.E. (1998). *The two sexes: Growing up apart, coming together — Family and public policy*. Cambridge, MA: Belknap Press/Harvard University Press.

Magnusson, D. (1988). *Individual development from an interactional perspective: A longitudinal study*. Hillsdale, NJ: Erlbaum.

MahadyWilton, M., Craig, W.M., & Pepler, D.J. (2000). Emotional regulation and display in classroom bullying: Characteristic expressions of affect, coping styles and relevant contextual factors. *Social Development, 9*, 226–245.

Moffitt, T.E. (1993). Adolescence-limited and life-course-persistent antisocial behaviour: A developmental taxonomy. *Psychological Review, 100*, 674–701.

Moffitt, T.E., Caspi, A., Rutter, M., & Silva, P.A. (2001). *Sex differences in antisocial behaviour: Conduct disorder, delinquency, and violence in the Dunedin Longitudinal Study*. Cambridge: Cambridge University Press.

Newton, C., & Wilson, D. (1999). *Circles of friends*. London: Folens.

O'Connell, P. (1999). Peer processes and bullying: Naturalistic observations on the playground. Doctoral dissertation, York University, Toronto.

O'Connell, P., Pepler, D., & Craig, W. (1999). Peer involvement in bullying: Issues and challenges for intervention. *Journal of Adolescence, 22*, 437–452.

Offord, D.R., Lipman, E.L., & Duku, E.K. (2001). Epidemiology of problems up to age 12 years. In R. Loeber & D.P. Farrington (Eds.), *Child delinquents: Development, intervention, and service needs* (pp. 95–116). Thousand Oaks, CA: Sage Publications.

Olweus, D. (1993). *Bullying at school: What we know and what we can do*. Oxford: Blackwell Publishers.

Pepler, D.J., & Craig, W. (1995). A peek behind the fence: Naturalistic observations of aggressive children with remote audio-visual recording. *Developmental Psychology, 31*, 548–553.

Pepler, D., Craig, W., Connolly, J., & Henderson, K. (2002). Bullying, sexual harassment, dating violence, and substance use among adolescents. In C. Wekerle & A.M. Wall (Eds.), *The violence and addiction equation: Theoretical and clinical issues in substance abuse and relationship violence* (pp. 153–168). Philadelphia: Brunner/Mazel.

Pepler, D.J., Craig, W., & O'Connell, P. (1999). Understanding bullying from a dynamic systems perspective. In A. Slater & D. Muir (Eds.), *Developmental Psychology: An Advanced Reader* (pp. 440–451). Malden, MA: Blackwell Publishers.

Pepler, D., Craig, W., O'Connell, P., Atlas, R., & Charach, A. (2004). Making a difference in bullying: Evaluation of a systemic school-based program in Canada. In P.K. Smith, D.J. Pepler, & K. Rigby (Eds.), *Bullying in schools: How successful can interventions be?* (pp. 125–139). Cambridge: Cambridge University Press.

Pepler, D.J., Craig, W.M., & Roberts, W.L. (1995). Social skills training and aggression in the peer group. In J. McCord (Ed.), *Coercion and punishment in long-term perspectives* (pp. 213–228). Cambridge: Cambridge University Press.

(1998). Observations of aggressive and nonaggressive children on the school playground. *Merrill-Palmer Quarterly 44*.

Pepler, D., Craig, W., Yuile, A., & Connolly, J. (2004). Girls who bully: A developmental and relational perspective. In M. Putallaz & J. Kupersmidt (Eds.), *Aggression, antisocial behavior, and violence among girls* (pp. 90–109). New York: Guilford Publications.

Pepler, D., King, G., & Byrd, W. (1991). A social cognitively based social skills training program for aggressive children. In D. Pepler & K. Rubin (Eds.), *The development and treatment of childhood aggression* (pp. 411–448). Hillsdale, NJ: Erlbaum.

Pikas, A. (1989). A pure concept of mobbing gives the best results for treatment. *School Psychology International, 10*, 95–104.

Robinson, G., & Maines, B. (1997). *Crying for help: The no blame approach to bullying*. Bristol: Lucky Duck Publishing.

Smith, P.K., Pepler, D.J., & Rigby, K. (Eds.). (2004). *Bullying in schools: How successful can interventions be?* Cambridge: Cambridge University Press.

Not Learning to Read: Diversity among Children with Reading Difficulties

John R. Kirby

And so to completely analyze what we do when we read
would almost be the acme of a psychologist's achievements, for
it would be to describe very many of the most intricate work-
ings of the human mind, as well as to unravel the tangled story
of the most remarkable specific performance that civilization
has learned in all its history. (Huey, 1908/1968, p. 6.)

When we think about diversity in Canadian schools and society, we should remember that there is diversity *among* exceptional learners — even among those described in broadly similar ways. My goal in this essay is to analyze *some* of the diversity among children with reading diffi- culties. Reading disabilities, dyslexia, and other forms of reading difficulty are among the most frequently encountered "excep- tional needs" in Canadian schools and society. Diversity among children with reading difficulties is important, and not only because every child deserves to be treated as an individual: dif- ferent types of reading difficulty have different sources, and to the extent that solutions are possible, different solutions. In seek- ing to improve Canadian education, it is essential that we equip Canadian teachers, special educators, and other professionals with the best available knowledge about reading difficulties and with the professional skills to continue enhancing their own life-long learning in this area.

Over the last 20 years, no aspect of education has generated as much argument, debate, and research as reading. The debates have been there for many years, but it is only in the last two decades that educational research has begun to settle some of the issues. Learning to read in English is no trivial matter, and it is clearly more difficult than learning to read in languages in which there is a more predictable relationship between the symbols and the sounds (Seymour, Aro, & Erskine, 2003). The result is that school is less pleasant and less profitable than it should be for many children. Parents and teachers, as well as the students themselves, are frustrated by the slow progress made by many, and by the inability of some children to make full use of their intelligence because of difficulty in reading. Early reading difficulties are likely to result in later school difficulties (Cunningham & Stanovich, 1997; Juel, 1988) and to put the student at increased risk of dropping out, social problems, and failure to find rewarding work (Perrin, 1990; Willcutt & Pennington, 2000; Willms, 1999). Recent OECD/Statistics Canada results indicate that as many as 40% of Canadian adults have serious literacy difficulties (OECD/Statistics Canada, 2000).

This essay will cover the following elements in relation to reading difficulties:

• a review of recent knowledge about reading development and reading difficulties,

• a review of recent research about different types of reading difficulty, and

• a discussion of the implications of these issues for Canadian education: What can we do to enhance the reading development of children and how can we prevent the development of reading difficulties?

Before this discussion begins, however, two preliminary matters need to be addressed. The first is the distinction between reading difficulties and reading disabilities, and the second is the nature of reading.

Reading Difficulties and Disabilities

First, I should explain what I mean by *reading difficulties* and some of the other terms that are used in this area. Children with reading difficulties are those who are experiencing more difficulty than most children of their age and general ability level in reading or learning to read. The difficulty should be relatively persistent and *not* primarily attributable to sensory impairment (e.g., uncorrected vision problems) or pervasively low mental ability or emotional disorders. My only reason for excluding these children is that their main difficulty lies elsewhere; including them in the *reading difficulty* group would make the job of understanding reading difficulties too huge and complex. Those who know this area of investigation will notice that I have *not* excluded children whose reading difficulties are associated with social or environmental disadvantage or with lack of appropriate instruction. This is deliberate, because these children are an important and pervasive aspect of the reading difficulties situation in Canadian schools, and because they resemble the other reading difficulty children in many ways.

Am I talking about children with *reading disabilities*? Yes, but I am referring not only to these children. In general terms, a reading disability is a more severe reading difficulty, one more immune to treatment than a reading difficulty. There is growing evidence that some reading disabilities are caused by measurable biological factors (including genetic factors and forms of brain injury caused by prenatal or postnatal damage), but we are not yet able to say so in all cases (perhaps because the causal factors are not yet measurable). Mention of biological factors may make some nervous, but biology is not destiny. The effects of many biologically based disorders can be minimized, sometimes more easily than the effects of some environmentally based difficulties, and biologically based treatments may develop in decades to come.

More to the point, it is not easy to distinguish between children with disabilities (in these terms) and those with difficulties. The most persuasive approach is to provide every child with the highest-quality literacy program possible; to offer those who struggle individualized, expert help; and to apply the term *disability* only to those who are still unable to make progress after this help is provided (Vellutino et al. 1996). This is the principle that I try to follow, but it is difficult to put into practice because the terms are not used consistently in the literature, and it is not usually clear how much remediation a given child has received. For those reasons, the terms are used interchangeably in this essay.

What Is Reading?

What do I mean by reading? I include everything from saying a sound that is associated with a letter up to extracting deeper meaning from a range of texts. Getting meaning (or perhaps *constructing* meaning) from text is the ultimate purpose of reading, and it is the main reason why we spend so much time on and feel so strongly about the importance of reading instruction. However, the ability to make meaning from text does not spring without tutoring from the child's brain. Reading is an *unnatural* skill, one for which our species is not biologically prepared. Unlike other skills, such as walking or talking, which our species has been doing for hundreds of thousands of years, reading is something that we invented relatively recently. The earliest recorded examples of writing date from about 3200 BCE (e.g., Olson, 1994); this is only slightly more than the blink of an eye in evolutionary history.

It is important to understand that reading involves a *code*, in which marks on a page stand for spoken words or sounds. There are three different kinds of reading codes, which vary in what the code elements (or symbols) stand for. The oldest kinds are logographies, such as Chinese, Japanese *kanji*, and Egyptian hieroglyphics, in which each character stands for a word or concept. The second kinds are syllabaries, in which each character or symbol stands for a syllable; examples include Korean, Japanese *kana*, and Mayan glyphs. The third kinds are alphabets, in which each character stands for a sound. Alphabets were the most recent to be developed, and all known alphabets are derived from one source (Canaanite) around 1200 BCE. (See Olson, 1994, for more on the history of reading.)

The path from the Canaanite to the English alphabets was long and tortuous, proceeding via the Phoenicians (from whom we have the terms *phonetic, phonics,* and *phonology*), the Greeks, and the Romans. At each stage in that journey, the sound-symbol system had to be adapted to include new sounds and dispatch unused ones. Some would say that the English alphabet should continue to change: for example, we have three symbols that make a /k/ sound (C, K, and Q) but have to cannibalize other letters to represent sounds for which we do not have single letters (/ch/, /sh/, and /th/).

One way to think of reading is as a hierarchy of processes, which at the lower levels deals with these code matters and which at the higher levels is more devoted to the extraction and creation of meaning. One such hierarchy is shown in Figure 1 (adapted from Kirby, 1988, and Kirby & Williams, 1991). The basic notion in this model is that reading can be seen as a series of types of processing, moving up, down, or in both directions. In *bottom-up* processing, lower-level information (such as the features that comprise letters and the letters that comprise words) is processed into the units one level up. In this way, a great deal of

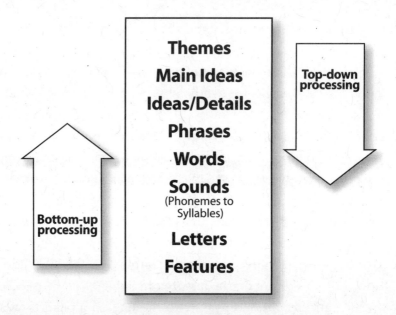

Themes
Main Ideas
Ideas/Details
Phrases
Words
Sounds
(Phonemes to Syllables)
Letters
Features

Top-down processing

Bottom-up processing

Figure 1. Hierarchy of Processes in Reading

information is compressed into a single unit. This compressing is based on rules or information contained in long-term memory; for instance, we use our previous knowledge to recode a sequence of 3 letters (C-A-T) as the single entity CAT, thereby saving 2 "spaces" in working memory. At higher levels, we may see four separate arguments and code them "right-wing agenda."

But reading is not entirely bottom-up; it also works *top-down*. At the word level, a child might use the sentence context (a cat having babies) to help decode an unfamiliar word (KIT-TEN); higher up, one could use a main idea (such as "this speaker is right wing") to help assign meaning to an unclear lower-level proposition (perhaps a statement on educational standards). Normally, reading is *interactive*, moving up and down in levels as we proceed through different parts of a text, and diverse texts with different purposes may elicit higher or lower levels in general.

So in response to the question *What is reading?*, I would answer *All of it*. Successful reading moves effortlessly (most of the time) between levels as appropriate, drawing upon stored information of many types. It involves constant packaging of information to form higher-level units and unpackaging to help identify lower-level units. It is important to understand that most of this happens without conscious awareness, because conscious awareness is very limited. If a reader paid attention to the letters in a word, it is unlikely that he or she would also be able to attend to the meaning of the sentence in which that word appeared (without rereading). It is important that the lower-level processes operate automatically, not absorbing conscious attention, so that this most limited resource can be devoted to the higher levels of processing.

What Have We Learned about Reading in the Past 20 Years?

The history of reading instruction in English has been characterized by a see-saw battle (or even "Reading Wars") between those advocating an emphasis upon the code and those emphasizing meaning or whole words (see, for instance, Crowder, 1982, chapter 10). Other languages with alphabetic writing systems have seen far less of this debate, especially in the cases of writing systems that are more *transparent* than English (i.e., writing systems in which there is a closer one-to-one correspondence between the letters on the page and the sounds associated with them). In those more transparent scripts (such as Spanish, Italian, German, and Finnish), children learn to read through code instruction relatively quickly (a year or less), so there is no need to consider more complex methods. In English, the process of learning to read is much slower (see Seymour et al., 2003, for comparative data) and less certain of success, so there is a constant search for alternative methods and a periodic "revolution" in instructional philosophy.

The next most recent revolution was the whole-language movement (Adams, 1990), which emphasized the importance of children constructing their own meaning from text and down-played (or even actively discouraged) teaching the code. The most recent revolution has been based on a promotion of "bal-anced literacy" (e.g., Pressley, 2002), in which code and meaning are each given emphasis. The balanced literacy approach has much to offer, because it accepts the importance of the code without forgetting the central and ultimate importance of con-structing meaning. (I should note that most who favour the code side would argue that they have never denied the importance of meaning and that many, or perhaps only *some*, who favour the whole-language approach would say that they have always allowed a place for the code.)

The importance of meaning has never been seriously doubt-ed, but the nature of what it means to *comprehend* text has not been specified very well until recently. We can certainly claim that more explicit and sophisticated theories of comprehension have constituted one of the key accomplishments of the last 20 years (e.g., Kintsch, 1999). In addition, some inroads into prac-tice have been made — in the teaching of strategies and metacog-nition, for instance (see Pressley, 2002, chapter 7, for examples) — but comprehension processes are still the subject of education-al talk more than of educational action.

The second area of accomplishment has been the discovery (or rediscovery) of the importance of the reading of words. Very detailed eye movement and other laboratory studies have shown that we pay an extraordinary amount of attention to individual words when we read (Adams, 1990; National Reading Panel, 2000; Rayner, Foorman, Perfetti, Pesetsky, & Seidenberg, 2001; Snow, Burns, & Griffin, 1998). As indicated in Figure 1 and the accompanying discussion, word reading is the absolutely essen-tial core of reading: if you fail to do it, you can't read; if you fail to do it well, you are very unlikely to read competently or to enjoy reading.

Content

⇩

Words

Orthographic route

Phonological route

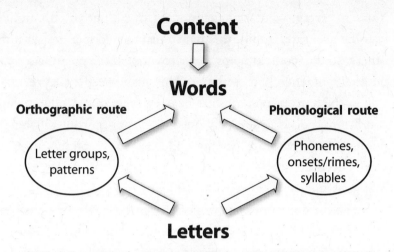

Letter groups, patterns

Phonemes, onsets/rimes, syllables

Letters

Figure 2. Word Recognition Processes

Word reading is illustrated in more detail in Figure 2. Conceptually, there are three ways to identify words. The two bottom-up routes involve either sounding out the letters on the page or more immediate recognition of the word as an orthographic unit. These two paths normally cooperate, so that units smaller than a word can be recognized (such as the *–at* of *hat, pat,* and *cat,* or the *–ight* of *right, night,* and *light*). Without going into the details, these two paths also seem to operate as a race, information proceeding along both as quickly as possible until one of the pathways reaches its goal (the identification of a word). Some words (especially in English) have to be recognized orthographically (e.g., irregular ones such as *yacht, answer,* and *two*), and unfamiliar or nonwords have to be sounded out (e.g., *stygian, tagliatelle,* or *brillig*).

The third path is the top-down one, by which knowledge of context (what has already been read, as well as knowledge of the topic) helps in word identification. For instance, in the sentence "The mother cat has three baby _____ ," you can guess the missing word (even if it is there and you cannot read it) from context. But try this sentence: "On top of the table there was a _____ ."

You can certainly guess at the missing word, but you are unlikely to be accurate. Again, this path normally cooperates with the others, so that context helps to narrow down the possible semantic and syntactic characteristics. This may speed word recognition as the bottom-up paths are nearing their goal. Under normal conditions, good readers rely on the bottom-up routes, whereas poor readers (who are usually children who cannot sound out words accurately and quickly) rely upon the top-down, contextual guessing route (Stanovich, 2000).

The third area of achievement in the past 20 years has been related to the cognitive processes underlying word reading — especially phonological processing, the "mental operations that make use of the phonological or sound structure of oral language" (Torgesen, Wagner, & Rashotte, 1994, p. 276). Children who develop reading disabilities or, less specifically, reading difficulties, very frequently have weaknesses or deficits in this area. Poor performance on measures of phonological processing is associated with concurrent and subsequent poor performance in reading, and instruction in phonological processing leads to improved reading performance (e.g., Goswami & Bryant, 1990; National Reading Panel, 2000; Snow, Burns, & Griffin, 1998).

Three aspects of phonological processing are known to determine individual differences in the rate of acquisition of reading skills: phonological awareness, phonological memory, and naming speed (Torgesen et al., 1994). *Phonological awareness* is an individual's sensitivity to the sound structure of words in his or her own language and the ability to manipulate the sounds within words. It is assessed with measures of rhyming, blending, segmenting, deleting, and rearranging sound units within words. Phonological awareness is critical for the development of skills in word recognition. *Phonological memory* is an individual's ability to retain and repeat in sequence series of sounds, and it is a component of what is known as working memory (which

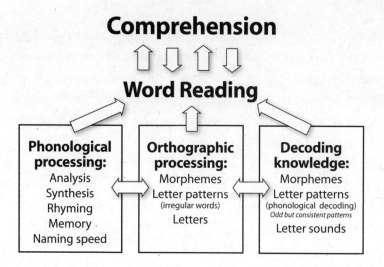

Figure 3. Reading and Prereading Processes

is also relevant to comprehension, considered below). The third component, *naming speed*, refers to the speed or efficiency with which individuals can retrieve and pronounce information stored in long-term memory; typically children are presented with a list of pictures, colours, digits, or letters and asked to name them as quickly as possible (Wolf & Bowers, 1999). These three aspects of phonological processing are critical for the acquisition of basic reading skills, and these skills are the foundation of subsequent reading development and learning from text.

The various reading and pre-reading processes are shown in Figure 3.

Are There Different Types of Reading Difficulties? — Recent Research

As Huey observed nearly one hundred years ago (see the quotation at the beginning of this essay) and as I have tried to outline on the preceding pages, reading is extraordinarily complex, its success depending on the cofunctioning of many distinct cognitive processes. Furthermore, because reading is a relatively recent invention of our species, we have not had time to evolve a specialized, modular mental mechanism to perform it. Instead, reading makes use of a variety of mental mechanisms that evolved to perform other functions (language, vision, etc.). It is more a wonder that we can read at all than that some of us have serious reading difficulties. And given the number of things that must go *right* for reading to work, there is no shortage of things that can go *wrong* to prevent reading from working efficiently. Over the years there have been many attempts to characterize the distinctions among reading difficulties. Most of these have failed, either because they lacked a solid theoretical foundation or because the empirical evidence was not strong. One distinction that has held up is the distinction between word-level and comprehension-level problems. For instance, whereas most children with reading difficulties/disabilities have difficulties in word reading, a small group of children has been identified who have normal word reading (and intelligence) but significantly lower reading comprehension (see Oakhill & Yuill, 1996, for more on this distinction).

The two distinctions that are currently most frequently used in the literature and in practice are the distinction between phonological and orthographic processing (the two bottom-up processes shown in Figure 2) and the distinction between phonological awareness and naming speed (two of the three aspects of phonological processing in Torgesen et al.'s, 1994 theory, see Figure 3). The first approach is called the dual route theory (Castles & Coltheart, 1993; Coltheart, 1978); the second, the double deficit theory (Wolf & Bowers, 1999). Both approaches have been used to define *subtypes* of children with reading disability (or difficulty).

Dual Route Theory

The dual route theory identifies the two bottom-up pathways that information may take toward word identification. The account that follows is based on the work of Castles and Coltheart (1993; Coltheart, 1978), and these studies should be consulted for more precise and extensive information.[1] One path, as was illustrated in Figure 2, goes from the letters on the page to the sounds associated with those letters and then to the word. So, for example, a beginning reader might see the letters C-A-T, make the associated sounds /k/ /a/ /t/, and pronounce or recognize the word CAT. The child has known the oral word CAT for years, and so the sounds are recognized as the word. Some letters can be processed in larger groups — for instance, C-H or T-H, some are associated with multiple sounds (e.g., the hard and soft sounds for G or C), and in English there is no simple one-to-one correspondence between letters and sounds. With practice, the letters in familiar words become linked, so that the word is recognized as a whole unit before the sounds are produced. (This is the beginning of the second, orthographic, path.) Because regular words (such as CAT) could be read by sounding out or as a whole unit, the phonological decoding factor must be tested with "words" that cannot be known by the readers. These are called *pseudowords*: series of letters that follow the general rules for English words but that are either not real words or are very rare and hence unfamiliar words.

The orthographic path has its roots in the visual system: from an early age, we learn to recognize objects and pictures and to apply names to them. As we begin to learn to read words, the first ones are probably learned as whole units, with only very sketchy details about the actual letters. For example, a child may learn to read the sign for McDonald's restaurants but may not be able to recognize the word without the golden arches. As words are learned through the phonological route (for instance, CAT in the previous paragraph), they become unitized and recognizable as single entities. This turns out to be essential in English, because we have so many words that do not have straightforward pronunciations. As more and more words are encountered, the list of direct-recognition words grows. Because regular words (those that follow standard phonics rules for pronunciation, such as CAT) can be either recognized as whole units or assembled by sounding out, it is necessary to test the orthographic factor with words that defy regular phonics rules, usually termed *irregular*, or *exception*, *words*. Many of these irregular or unpredictable words are some of the earliest and most frequently encountered (for instance, OF, ONE, TWO, DO, GO, I).

The dual route theory began with the observation that some acquired dyslexics (those who have received some damage to the brain) rely more on the phonological than the orthographic pathway and others rely more on the orthographic pathway (Coltheart, 1978). The former have been called *surface dyslexics* and the latter, *phonological dyslexics*. However, because the term *surface* is not very informative, I will refer to them as *orthographic dyslexics*, and because there are other areas of phonological difficulties, I will call the phonological group *phonological decoding dyslexics*. (Note that I am using the term *dyslexic* because of its use in the literature; I am not making assumptions about how permanent the difficulty is, what its source is, or whether it is changeable through instruction.)

The results from brain-damaged individuals indicate that the two paths of the dual route model can be damaged or maintained separately (Castles & Coltheart, 1993). If these two groups can be identified in developmental dyslexics (those without apparent damage to their brains, who make up the vast majority of the children with reading difficulties), there should be implications for assessment and instruction. However, one of the difficulties with the dual route approach is that both factors (irregular word reading and pseudoword reading) require some degree of reading ability, so they are not useful measures for early identification. Thus, there is interest in determining the precursors of the two types of processes: if children with weaknesses could be identified at the beginning of schooling, extra support could be provided before reading difficulties begin and the experience of failure sets in. It is also interesting to ask how children with phonological decoding or orthographic difficulties progress in reading. Do they fall further and further behind — the so-called Matthew effect (Stanovich, 1986) or do they begin to catch up with their peers (Phillips, Norris, Osmond, & Maynard, 2002)?

Castles and Coltheart (1993) developed a regression technique for identifying children with phonological decoding and orthographic dyslexia. This method has been subsequently used by a number of other researchers (Manis, Seidenberg, Doi, McBride-Chang, & Petersen, 1996; Samuelsson, Finnström, Leijon, & Mård, 2000; and Stanovich, Siegel, & Gottardo, 1997). Briefly, the technique involves regressing measures of two distinct forms of reading skill upon each other, to identify those children who perform unusually badly (below the 90% confidence interval of the regression line) on either measure, given their ability on the other measure. Castles and Coltheart calculated their regression equation from a sample of normally achieving children and applied it to a group of children showing reading difficulties. Children with phonological decoding dyslexia are able to read exception (irregular) words adequately but show greater difficulty in reading pseudowords. Exception words (such as *two, answer,* and *yacht*) are thought to require orthographic processing, so those with phonological decoding problems should not be affected. Pseudowords (such as *gif* or *tef*), which follow the pattern of English words but are not in fact words, are thought to require phonological skills alone; visual memory cannot provide a pronunciation of them, so children with phonological decoding dyslexia would not be able to use their intact orthographic skills to compensate for their phonological weaknesses. Children with orthographic dyslexia showed the opposite pattern: adequate reading of pseudowords, but low ability to read irregular words.

Kirby, Etmanskie, and Parrila (2000) used data from approximately 150 children in a six-year longitudinal study of reading development to investigate the dual route model. From kindergarten (age 5) to Grade 5 (age 10), children were annually administered a battery of cognitive, linguistic, reading, and spelling measures; the number of children and the measures administered varied from year to year. The children came from a broad range of schools and represented a full range of abilities. The study was based on the children who participated in Grade 3, whose performance was tracked backward and forward in time as long as they were in the study.

Whereas Castles and Coltheart (1993) used a regression line from normally achieving children and imposed it on a sample of children with reading disabilities, Kirby, Etmanskie, and Parrila used the technique to investigate the subtypes within a broad sample of children,[2] including some who were likely to develop

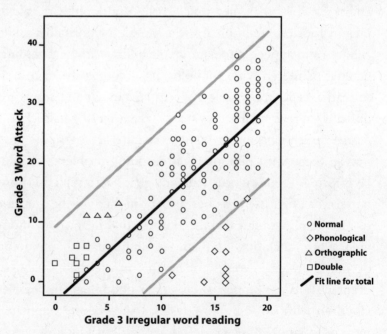

Figure 4. Identification of Children with Phonological Decoding Difficulties (Grade 3)

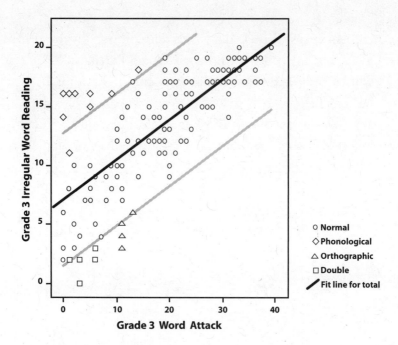

Figure 5. Identification of Children with Orthographic Difficulties (Grade 3)

reading difficulties. The Irregular Word Reading (from Castles & Colt-heart, 1993) and Word Attack (from Woodcock, 1987) scores were used to identify the various groups of readers. In the Irregular Word Reading test, children were asked to read 20 words considered to be irregularly spelled, presented one by one, and their score was the number correct. In Word Attack, children were asked to read pseudowords, and again their score was the number correct. The identification of 11 children with phonological decoding difficulties (Figure 4) was straightforward. However, Figure 5 shows that the identification of children with orthographic difficulties was more complex. Of the 10 children identified, 6 performed extremely poorly on Word Attack, as well as on Irregular Word Reading; it was decided to term these *double difficulty children*. The result was four groups: phonological decoding, orthographic (termed *surface* by Kirby et al., 2000), double difficulty, and normally achieving children. We then followed these children backward and forward in time, to observe the precursors and consequences of their diagnosed difficulties.[2] In the rest of this section, some of Kirby, Etmanskie, and Parrila's (2000) findings will be described. (For a fuller exposition, the study itself should be consulted.)

What is the origin of phonological decoding difficulties? In Figure 6, we can see that the children with phonological decod-

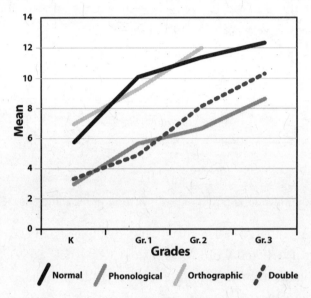

Figure 6. Performance of Subtypes on Blending Phonemes

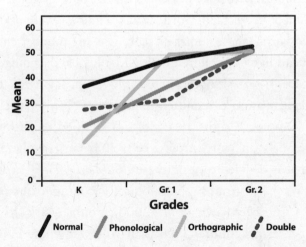

Figure 7. Performance of Subtypes on Letter Recognition

ing difficulties in Grade 3 (both the single and the double difficulty groups) had performed poorly on Blending Phonemes since kindergarten. This task, in which children are presented with a series of sounds and asked what word they form, is a standard measure of phonological awareness (Torgesen, Wagner, & Rashotte, 1994). Other phonological awareness measures showed the same pattern. As suspected or assumed by many, poor phonological awareness is the precursor, and may be the cause, of phonological decoding difficulties. It is clear that these children could have been diagnosed much earlier than Grade 3, without using a reading measure.

What is the origin of orthographic difficulties? Figure 7 shows that the three difficulty groups, and especially the orthographic (surface) children, had lower letter recognition scores than the normally achieving children in kindergarten, but this had disappeared by Grade 2. It is not surprising that after several years in school, they had learned to recognize most of the upper and lower case letters. Letter recognition is an orthographic task (though a very basic one), so it is not surprising that the

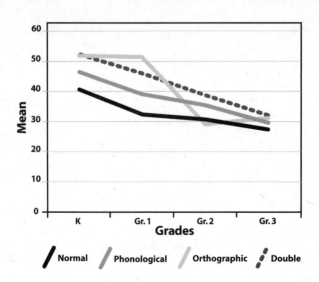

Figure 8. Performance of Subtypes on Picture Naming Speed

orthographic (surface) group did poorly in kindergarten. The double group was still doing poorly in Grade 1.

Another possible source of orthographic difficulty is naming speed (Wolf & Bowers, 1999). Figure 8 indicates that the two groups with orthographic difficulties (the surface and double groups) were very slow in picture naming in kindergarten and Grade 1, although they had caught up with the normally achieving children by Grade 2. Naming speed will be discussed in greater detail in the discussion of the double deficit theory (see next section), but for the moment, it is worth noting that orthographic difficulties may be preceded by slower naming speed. It is also worth noting that although naming speed becomes faster with development for all groups, the initially slow naming speed may be the indicator that something is not working optimally. It is possible that naming speed's effect is mediated by its effect on orthographic processing.

Finally, what is the consequence for reading development of having one of the identified types of reading difficulty? Figure 9

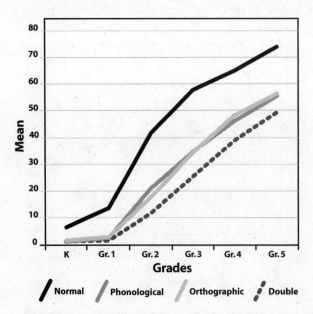

Figure 9. Performance of Dual Route Subtypes on Word Identification

examines the developmental course of scores on the Word Identification subtest of the Woodcock Reading Mastery Tests — Revised (1987) for the four groups of children identified previously. Word Identification is one of the most commonly used measures of reading skill, and although it only asks children to read isolated words (presented by themselves, not in continuous text), scores on it correlate well with other measures, including reading comprehension. Figure 9 shows clearly that the groups with difficulties were distinct as early as kindergarten and that the double group performed worse than the two single-difficulty groups, who in turn performed worse than the normally achieving children. While there is no sign that the difficulty groups are falling further and further behind, there is equally no indication that they are catching up. The difficulty groups are reaching levels by Grade 5 that the normally achieving attained in Grade 3 or earlier. Kirby, Etmanskie, and Parrila found the same pattern of results for the Woodcock Passage Comprehension scores.

So what have we learned from the dual route approach to reading disabilities/difficulties? First, the approach does identify an appropriate number of children, and they seem to have the expected characteristics. Second, the children with difficulties were clearly identifiable in earlier grades, at least as early as kindergarten; this has implications for early assessment. Lastly, it is clear that the problems identified in Grade 3 are serious: they result in enduring and significant lags in reading development, of about two years. The nature of the children's reading difficulties, and the presumed underlying causes, suggest that they need very different reading instruction.

The dual route theory is difficult to apply to younger children, because few of them have the basic reading skills assessed in the dual route approach. A more promising theory for early identification is the double deficit theory (Wolf & Bowers, 1999).

Double Deficit Theory

Wolf and Bowers (1999) developed an alternative theory that also identifies two cognitive processes essential for reading success. Their candidates are phonological awareness and naming speed, both of which we encountered in the description of the Kirby, Etmanskie, and Parrila (2000) study in the previous section. *Phonological awareness* consists of an individual's sensitivity to the sound structure of words in his or her own language and the ability to manipulate the sounds within words; it is widely seen as essential to learning the alphabetic principle (that scripts like English represent individual sounds in oral language with letters and that changing letters changes the sounds and thus the words) and phonic decoding.

Naming speed measures how quickly an individual can name a series of visually presented items, such as colours, pictures, digits, or letters. Naming speed is not understood as well as phonological awareness; various theories state that it measures lexical access speed (that is, how quickly the stimulus is identified in the brain), general mental timing, or the orchestration of complex processes (see Kirby, Parrila, & Pfeiffer, 2003, or Wolf & Bowers, 1999, for more on this). Slow naming speed is thought to result in slow word identification and thus in lessened fluency and lower reading comprehension.

According to the double deficit approach, there are three deficit or difficulty groups: those with a phonological awareness deficit (PAD), a naming speed deficit (NSD), or a double deficit (DD). Children with neither deficit are termed normally achieving or double asset (DA). Wolf and Bowers (1999) summarized extensive evidence that all three deficit groups have reading problems, but that the DD children have the most severe reading difficulties.

Kirby, Parrila, and Pfeiffer (2003) reported a six-year longitudinal study of reading development in children whose phonological awareness and naming speed were assessed in kindergarten. The data set was largely the same as that used in the dual route study by Kirby, Etmanskie, and Parrila (2000), but the addition and loss of participants from year to year make comparison between studies difficult. Kirby, Parrila, and Pfeiffer analyzed their data in two ways, by using the two kindergarten scores first to predict subsequent reading development and second to form the four diagnostic groups (PAD, NSD, DD, and DA) and to observe their progress.

In the first analyses, they found that phonological awareness was the more powerful predictor of reading development in kindergarten and Grade 1 but that naming speed became more powerful by Grade 3 — after controlling for the effects of their participants' verbal and nonverbal mental ability and letter knowledge in kindergarten. This was true for both word reading and reading comprehension. These results support and extend those of other investigators and emphasize the importance of these two dimensions in understanding reading development.

Although the regression analyses described above provide a more precise picture, examining reading development in terms of the four diagnostic groups is more informative about how diagnostic screening could be used in special education.[15] Figure 10 shows the four double deficit groups' performance over the six years of the study on Word Identification. Again it is clear that the groups were distinct in reading skills from the beginning, that the double deficit children fared the worst, and that there is no sign of either divergence or catching up over time. The only exception to this, interestingly, is the PAD group, who were reading poorly in the early years, but by Grade 5 were not as far behind as the NSD or DD children.

There are probably two factors at work here: First, teachers were becoming more aware of phonological awareness as this study was being conducted, so it is likely that many of the children who were weak in phonological awareness at the beginning were receiving instruction that helped them overcome their weakness. (There is no shortage of research indicating that instruction in phonological awareness contributes to reading development [e.g., National Reading Panel, 2000].) The second factor is that phonological awareness was measured in kindergarten, before the children had received any formal reading instruction. There are very likely two sorts of children who receive low phonological awareness scores in kindergarten: those who have genuinely low potential in this area and those who have not had sufficient exposure to reading and analytic language. The former children are likely to continue to struggle in phonological awareness and reading; the latter should merely have a delayed start and should make good progress once exposure and instruction begin.

Inspection of Figure 10 shows that the DD children reached reading levels in Grades 4 and 5 that the DA children had attained 1.5 to 2 years earlier. These results are roughly comparable to those obtained in the dual route approach, even though many more children were included in the double deficit groups.

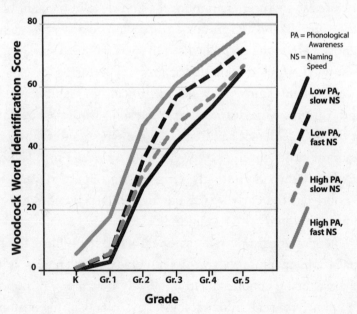

Figure 10. Performance of Double Deficit Subtypes on Word Identification

Kirby, Parrila, and Pfeiffer (2003) also observed the development of serious reading difficulties in the four groups. Using a criterion of being behind grade norms by 2 years by grade 5, they found that 43% of the DD, 25% of the NSD, 6% of the PAD, and none of the DA qualified.

Finally, what were the relations between the two studies and the two sets of subtypes? These questions are difficult to answer, because many more children were "identified" in the double deficit study and because a number of the children identified as dual route subtypes in Grade 3 were not in the study in kindergarten. Nevertheless, some relationships can be seen. Of the 5 children with later phonological decoding problems, 3 had earlier had phonological awareness problems; of the 3 with later orthographic problems, 2 had earlier had naming speed problems. Stated differently, the children with later phonological decoding problems had kindergarten phonological awareness scores that were more than half a standard deviation lower than those of the children who later had orthographic problems. Conversely, those who later had orthographic problems had kindergarten naming speed scores that were more than half of a standard deviation slower than those of the children who later had phonological decoding problems. (The standard deviations are those of the overall sample.) Looked at the other way, the children with poorer phonological awareness scores in kindergarten later had lower pseudoword reading scores than those with better phonological awareness scores, and those who had slower naming speeds in kindergarten later read fewer irregular words than those who had been faster. There is a clear suggestion here that early difficulties in phonological awareness lead to later problems in phonological decoding, and early slowness in naming speed leads to later orthographic problems.

What can we learn from this double deficit study? As in the dual route study, the approach succeeded in identifying children with the appropriate characteristics, but this time the identification was *prospective* — before reading instruction had begun. Because of the different methods, more children were identified; this clearly leads to *overidentification*, because not all of the identified children later developed reading disabilities. However, this may be a less serious problem than underidentification or no identification at all; I elaborate on this in the final section. On average, the identified children showed much poorer reading development, with little sign of catching up to their normally achieving (double asset) peers, and the reading difficulties they encountered were relatively severe. Perhaps most importantly, it is clear that the subtypes of the double deficit approach are related to the subtypes of the dual route approach: low phonological awareness is the precursor of poor phonological decoding, and slow naming speed leads to poor orthographic processing.

Implications of Reading Development and Reading Difficulties for Canadian Education

The studies described above and related studies have implications that can be grouped into four categories: preschool education, early assessment, educational intervention, and teacher education.

Preschool Education

The conclusion of these and many other studies (e.g., National Reading Panel, 2000) is that differences in oral language skills appear among children before reading instruction begins, and these differences predict children's later reading success and failure. As all kindergarten teachers know, great differences exist among children at kindergarten entry in early or prereading skills: some are already reading, while others seem to have encountered few books. Although some may think that kindergarten is too early to begin to worry about children's academic skills, I fear that it is too late. The foundation of those language skills is built from birth, and there is no reason why much the

330

same should not be said for reading. We need to think about children's preschool learning about language and reading, to help ensure that more children come to school equipped to benefit quickly from reading instruction. The present studies and many others (e.g., Cunningham & Stanovich, 1997) demonstrate that starting poorly is a powerful predictor of later failure.

What can be done to help ensure that children are better equipped for reading before they go to school? The obvious response is to advise parents on how to stimulate their children's language and reading development. We are not shy in advising parents about prenatal care, postnatal nutrition, medical care, vaccinations, and so on, so why not extend this approach to language and reading? One major impediment is that many parents are not able to act on the advice, due to a combination of personal skills and resources. Hart and Risley (1995; see also Kirby, 1997) found great differences among children in the amount and richness of oral language to which they were exposed. It may not be feasible for parents with low language skills to offer a rich language environment to their children; one solution may be high-quality and publicly supported daycare (see Kirby, 1997, for more on this).

Hart and Risley's (1995) results suggest that amount and variety of language experience are the important features of an environment for stimulating language development, experienced in the context of positive, supportive parenting. With regard to reading development, the standard advice to parents has been to read to their children. Recent research shows that this may not be enough: reading is important, but the *way* a parent reads to a child may be more important (e.g., Evans, Shaw, & Bell, 2000; Sénéchal & LeFevre, 2002). For example, it is important that reading be a shared activity, rather than one imposed upon an uninterested child; a parent reading out loud while a child runs around the room may be no improvement over television. With respect to specific prereading skills, there is evidence that learning the names of the letters and the sounds that they make and learning to recognize a few simple words contribute to a stronger foundation for learning to read (Kirby & Hogan, in press; Stephenson, Parrila, Georgiou, & Kirby, 2006). These tasks are within the resources of all but the least able parents.

Early Assessment

The evidence reported here and in many other sources indicates (a) that many reading difficulties are identifiable as early as entry to kindergarten and (b) that children who begin poorly are likely to continue to do poorly in school (e.g., Cunningham & Stanovich, 1997). These findings point to the need for early assessment. It is essential that early assessment be done as gently as possible, given the ages of the children and the anxieties of their parents. It is also important that any assessment be sensitive to the children's cultural and economic environments.

How should assessment be organized? The best of all worlds would have a cascade of assessments, beginning in a family doctor's office as oral language is beginning and continuing with yearly gentle and unobtrusive assessments of language and prereading skills. For most children, this would take a few minutes a year and lead at worst to a few suggestions about language activities in the home. For children demonstrating difficulties, there would need to be more intense followup assessments administered by specialists and leading to more focused and specialized interventions. All such preschool assessments and interventions should attend to the languages of the home (so that children are not misdiagnosed) and to the family's resources. Families with few or inadequate resources should be offered assistance, in forms such as subsidized, high-quality childcare, access to parent tutors/mentors, and advice on library access. Most important, these early assessments and interventions should link seamlessly to the education system. Children's needs should not have to be reassessed at school entry as though nothing is known about them; instead, they should be continuously assessed. Interdisciplinary and cross-age teams (consisting of, for instance, teachers, special educators, speech therapists, and medical personnel as required) should consider children's cases on an ongoing basis.

What aspects of "language and prereading skills" should be assessed and how? Based on what I have presented above, it should come as no surprise that I advocate early assessments of phonological awareness, naming speed, and letter knowledge. Other basic phonological skills, such as memory and pronunciation, should be included, as well. There are other matters, too, including vocabulary and grammar, which would need to be addressed. With regard to the family, some assessment should be made of the literacy resources and activities in the home.

Educational Intervention

Early assessment is justifiable only if it leads to early intervention. Again, early interventions should be linked as seamlessly with the child's regular life as possible, so that there is no unnecessary sense of being stigmatized. Parents should be able to carry out most of the basic activities, and well-trained childcare workers should be able to handle most others. Some specialized interventions, such as speech therapy, would have to be carried out by specialists. Preschool interventions should connect smoothly with school programs.

What should be taught? This, of course, depends on the early assessments. For instruction to work, many important noncognitive factors in reading have to exist, including opportunity, interest, and motivation. Children lacking in vocabulary, or whose grammar and pronunciation are poor, may need continuing work in those areas. But the main focus of this essay has been upon the key areas of weakness or even deficiency in children with reading difficulties or disabilities: phonological processing (especially phonological awareness), naming speed, and orthographic processing (including letter knowledge). I suggest that these are the major areas of weakness, and they should therefore be the major targets of intervention.

Many programs indicating how to teach phonological awareness already exist (see, for example, National Reading Panel, 2000). Naming speed has not often been the target of instruction, but recently there has been an increase in the teaching of reading fluency, which may be one of the major consequences of naming speed (see, for example, Wolf & Katzir-Cohen, 2001). Orthographic processing may be the least well understood of the group: from the learning of letters to the processing of complex letter sequences, much remains to be learned.

Teacher Education

Finally, what can we say about teacher education? A great deal has been learned about reading and reading disabilities in the last 20 years, but how much of this has been incorporated into teacher education? My impression is "not much" and "not deeply." A great deal of teacher education is hurried, with a focus on immediate skills. To apply much of the recent research knowledge would require more background knowledge than most new teachers have, and acquiring that knowledge may take more time than they choose to devote to this activity. It may take a major reconceptualization of teacher education to build in the required extensive knowledge about oral and written language, cognitive processes, and text processing, not to mention the ability to read recent research critically (see, for example, Stanovich, 1994; 2003). A reconceptualization of the roles and responsibilities of teachers may also be needed.

It may be that much of the required knowledge can be held and explained by a small number of master or lead teachers, acting as consultants to other teachers. If that is to be the path, a considerable burden will be placed on the education of those lead teachers. And it may be a good idea to start doing it sooner than later.

Diversity in Not Learning to Read

The purpose of this essay has been to review some of the diversity that exists among children variously described as reading disabled and poor readers. These different subgroups require different forms of instruction, and they have to be identified through more sophisticated early assessment. Great progress has been made in the last 20 years. Consider, for instance, phonological awareness, which was known only to a few laboratory researchers in 1980; I now hear many experienced teachers discussing it, and almost all of my teacher education class in 2004 had heard of it and knew something of its relevance to reading. We should be optimistic that further progress will be as successful. As E.B. Huey indicated in the quotation at the beginning of this essay, a complete psychology of reading would unravel some of the most complex workings of the human mind. We are not close to reaching Huey's "acme," but we are much closer than we were in his time. We should not wait for this task to be completed before we apply the knowledge we have gained to improve children's literacy levels.

NOTES

I would like to thank the Social Sciences and Humanities Research Council of Canada and the Canadian Language and Literacy Research Network for the funding that supported the research presented in this essay. Many colleagues and students have contributed in many ways to this work. I'd especially like to thank colleagues J.P. Das, Hélène Deacon, Rauno Parrila, Robin Sidhu, and Lesly Wade-Woolley, and students Philippa Beggs, Joanna Catterson, Christina Colasante, Jennifer Curry, Jennifer Dawson, Jill Etmanskie, Catherine Fermoyle, Marjorie Hitschfeld, Rhonda Martinussen, and Shannon Pfeiffer. This research would have been impossible without the participation and cooperation of many children, parents, teachers, schools, and schoolboards: a big thank you to all of you, and I hope you continue to support literacy research.

1   Although the experimental results that support the dual route theory are not challenged, some authors do challenge the interpretation that there are distinct pathways; see Plaut, McClelland, Seidenberg, & Patterson, 1996, for more about this.

2   The numbers of participants in each group decreased with distance from Grade 3, as some had joined the study after kindergarten, and some left before Grade 5. The numbers of participants in the groups, from kindergarten to Grade 5 were: phonological decoding: 3, 10, 10, 11, 11, 7; orthographic: 3, 3, 2, 5, 5, 5; double: 3, 6, 6, 7, 7,7.

3   The numbers of children in the four groups varied from kindergarten to Grade 5 as follows: in the DD group, n went from 24 to 15, 11, 10, 9, and 7 across years; in the PAD group, n went from 25 to 22, 19, 19, 18, and 17; in NSD, it went from 25 to 19, 16, 12, 9, and 8; and in the DA group n went from 25 to 19, 18, 19, 14, and 14.

REFERENCES

Adams, M.J. (1990). *Beginning to read: Thinking and learning about print.* Cambridge, MA: MIT Press.

Castles, A., & Coltheart, M. (1993). Varieties of developmental dyslexia. *Cognition, 47,* 149–180.

Coltheart, M. (1978). Lexical access in simple reading tasks. In G. Underwood (Ed.), *Strategies of information processing* (pp. 151–216). London: Academic Press.

Crowder, R.G. (1982). *The psychology of reading.* Oxford: Oxford University Press.

Cunningham, A.E., & Stanovich, K.E. (1997). Early reading acquisition and its relation to reading experience and ability ten years later. *Developmental Psychology, 33,* 934–945.

Evans, M.A., Shaw, D., & Bell, M. (2000). Home literacy activities and their influence on early literacy skills. *Canadian Journal of Experimental Psychology, 54,* 65–75.

Goswami, U., & Bryant, P.E. (1990). *Phonological skills and learning to read.* Hove, UK: Erlbaum.

Hart, B., & Risley, T.R. (1995). *Meaningful differences in the everyday experiences of young American children*. Baltimore, MD: Paul H. Brookes.

Huey, E.B. (1908/1968). *The psychology and pedagogy of reading*. Cambridge, MA: MIT Press.

Juel, C. (1988). Learning to read and write: A longitudinal study of 54 children from first through fourth grades. *Journal of Educational Psychology, 80*, 437–447.

Kintsch, W. (1999). *Comprehension: A paradigm for cognition*. Cambridge: Cambridge University Press.

Kirby, J.R. (1988). Style, strategy, and skill in reading. In R.R. Schmeck (Ed.), *Learning styles and learning strategies*. New York: Plenum Press.

——— (1997). Measuring environment: Meaningful differences in language experience. *Canadian Journal of Education, 22*, 323–329.

Kirby, J.R., Etmanskie, J.M., & Parrila, R.K. (2000, July). The development of two forms of reading difficulty. Paper presented to the International Congress of Psychology, Stockholm, Sweden (available from the first author).

Kirby, J.R., & Hogan, B.E. (in press). Family literacy environment and early literacy development. *Exceptionality Education Canada*.

Kirby, J.R., Parrila, R., & Pfeiffer, S. (2003). Naming speed and phonological processing as predictors of reading development. *Journal of Educational Psychology, 95*, 453–464.

Kirby, J.R., & Williams, N.H. (1991). *Learning problems: A cognitive approach*. Toronto: Kagan and Woo.

Manis, F.R., Seidenberg, M.S., Doi, L.M., McBride-Chang, C., & Petersen, A. (1996). On the bases of two subtypes of developmental dyslexia. *Cognition, 58*, 157–195.

National Reading Panel (2000). *Teaching children to read: An evidence-based assessment of the scientific literature on reading and its implications for reading instruction*. Bethesda, MD: National Institute of Child Health and Human Development.

OECD/Statistics Canada. (2000). *Literacy in the information age. Final report of the International Adult Literacy Survey*. Ottawa: Minister of Industry.

Oakhill, J., & Yuill, N. (1996). Higher order factors in comprehension disability: Processes and remediation. In C. Cornoldi & J. Oakhill (Eds.), *Reading comprehension difficulties: Processes and intervention* (pp. 69–92). Mahwah, NJ: Lawrence Erlbaum Associates.

Olson, D.R. (1994). *The world on paper*. Cambridge: Cambridge University Press.

Perrin, B. (1990). *Literacy Counts*. Ottawa: National Literacy Secretariat.

Phillips, L.M., Norris, S.P., Osmond, W.C., & Maynard, A.M. (2002). Relative reading achievement: A longitudinal study of 187 children from first through sixth grades. *Journal of Educational Psychology, 94,* 3–13.

Plaut, D.C., McClelland, J.L., Seidenberg, M.S., & Patterson, K. (1996). Understanding normal and impaired word reading: Computational principles in quasi-regular domains. *Psychological Review, 103,* 56–115.

Pressley, M. (2002). *Reading instruction that works* (2nd ed.). New York: Guilford.

Rayner, K., Foorman, B.R., Perfetti, C.A., Pesetsky, D., & Seidenberg, M.S. (2001). How psychological science informs the teaching of reading. *Psychological Science in the Public Interest, 2*(2), 31–74.

Samuelsson, S., Finnström, O., Leijon, I., & Mård, S. (2000). Phonological and surface profiles of reading difficulties among very low birth weight children: Converging evidence for the developmental lag hypothesis. *Scientific Studies of Reading, 4,* 197–217.

Sénéchal, M., & LeFevre, J. (2002). Parental involvement in the development of children's reading skill: A five-year longitudinal study. *Child Development, 73,* 445–460.

Seymour, P.H.K., Aro, M., & Erskine, J.M. (2003). Foundation literacy acquisition in the European orthographies. *British Journal of Psychology, 94,* 143–174.

Snow, C.E., Burns, M.S., & Griffin, P. (Eds.). (1998). *Preventing reading difficulties in young children*. Washington, DC: National Academy Press.

Stanovich, K.E. (1986). Matthew effects in reading: Some consequences of individual differences in the acquisition of literacy. *Reading Research Quarterly, 21,* 360–407.

(1994). Romance and reality. *Reading Teacher, 47,* 280–291.

(2000). *Progress in understanding reading: Scientific foundations and new frontiers*. New York: Guilford.

(2003). Understanding the styles of science in the study of reading. *Scientific Studies of Reading, 7,* 105–126.

Stanovich, K.E., Siegel, L.S., & Gottardo, A. (1997). Converging evidence for phonological and surface subtypes of reading disability. *Journal of Educational Psychology, 89,* 114–127.

Stephenson, K.A., Parrila, R.K., Georgiou, G.K., & Kirby, J.R. (2006). Effects of home literacy, parents' beliefs, and children's task-focused behavior on emergent literacy and word reading skills. Manuscript submitted for publication.

Torgesen, J.K., Wagner, R.K., & Rashotte, C.A. (1994). Longitudinal studies of phonological processing and reading. *Journal of Learning Disabilities*, 27, 276–286.Vellutino, F.R., et al. (1996). Cognitive profiles of difficult to remediate and readily remediated poor readers: Early intervention as a vehicle for distinguishing between cognitive and experiential deficits as basic causes of specific reading disability. *Journal of Educational Psychology*, 88, 601–638.

Wagner, R.K., Torgesen, J.K., Laughon, P.L., Simmons, K., & Rashotte, C. (1993). Development of young readers' phonological processing abilities. *Journal of Educational Psychology, 85*, 85–103.

Willcutt, E.G., & Pennington, B.F. (2000). Psychiatric comorbidity in children and adolescents with reading disability. *Journal of Child Psychology and Psychiatry, 41*, 1039–1048.

Willms, J.D. (1999). Quality and inequality in children's literacy: The effects of families, schools, and communities. In D.P. Keating & C. Hertzman (Eds.), *Developmental health and the wealth of nations* (pp. 72–93). New York: Guilford Press.

Wolf, M., & Bowers, P.G. (1999). The double-deficit hypothesis for the developmental dyslexias. *Journal of Educational Psychology, 91*, 415–438.

Wolf, M., & Katzir-Cohen, T. (2001). Reading fluency and its intervention. *Scientific Studies of Reading, 5*, 211–238.

Woodcock, R.J. (1987). *Woodcock Reading Mastery Tests — Revised*. Circle Pines, MN: American Guidance Service.

Educating Gifted Children:
Frameworks for Debate

Marion Porath

This essay focuses on building capacity for diversity as it pertains to learners who are gifted. These learners are developmentally advanced in one or more areas (intellectual, academic, artistic, social, emotional, and/or physical). They may also be extraordinarily creative. Our schools tend to focus on intellectual, academic, and physical giftedness; some attend to artistic giftedness. Diversities of thought and development are the hallmarks of gifted learners and have been the focus of research and practice. Diversities of language, background, and culture are also relevant to understanding giftedness. These diversities receive relatively little attention in research and practice. All of the diversities discussed in this volume are important in truly understanding the complexity of giftedness.

The essay begins with a discussion of diversity and giftedness, highlighting the range of diversity among gifted learners. Then, to provide background for frameworks for debate on the education of gifted learners, current issues are presented, followed by an overview of current educational and social contexts relevant to building capacity for gifted learners in our schools. Frameworks for debate that focus on teaching and learning are suggested, including a focus on the nature of optimal learning environments. I conclude with guiding questions pertaining to

341

the direction of education in the 21st century and to policy and practice for gifted learners.

Diversity and Giftedness

Diversity in thought and development make the population of gifted learners a highly heterogeneous one. When the diversities of language, background, and culture are added, the heterogeneity increases considerably. Two comparisons are relevant to understanding giftedness and diversity. First, *between-group diversity* distinguishes gifted learners. Gifted students have greater capacity for learning, learn faster, reason in a more complex and abstract way, and are developmentally advanced, as compared to their chronological age peers of average ability. Second, gifted students are characterized by *within-group diversity*. This diversity is profound across intellectual (general intelligence and specific abilities) (Lubinski & Benbow, 2000; Robinson, Zigler, & Gallagher, 2000) and nonintellectual (motivation and self-concept) attributes (Lubinski & Benbow, 2000). Research on gifted learners has failed to attend to the significant variability evident in studies that compare gifted and average children. These studies focused instead on differences between groups that are based on averages (Robinson, 1987) that obscure the important inter- and intra-individual differences that characterize gifted learners.

Both between-group and within-group comparisons are essential to consider in planning educational environments and instructional modifications. Between-group diversity will be discussed further later in the essay with regard to teaching, learning, and optimal educational environments. Within-group diversity is discussed in detail here because of its importance in understanding gifted learners. Because of current labelling and funding practices in Canada, gifted learners are often viewed as a homogeneous group. We must get beyond categorical thinking in order to understand the complexity of giftedness in a multicultural society.

Within-Group Diversity

Diversity *among* gifted learners can be described in several ways. Statistically, there is a distribution within the normal distribution of intellectual ability. Within the top 1% (IQ from about 135 to above 200), another distribution is evident, with a range of over 70 points (Lubinski & Benbow, 2000).

Significant variability is also evident in the academic profiles of gifted children; it is greater among the top 5% than it is in the average population (Keating, 1991). Matthews (1997) studied linguistic, logical-mathematical, and social-emotional development among early adolescents with relatively homogeneous IQs and found significant differences in domain-specific patterns of achievement. In addition, variability in creativity, social development, and motivation as evidenced in drive, capacity for work, and perseverance is apparent among gifted learners (Lubinski & Benbow, 2000).

When all of the above factors are considered together, they highlight the complexity of gifted children's learning, motivational, and behavioural profiles. This complexity needs to be matched by correspondent complexity in gifted children's learning *environments*. (The plural is used here to emphasize that no one learning environment is likely to meet all of a gifted child's needs.) Complex learning environments include options for learning and representation of knowledge, provocations for learning (Project Zero & Reggio Children, 2001), and opportunities to apply and extend essential academic skills. Educational environments are critical in providing the experiences that optimize potential and will be discussed in more detail later in the essay.

Additional Considerations and Issues Relevant to Diversity and Giftedness

Research and practice in gifted education primarily reflect the values and learning abilities of white, middle-class, academic achievers. However, subgroups of gifted students exist who need additional targeted efforts to help them reach their potential and avoid psychosocial problems (Lupart & Odishaw, 2003). They include highly gifted students (usually defined as having an IQ > 145), highly creative students, gifted females, gifted students with disabilities, gifted students who are underachieving, and gifted students with cultural and linguistic backgrounds that differ from the mainstream. These subgroups may be neglected, underserved, and misunderstood (Lupart & Odishaw, 20003).

Highly Gifted Students

Highly gifted students — students whose intellectual ability is found in 1 of approximately 10,000 children — are at greater risk for psychosocial problems than gifted students whose IQs are lower and students of average ability. About 25% of highly gifted students are vulnerable, as compared to about 10% of other gifted students and about 10% of average students (Janos & Robinson, 1985). It is very difficult to meet like-minded peers when one's intelligence is so different from average. Highly gifted students' educational experiences are likely to be significantly out of step with their developmental levels; advancement of at least several grade levels in core academic subjects and exceptional ability to learn makes sufficient curricular challenge very difficult to accomplish in regular classrooms.

Highly Creative Students

Highly creative students are also unlikely to have satisfying educational experiences. Teachers favour students whom they perceive as socially responsible, and creative students are unlikely to be perceived in this way (Wentzel, 1993). Creative students ask many questions, resist school norms, and like to do things in unusual ways. They are not "ideal" students from many teachers' points of view (Scott, 1999), and their creativity is likely to be stifled in classrooms that do not value the exploration of ideas.

Gifted Females

Gifted girls are, in general, highly socially intelligent (Fischer, Knight, & Van Parys, 1993) in addition to being very able intellectually and academically. When they enter school, they may adapt easily to prevailing norms for achievement and behaviour, having figured out very quickly what the expectations are for a group of five-year-olds. For this reason, their abilities may not be recognized. As they progress through school and enter early adolescence, their social intelligence and interest in the social domain come to play again. At this point in their development, gifted girls may feel torn between intellectual achievement and social acceptance, often opting for the latter (Kerr, 1994). They often experience pressure *not* to achieve and have difficulty reconciling their identities as females and gifted students.

Despite social pressures, gifted girls demonstrate stellar achievement overall. However, they tend to "disappear." Their professional accomplishments and financial rewards do not equal those of men (Reis, 2003), particularly in the field of mathematics and science (Cannon & Lupart, 2001). It may be that gifted women hold different standards for accomplishment than those typically considered (Reis); however, longitudinal studies show that many female students may not develop their potential (Cannon & Lupart, 2001). Their achievements may also be more private than public. Inzlicht and Ben-Zeev (2003) showed that highly able female college students who were paired with male students to complete a task chose to underperform in public situations, as compared to situations where they were paired with other females and performance requirements were more informal.

Gifted Students with Disabilities

Giftedness can and does coexist with physical, sensory, and/or learning disabilities. Unfortunately, many are unable to conceive of giftedness and learning disability coexisting in the same individual, possibly because they understand intelligence as a unidimensional phenomenon. Similarly, physical or sensory disability may blind us to intellectual capability. The achievements of individuals like Stephen Hawking, Helen Keller, and Albert Einstein are often used to illustrate the reality of the coexistence of gifts and disabilities. However, this reality is more common than it may seem if we focus only on individuals who have achieved prominence. Many students struggle to realize their potential in the face of educational programs that focus on their "weaknesses" and neglect their strengths. Multidimensional conceptions of intelligent behaviour and the demonstration of knowledge (e.g., Gardner, 1983; Project Zero & Reggio Children, 2001) can broaden our notions of how ability is expressed and contribute to educational programs that build students' capabilities.

Gifted Students Who Are Underachieving

Students are described as "underachievers" when they are perceived or have been assessed as having high potential but are not achieving in school to a level commensurate with their ability. However, the term "underachievement" has been criticized as inappropriate. Neumeister and Hébert (2003) propose "selective achievement" and Delisle and Galbraith (2002) propose "selective consumer," suggesting that "underachieving" gifted students are making informed decisions about where to direct their efforts. Some gifted learners may have a different value system vis-à-vis learning and education, and the terms suggested by Neumeister and Hébert and Delisle and Galbraith seem to honour this possibility (Richardson, 2004). Matching students' learning style preferences with instructional style and classroom environment enables learning. Hence, consideration of their educational values and needs in this match may help "underachieving" students achieve.

Gifted Students with Cultural and Linguistic Backgrounds Different from the Mainstream

In Canada, we still have much to learn about what counts as intelligent performance and what is recognized as giftedness in the many cultures that make up our society. When cultural values resemble those of the school system (i.e., verbal and logical-mathematical skills and reasoning) (Gardner, 1983), gifted learners fare best. Recent research on culture and competence suggests that there are other rich and varied ways of demonstrating competence. For example, the book *Culture and Competence,* edited by Sternberg and Grigorenko (2004), includes chapters concerning cultural perspectives on competence, the culturally situated nature of competence, the influence of schooling on competence, intellectual and social aspects of competence, and intercultural competence. This work is important to consider as our society becomes increasingly diverse and global in nature.

It is also essential to understand Aboriginal conceptions of giftedness and to reflect these conceptions in practice and to understand and apply Aboriginal values regarding community and social practices. Nevertheless, there is little representation of Aboriginal students in gifted programs in Canada. Non-Aboriginals are just beginning to understand what is valued as competence in Aboriginal communities (see, for example, Grigorenko et al., 2004; Struthers, 2003). When Aboriginal values are respected and incorporated into educational planning (e.g., mentorships in the community, project-based approach to learning, wide range of educational options that match students' needs), students experience more academic success (Matthews, 1994). Collaboration between school systems and Aboriginal communities is vital for understanding what is valued as competence and what environments support optimal learning.

The Educational Context

Canadian education consists of two systems: "regular" and "special" education. These systems function largely independently of each other, rather than collaboratively (Lupart & Webber, 2002). Somewhat paradoxically, a philosophy of egalitarianism prevails in this dual system. However, as Winner (2000) emphasizes, "Schools cannot be truly egalitarian unless they acknowledge learning differences, including those differences possessed by students of high ability" (p. 166). When the current focus on educational standards is added to the mix, students whose thinking and development do not conform to average expectations are not well served by the majority of educational settings. Wilson (1996) emphasized that an exclusive focus on educational standards can distract efforts to meet the needs of students. Results of assessments, including large-scale assessments that focus on local, provincial, national, and/or international standards, should be used to customize education rather than to standardize it (Wilson, 1996).

There is need for systemic change (Lupart & Webber, 2002) that includes recognition of the relevance of diversity to education and a focus on teaching and learning (Donovan, Bransford, & Pellegrino, 1999). Current research on learning notes the importance of engagement of students' initial understandings, student ownership of learning goals and their progress toward those goals, and provision of opportunities to master both factual and conceptual knowledge (Donovan et al., 1999).

The knowledge structures of experts are complex, and instruction that has as its objective the nurturance of expertise incorporates meaningful conceptual material (Bereiter & Scardamalia, 1986). Conversely, instruction that fails to incorporate conceptual material can lead to cumulative deficits in achievement (Meichenbaum & Biemiller, 1998). This outcome was illustrated powerfully by Jeanne Bamberger (1986) in her study of gifted adolescent musicians. These young musicians went through a "mid-life crisis" when called upon to learn formal theoretical musical concepts. Having experienced a largely skills-based approach to musical instruction since early childhood, they were unprepared for the demands to think more deeply about music and became frustrated and unmotivated.

Focus on Teaching and Learning

Current research on teaching and learning emphasizes a focus on students' perspectives and ways of thinking. This focus provides a solid foundation for subsequent learning. Without engagement of students' initial knowledge, what is learned is at risk of sitting as an "educational overlay" that is not incorporated into students' mental structures as deep, fully understood knowledge (Jordan & Porath, 2006). This engagement is just as important for gifted students as it is for other learners. Gifted students generally know a lot about a variety of topics and express their knowledge in mature ways. However, these abilities are primarily skill based (e.g., advanced vocabulary and general knowledge, mathematics computation) and are often considerably more advanced than their conceptual knowledge (Fischer & Canfield, 1986; Porath, 1992, 1996, 1997) (e.g., narrative plot structure, mathematical principles, scientific concepts like density). This pattern of development makes the need to uncover and engage gifted learners' conceptual knowledge vital in ensuring an appropriate education.

The Role of Developmental Theory

Developmental theory can be helpful in understanding advanced development. Work in the neo-Piagetian tradition (Case, 1985, 1992a; Case & Okamoto, 1996) has mapped development from birth to adolescence in a number of domains (e.g., mathematical, logical reasoning, narrative, social-emotional, and visual-spatial).

Stages and substages of development and the growth of conceptual thinking in each domain across each stage are articulated. The latter is captured by descriptions of the *central conceptual structure* in each domain. These structures are "blueprints" of children's understanding. *Structure* is defined as an internal mental entity consisting of the relations among a number of concepts. *Conceptual* refers to the semantic nature of the relations: the meanings, representations, or concepts that children assign to external entities in their world. Since a structure is believed to form the basis of a wide range of more specific concepts and to play a role in enabling children to make the transition to a new stage of thought, it is defined as *central* (Case, 1992a). These structures provide the "conceptual glue" for skills. For example, the conceptual knowledge described above (e.g., plot structure, mathematical principles, and scientific concepts) is central to writing expert stories, reasoning well mathematically, and understanding science deeply rather than simply applying an algorithm. When skills can be "glued" to a concept, expert understanding results (e.g., using expressive, evocative vocabulary to communicate plot).

Work with gifted learners (Porath, 1992, 1996, 1997, 2001) shows that central conceptual understanding is usually less advanced — generally between one and two years above age expectations — than are skills, which may be several years or more above age expectations. Development of central conceptual structures is linked to maturation (frontal lobe development) (Case, 1992b). When viewed through a neo-Piagetian lens, gifted children's development is distinguished by their ability to grasp central conceptual understandings quickly and then use them flexibly and creatively.

Understanding Learners' Minds

Vygotsky's work on disability (disability being conceived as any difference from the "norm") is informative in thinking about helping all students learn (Gindis, 1999). Vygotsky believed that it is up to society and schools to find the "way in" to students' ways of thinking. The "problem" does not reside in the student, but in our ability to understand how the student learns. Gifted students can be challenging to teach. They may make intuitive leaps when solving problems, think in unexpected ways, have gaps in their knowledge and/or a disability that affects certain aspects of their learning, and/or be resistant to mastery of basic skills. Finding the "way in" is made easier when we make the effort to understand what knowledge they bring to school.

Paley (1986) made great strides in understanding her students when she practised "listening to what the children say." If we add to this practice the belief in children's competence that is the hallmark of the world-famous schools of Reggio Emilia, Italy (Project Zero & Reggio Children, 2001) and knowledge of students' cultural, intellectual, historical, and political legacies (Delpit, 2003), a truly *learner-centred* philosophy of teaching will be the result (as opposed to a *teacher-centred* philosophy focusing on the curriculum and the delivery of predetermined knowledge to students).

Contemporary education is increasingly learner-centred (Fried, 2001), focusing on the capabilities and needs of the students as starting points for instruction. Education that honours the constructive nature of understanding sustains children's excitement in learning and extends their achievements (Freeman, 2000; Robinson, Abbott, Berninger, Busse, & Mukhopadhyay, 1997). It also makes teaching much more rewarding (Jordan & Porath, 2006). To this end, an examination of one's own beliefs about teaching is worthwhile, particularly when one teaches gifted learners with their complex developmental, motivational, and social-emotional profiles. How we think about others' minds and the way minds develop determines how we teach. Bruner (1996, pp. 53–63) presented four *models of mind* and their pedagogical consequences.

1. If we see children as imitative learners who need to acquire "know-how," we assume a modelling role in teaching. We teach children the skills they need to function in particular social-cultural settings by showing them and having them practise the skills. This model of mind does not focus on teaching for understanding (or "knowing that") but on skill sets only.

2. If we believe that children learn from didactic exposure, we take the position that there are knowledge sources, including the teacher's mind, that allow children to "look up" or "hear" what they need to know. In this model, "knowing how" is assumed to result from "knowing that." This model of mind conceives the learner's mind as a tabula rasa waiting to be filled with facts dispensed by teachers, books, and other sources of knowledge.

3. If we see children as thinkers, then we teach in a way that reflects our curiosity about children's perspectives on learning, the curriculum, and school as a social-cultural milieu. This model of mind assumes the child's capacity to reason and engage in discussion with others, and this results in learning. Underlying this approach to education is the teacher's effort to understand how children think, how they think about their own thinking, and how they remember and organize knowledge and learning.

4. If we see children as needing to distinguish their own knowledge from the objective knowledge in their culture, then we teach in a way that unites the previous perspective — children as thinkers — with study of the past. We help children to understand what distinguishes "personal knowledge" from knowledge that has a history — "what is taken to be known" in our culture. We also strive to utilize children's ways of knowing in our instruction. We strive to

build instructional bridges (McKeough & Sanderson, 1996) to help them unite their own conceptions of knowledge and those of the culture.

Teaching is a complex activity, in which all four models of mind are used. It is the primary focus of pedagogy that is important. That is, if one takes the perspective that children are thinkers who need support in uniting their own knowledge with that of the culture, then efforts to teach skills and to utilize knowledge sources are directed toward that goal.

The Social Context

We live in a time of profound social change characterized by a shift from industrial capacity to knowledge generation and intelligent use of information (Keating & Hertzman, 1999). Contemporary society has been characterized as a *learning society*, "a society capable of adapting to technological and social change rapidly enough and well enough to maintain or re-create the supports for healthy human development" (Keating & Hertzman, p. 5). As this capability is dependent on collaborative knowledge building and innovation, socially distributed intelligence (Keating, 1999) is essential. It is no longer adequate to teach children to learn individually; we must also engage and support them to learn in groups and share their expertise so that shared competence results.

Learning environments that serve gifted learners well take into account the current educational and social contexts and recognize the multiple ways in which diversity is manifest among gifted learners. Before considering what those environments might look like, some conceptual groundwork relevant to giftedness needs to be laid.

Aspiring to Optimal Learning Environments for Gifted Learners: Some Conceptual Groundwork

Optimal learning environments for gifted learners require, first, consideration of those whom the environments are designed to support. Who is gifted? What is the meaning of the term? How does giftedness translate into education? What does it mean to "accelerate" learning? Second, developmental considerations are relevant. What is the course of development of giftedness in different domains? Are environments for young gifted children comparable to those for gifted adolescents? Once these questions are considered, we can think about educational implications.

What Is Giftedness?

There is value in using the widely accepted term "gifted." It provides a common reference point for discussion. However, current terminology is imprecise, making determination of who is gifted difficult. First, the term "gifted" implies a categorical type. As discussed earlier, the "gifted" population is much too diverse to be considered a categorical type (Lubinski & Benbow, 2000). Furthermore, a categorical approach implies that there is an agreed-upon definition of giftedness and a well-defined point at which someone either "is gifted" or is not (an absolutist conception). This approach fails to consider what is valued in different societies and cultures; developmental, educational, and environmental influences on intelligent behaviour; and the fact that we do not know the limits of human potential. If the idea and development of giftedness are constrained by arbitrary cut-off points, we are in danger of constraining this potential.

Even if one were to use a traditional North American definition and consider "gifted" to mean an IQ in the top 2% of the population, there is such developmental diversity among children and adolescents with high IQs — academic, creative, social, and motivational (Lubinski & Benbow, 2000; Matthews, 1997) — that it makes the definition of little use in fostering development in a holistic fashion. For almost a century, since Terman's (1925) pioneering work with children of high IQ, giftedness has been understood as high general intelligence ("g"). This has resulted in a unidimensional view of ability. Moreover, the "g" perspective on giftedness is understood by many as a "quality of mind," an understanding that fuels charges of elitism that impact on the stability of and support for gifted education (Keating, 1991). While "g" is empirically supported (Gottfredson, 1997) and does have the advantage of raising awareness about exceptionally high intellectual ability, it is not easily translated into educational objectives (Keating, 1991).

The term "gifted" is itself being questioned. It connotes elitism and educational privilege (Keating, 1991; Porath, 2002) and reflects a unidimensional view of intelligence. As educational psychologists Bruce Shore and Reva Friedman have put it:

> Scholarship in the field is moving away from the term, and practice is beginning to respond with multiple views of high ability, some of them linked to the domain of activity, some to creativity, and all to the realization that the nurturance of high potential in a human being involves both unfettering potential that is within the person and adding knowledge and skills that were not there before (Shore & Friedman, 2000, p. xv).

If we take the time to rethink and reframe the language we use in light of current knowledge, we can facilitate reconceptualization of giftedness in a way that leads to meaningful educational planning. If we see giftedness as a "set of maximal expectations toward which ... efforts can be focused" (Shore & Friedman, 2000, p. xvi), we raise the bar for all learners. If giftedness is ignored, we impose an "artificially lowered ceiling ... on general educational expectations" (Shore & Friedman, p. xvii).

What Is Acceleration?

"Acceleration" is another term used in reference to highly able learners, who make rapid progress through the curriculum. It implies "speeding up" the learning process and is often perceived to connote a negative educational strategy (Southern & Jones, 1991). It does not require reconceptualization so much as it requires replacement with a more accurate term because acceleration actually is developmentally based instruction. The central objective of developmentally based instruction is "tuning the learning environment to the knowledge to be conveyed as well as to the learning capabilities of the students" (Larkin, 1994, p. xii). In accomplishing this objective, an *optimal match* is achieved between the curriculum, the learning environment, and learners' minds (Donaldson, 1979; Keating, 1991; Robinson & Robinson, 1982). School systems aim for an optimal match for most learners; however, the concept appears to break down where advanced development is concerned.

If we take seriously the notion that all children come to school at a point on their own individual developmental pathway, then we must plan accordingly. There are multiple pathways to, and demonstrations of, giftedness in any one domain (Fischer, Knight, & Van Parys, 1993; Golomb, 1992; Porath, 1993, 2000; Robinson, 1993). We must plan for different developmental timetables, different backgrounds, different levels of expertise, and different ways of learning. Learning environments that consider these differences in children's ways of knowing and learning support them in reaching *their* potential — not in reaching a preconceived, arbitrary, age-grade-bound notion of where they "should be."

Creating Rich Educational Environments

Implicit in developmentally based instruction is the important role of the learning environment and how it is matched to learners' capabilities. This is a critical aspect of meaningful education for gifted learners. Jackson (2000) asks the important question of where we direct our efforts on behalf of gifted learners. Do we continue to try to disentangle the complexity of giftedness through efforts to refine the definition and articulate influences on giftedness, as has been done via extensive discussion of different conceptions of giftedness (see, for example, Sternberg & Davidson, 1986) and complex modelling of giftedness (e.g., Gagné, 1999)? This is not to say that these efforts are misguided or unimportant. They have contributed to our understanding of the multiple ways in which children demonstrate giftedness and the complexity of influences on giftedness. It is, rather, to suggest (as Jackson does) that there is another question we should consider. This question is particularly important for educational decision making.

Jackson's (2000) second question regarding targeted efforts on behalf of gifted learners is whether, instead of trying to determine the complexity of giftedness, we should aim for complexity in educational environments, allowing for complex *determination* of giftedness, rather than trying to disentangle the concept. Directing our efforts to creating complex environments is favoured by Renzulli (2002), who argues that giftedness, creativity, and high commitment to task will be observed only if children have the benefit of rich environments that afford opportunities for them to demonstrate their abilities.

Similarly, Barab and Plucker (2002) emphasize smart *contexts* rather than smart *people* in determining intelligent behaviour. According to their conception, intelligence is situated in context. Complex determination of giftedness, in addition to offering highly intelligent learners rich contexts in which to develop their abilities, would support highly competent individuals in expressing their competence if they are disabled, have cultural or linguistic backgrounds that are different from the mainstream culture, are not demonstrating competence because of gender-related issues, and/or are "underachieving."

A focus on "smart contexts" is consistent with a *relativistic* conception of giftedness that takes into account different patterns and pathways in children's development, developmental trajectories in different domains (e.g., music may be mastered in adolescence but mastery of philosophy takes much longer) (Brazelton & Greenspan, 2000; Feldman, 1986), and the possibilities that giftedness can wax and wane over time and be expressed in different ways over the course of development (Jackson, 2000). This conception is much more in tune with the way children develop and learn than the *absolutist* conception of giftedness that has prevailed for almost a century, leaving a legacy of stasis — intellectual ability defined by IQ as stable and predictive of adult success. A dynamic view of children in context will inform our thinking to a much greater extent (Jackson, 2000).

When designing educational environments, as with the design of instruction, it is important to acknowledge students' contributions. Not only should we "listen to what the children say" (Paley, 1986), but we should also "watch what the children do." We need to study young people at work (Renzulli, 2002) and acknowledge that gifted children may play an important role in creating environments that sustain them (Robinson, 1987).

The Environment as the "Third Teacher"

Educational environments are critical in providing the experiences that optimize potential. Teachers in the world-renowned schools of Reggio Emilia, Italy, refer to the environment as the "third teacher" (Strozzi, 2001). In addition to the teacher and learning materials (books, computers, etc.), the structure, complexity, and aesthetics of educational environments can facilitate learning and awaken learners to new possibilities (Barbour &

Shaklee, 1998). The expression of knowledge is affected by the way we arrange our classrooms (considering space, light, and design) and the manner in which we display materials. Brazelton and Greenspan (2000) refer to the nature/nurture interaction as a "key in a lock" (p. 81). The right experiences can open up the "lock" of nature and help children realize their potential.

Are our classrooms aesthetic places? Do they convey a sense of welcome and invite students to engage in learning? Are materials arranged provocatively? Do they invite experimentation and foster creativity? If we provide complexity in educational environments, we allow for complex determination of ability (Jackson, 2000).

Developmental Considerations: The Early Years

The early years are "critically formative"; however, a significant body of research focused on gifted young children has yet to accrue (Robinson, 1993, 2000). Giftedness does not simply "happen" in middle childhood. Precocity in development can be evident in infancy. Retrospective parental reports of unusually advanced development in infancy (e.g., Feldman, 1986) are often deemed unreliable; however, observations and behavioural ratings of infants have been linked prospectively to intellectual and academic giftedness (e. g., Gottfried, Gottfried, Bathurst, & Guerin, 1994; Louis & Lewis, 1992). Linguistic and mathematical precocity are apparent in very young children and tend to be stable over time (Dale, Robinson, & Crain-Thoresen, 1995; Robinson, Abbott, Berninger, & Busse, 1996).

Research on the early emergence and stability of exceptional capabilities strongly suggests that provision of an optimal curricular match to advanced abilities in early childhood settings is essential to nurture young children's curiosity, motivation, and accomplishment (Keating, 1991; Robinson et al., 1996). Well-designed programs in stimulating environments sustain children's excitement in learning and extend their achievements (Robinson, Abbott, Berninger, Busse, & Mukhopadhyay, 1997).

Well-designed programs also support healthy social and emotional development (Keating, 1991). Without a challenging school program, young gifted students may "act their age," with the result that social behaviour becomes the educational focus. However, behaviours perceived as problematic often disappear when sufficient academic challenge is provided (Keating, 1991). Without such challenge, a significant aspect of gifted children's development is ignored. Cognitive development must not wait until the middle of elementary school (a usual time to institute provisions for gifted learners). If it does, a powerful negative message is communicated to children — your knowledge and thinking are not valued here.

A "nurturant resourceful environment" (Meichenbaum & Biemiller, 1998, p. 13) is necessary to support high motivation to learn. Children need to be helped and supported to be interested (Bereiter & Scardamalia, 1986). Intensive early support and meaningful education matched to a child's developmental levels result in high levels of competence and satisfaction (Bloom, 1985).

Developmental Considerations: Middle Childhood and Adolescence

It is important to consider the nature and structure of conceptual understanding that gifted learners demonstrate, as discussed earlier. The importance of including conceptual knowledge in educational programs is underscored by research on expertise. The knowledge structures of experts are complex; instruction that has as its objective the nurturance of expertise incorporates meaningful conceptual material (Bereiter & Scardamalia, 1986), in addition to skills. Instruction focused on skills only does not provide the "conceptual glue" that gives deeper meaning to what we learn. Deep understanding should be emphasized from early childhood on, thereby providing a strong foundation for later learning.

Failure to incorporate conceptual material can lead to cumulative deficits in achievement (Meichenbaum & Biemiller, 1998) that become evident as children become older. As Bamberger (1986) found in her study of gifted adolescent musicians (described earlier), an early skills-based approach to musical instruction failed to prepare them for conceptual thinking. The "mid-life" crisis phenomenon also has social-emotional implications for gifted learners who have likely experienced considerable success in school, often due to their quick mastery of a skills-based curriculum. If they have never been challenged to think about the concepts that underpin skills and give them meaning — that is, to apply, analyze, synthesize, and/or evaluate their knowledge — later efforts to engage them in such thinking often meet with defensiveness, unwillingness to participate, and/or self-doubt.

Keeping in mind that, given their variable developmental profiles, theories of adolescent development are relevant to some aspects of gifted adolescents' education, it may also be the case that theories or models of adult development will provide useful guidance in educating gifted adolescents. For example, Lubinski and Benbow (2000) suggest that theories and models of adult career development are appropriate for gifted adolescents because they are developmentally ready for the decision-making processes emphasized in these models. (Similarly, gifted elementary school children may benefit from the sort of career development foci typically offered to adolescents. A six-year-old boy once told me he had three careers in mind, each building on the expertise of the preceding one: "People have more than one career nowadays, you know." This is sophisticated thinking that deserves a sophisticated response.)

Giftedness across the School Years

When faced with compelling advanced developmental needs, the predictive question of subsequent educational and/or professional performance is not relevant; however, an optimal match between school program and abilities is. In this regard, all learners need school environments that respect their competence, offer them appropriate curriculum, and value their input. The curricular content and approaches to teaching and learning will likely change across the school years, but learners' needs for an optimal match between their abilities and their program will not.

When learners are viewed as competent; their ideas are taken seriously; and their teachers, parents, and community have high expectations for them, the result is highly engaged learners who think deeply (Katz, 1993). This principle is illustrated powerfully in the schools of Reggio Emilia, Italy. Part of the success of this approach, replicated elsewhere in Italy and adapted in Canada and the United States (see, for example, Project Zero & Reggio Children, 2001), stems from a conception of children as full members of society and responsiveness to regional beliefs and priorities (New, 2001). Central to the success of schooling is the image of the child/adolescent as strong and competent and the projection of that belief to students (Willms, 1999).

Excellence is promoted in particular social and cultural settings; it is the result of both individual competence and "smart contexts" (Barab & Plucker, 2002). The latter emphasize, like an optimal match, meaningful student-environment transactions that are dynamic in nature, take place in rich contexts, and encourage participation in valued social practices (Barab & Plucker, 2002). Ferrari (2002) suggests that the important educational question to ask is this: "What sort of social and personal conditions promote excellence, and what sort of actions can educators take to assure that students will learn to become excellent in ways that both they and society value?" (p. viii).

Education in a Learning Society

Ferrari's question, together with consideration of the high degree of adaptability necessary to live successfully in a learning society, provides an important focus for debate on how we can best educate all children to their fullest potential. Similarly, Keating's (1999) notion of socially distributed intelligence as essential for the collaborative endeavours that characterize a learning society needs to be incorporated into planning for education in the 21st century.

Excellence

Children need to understand excellence — what it means in different disciplines and what it means to them personally. In order to achieve excellence, they must understand what counts as excellence. They also need to understand the general and personal conditions that promote excellence. If teachers emphasize mastery goals directed at increasing individual personal competence in a subject, then students strive for increased competence through effort. Mastery goals are linked to engagement with learning and the absence of an evaluation focus that places a high degree of emphasis on grades and performance evaluation (Ames, 1992; Dweck, 1986). Classrooms focused on mastery make criteria for excellence clear, support students in achieving to their potential, and help students reflect on their own development as learners. Teachers in these classrooms model their own engagement with learning.

Intersubjectivity

Critical to the development of socially distributed intelligence and full participation in a learning society is the capacity to understand and interact effectively with others. Effective interpersonal relationships in a world of rapidly changing educational, political, cultural, and professional structures are crucial (Keating, 1995).

Bruner (1996) argued that day-to-day life requires everyone to be a psychologist. We need to have theories about why others act the way they do in order to live life effectively. Bruner emphasized the study of *intersubjectivity* — "how people come to know what others have in mind and how they adjust accordingly" (p. 161) — as a central objective for contemporary research.

We need to educate for human understanding. Our responsibility is "to create a context where words such as creativity, change, innovation, error, doubt, and uncertainty, when used on a daily basis, can truly be developed and become real" (Rinaldi, 2003, p. 3). We need to work toward highly evolved teaching-learning relationships. To accomplish these goals, intersubjectivity needs to be legitimized in the curriculum (Bruner, 1996) and recognized as a form of giftedness (Csikszentmihalyi & Larson, 1984; Horowitz & O'Brien, 1986; Keating, 1995).

Identities of Achievement

The concept of *identities of achievement* (Perry, 2003) summarizes well our aim as educators. Students need to feel competent, to be valued for their ideas, and to understand what defines them as competent within a framework of sociocultural values — in short, they need to have an identity of achievement. This means that we must refrain from making decisions about the limits of children's potential — that is, from attempting to determine their capacity (Delpit, 2003). We do not know the limits of human potential, and we need to affirm students' abilities to themselves and to their communities (Delpit, 2003) to begin to grasp what that potential might be.

On a societal level, investment in human capital (education, health, and nutrition) is essential (Willms, 2002) to creation of a learning society that aims to provide its learners with identities of achievement. Within such a societal context, educators and policymakers can frame discussions about the nature and nurture of giftedness within social, cultural, intellectual, and philosophical contexts.

Excellence and Teacher Ownership

The points made regarding excellence are also relevant to teaching. In order to accomplish the objectives set out in this essay, teachers need to understand what constitutes excellent teaching and what supports excellence in their own practice. They need to be valued for their identities of achievement and for their contributions to educational change. A top-down model of educational change is not a viable one (Lupart & Webber, 2002); teacher input and leadership must be valued in our efforts to achieve "smart" educational systems that take into account a dynamic interaction between learners, society and culture, and educational environments (Barab & Plucker, 2002). Along with teacher ownership of change must come time to allow for innovation to be respected and take root and to study the effects of the implementation of changes to systems.

Many teachers have the kind of knowledge contained in good case studies — the case knowledge that Jackson (2000) described as being valuable in helping us understand the developmental course of giftedness. Expert teacher knowledge can help us develop smart classrooms and smart systems that value and encourage all learners. It is important not only to study young people at work (Renzulli, 2002) but also to study exemplary teachers at work within the framework of a reciprocal relationship between education and psychology. Knowledge based on our practice and experience is important, but "it must be compared to knowledge from other sources, connected with knowledge based in research, and interwoven with knowledge derived from theoretical perspectives to be made useful" (Snow, 2001, p. 8). This is not a unidirectional connection, however. The personal knowledge of excellent teachers, when made systematic, can enrich research-based and theoretical knowledge.

Teachers can also research their own practice, asking questions like:

• What do students think about _____?

• What is the relationship of _____ to the curriculum?

• Which ideas build on which others and how?

• Which ideas get in the way and how?

• How does a specific representation of thoughts influence how the thoughts develop further?

• How do my pedagogical practices enhance or constrain student learning?

(Duckworth, 1987; Jordan, Porath, & Bickerton, 2003).

Continued research into the diversities relevant to understanding gifted learners; teacher research focused on investigating their practice; and debate on policy, practice, and what counts as excellence in the diverse communities that characterize Canada will facilitate realization of an optimal match between the goals of a learning society and its learning environments.

REFERENCES

Ames, C. (1992). Classrooms: Goals, structures, and student motivation. *Journal of Educational Psychology, 84,* 261–271.

Bamberger, J. (1986). Growing up prodigies: The midlife crisis. In D.H. Feldman (Ed.), *Developmental approaches to giftedness* (pp. 265–279). San Francisco: Jossey-Bass.

Barab, S.A., & Plucker, J.A. (2002). Smart people or smart contexts? Cognition, ability, and talent development in an age of situated approaches to knowing and learning. *Educational Psychologist, 37,* 165–182.

Barbour, N.E., & Shaklee, B.D. (1998). Gifted education meets Reggio Emilia: Visions for curriculum in gifted education for young children. *Gifted Child Quarterly, 42,* 228–237.

Bereiter, C., & Scardamalia, M. (1986). Educational relevance of the study of expertise. *Interchange, 17*(2), 10–19.

Bloom, B.S. (Ed.). (1985). *Developing talent in young people.* New York: Ballantine.

Brazelton, T.B., & Greenspan, S.I. (2000). *The irreducible needs of children: What every child must have to grow, learn, and flourish.* Cambridge, MA: Perseus.

Bruner, J. (1996). *The culture of education.* Cambridge, MA: Harvard University Press.

Cannon, M.E., & Lupart, J.L. (2001, April). *Gender differences in grades 7 and 10 students towards science, math, computers and future career choices.* Paper presented at the NAMEPA/WEPAN Conference, Alexandria, Virginia.

Case, R. (1985). *Intellectual development: Birth to adulthood.* New York: Academic Press.

(1992a). *The mind's staircase: Exploring the conceptual underpinnings of children's thought and knowledge.* Hillsdale, NJ: Erlbaum.

(1992b). The role of the frontal lobes in the regulation of cognitive development. *Brain and Cognition, 20,* 51–73.

Case, R., & Okamoto, Y. (1996). The role of central conceptual structures in the development of children's thought. *Monographs of the Society for Research in Child Development, 61*(1–2, Serial No. 246).

Csikszentmihalyi, M., & Larson, R. (1984). *Being adolescent.* New York: Basic Books.

Dale, P.S., Robinson, N.M., & Crain-Thoreson, C. (1995). Linguistic precocity and the development of reading: The role of extralinguistic factors. *Applied Psycholinguistics, 16,* 173–187.

Delisle, J.R., & Galbraith, J. (2002). *When gifted kids don't have all the answers: How to meet their social and emotional needs.* Minneapolis, MN: Free Spirit.

Delpit, L. (2003). 2003 Dewitt Wallace-*Reader's Digest* distinguished lecture: Educators as "seed people" [TS: **Replace these straight quotes with smart quotes.**] growing a new future. *Educational Researcher, 17*(32), 14–21.

Donaldson, M. (1979, March). The mismatch between school and children's minds. *Human Nature,* 155–159.

Donovan, M.S., Bransford, J.D., & Pellegrino, J.W. (Eds.). (1999). *How people learn: Bridging research and practice.* Washington, DC: National Academy Press.

Duckworth, E. (1987). *"The having of wonderful ideas" and other essays on teaching and learning*. New York: Teachers College Press.

Dweck, C.S. (1986). Motivational processes affecting learning. *American Psychologist, 41*, 1040–1048.

Feldman, D.H. (1986). *Nature's gambit: Child prodigies and the development of human potential*. New York: Basic Books.

Ferrari, M. (Ed.). *The pursuit of excellence through education* (pp. 3–20). Mahwah, NJ: Erlbaum.

Fischer, K.W., & Canfield, R.L. (1986). The ambiguity of stage and structure of behavior: Person and environment in the development of psychological structure. In I. Levin (Ed.), *Stage and structure: Reopening the debate* (pp. 246–267). Norwood, NJ: Ablex.

Fischer, K.W., Knight, C.C., & Van Parys, M. (1993). Analyzing diversity in developmental pathways: Methods and concepts. In R. Case & W. Edelstein (Eds.), *The new structuralism in cognitive development: Theory and research on individual pathways* (pp. 33–56). Basel: Karger.

Freeman, J. (2000). Teaching for talent: Lessons from the research. In C.F.M. van Lieshout & P.G. Heymans (Eds.), *Developing talent across the life span* (pp. 231–248). Hove, East Sussex: Psychology Press.

Fried, R.L. (2001). Passionate learners and the challenge of schooling. *Phi Delta Kappan, 83*, 124–136.

Gagné, F. (1999). My convictions about the nature of abilities, gifts, and talents. *Journal for the Education of the Gifted, 22*, 109–136.

Gardner, H. (1983). *Frames of mind: The theory of multiple intelligences*. New York: Basic Books.

Gindis, B. (1999). Vygotsky's vision: Reshaping the practice of special education for the 21st century. *Remedial and Special Education, 20*, 333–340.

Golomb, C. (1992). *The child's creation of a pictorial world*. Berkeley: University of California Press.

Gottfredson, L. (1997). Why g matters: The complexity of everyday life. *Intelligence, 24*, 79–132.

Gottfried, A.W., Gottfried, A.E., Bathurst, K., & Guerin, D.W. (1994). *Gifted IQ: Early developmental aspects — The Fullerton longitudinal study*. New York: Plenum Press.

Grigorenko, E.L., Meier, E., Lipka, J., Mohatt, G., Yanez, E., & Sternberg, R.J. (2004). Academic and practical intelligence: A case study of the Yup'ik in Alaska. *Learning and Individual Differences, 14*, 183–207.

Horowitz, F.D., & O'Brien, M. (1986). Gifted and talented children: State of knowledge and directions for research. *American Psychologist, 41,* 1147–1152.

Inzlicht, M., & Ben-Zeev, T. (2003). Do high-achieving female students underperform in private? The implications of threatening environments on intellectual processing. *Journal of Educational Psychology, 95,* 796–805.

Jackson, N.E. (2000). Strategies for modeling the development of giftedness in children. In R.C. Friedman & B.M. Shore (Eds.), *Talents unfolding: Cognition and development* (pp. 27–54). Washington, DC: American Psychological Association.

Janos, P.M., & Robinson, N.M. (1985). Psychosocial development in intellectually gifted children. In F.D. Horowitz & M. O'Brien (Eds.), *The gifted and talented: Developmental perspectives* (pp. 149–195). Washington, DC: American Psychological Association.

Jordan, E., & Porath, M. (2006). *Educational psychology: A problem-based approach.* Boston: Allyn & Bacon.

Jordan, E., Porath, M., & Bickerton, G. (2003). Problem-based learning as a research tool for teachers. In A. Clarke & G. Erickson (Eds.), *Teacher inquiry: Living the research in everyday practice* (pp. 141-153). London: RoutledgeFalmer.

Katz, L.G. (1993). What can we learn from Reggio Emilia? In C. Edwards, L. Gandini, & G. Forman (Eds.), *The hundred languages of children: The Reggio Emilia approach to early childhood education* (pp. 19–37). Norwood, NJ: Ablex.

Keating, D.P. (1991). Curriculum options for the developmentally advanced: A developmental alternative to gifted education. *Exceptionality Education Canada, 1*(1), 53–83.

(1995, June). *Building the learning society: Education's critical role.* Invited address. Canadian Society for the Study of Education, Université de Québec, Montréal.

(1999). The learning society: A human development agenda. In D.P.

Keating & C. Hertzman (Eds.), *Developmental health and the wealth of nations: Social, biological, and educational dynamics* (pp. 237–250). New York: Guilford.

Keating, D.P., & Hertzman, C. (1999). *Developmental health and the wealth of nations: Social, biological, and educational dynamics.* New York: Guilford.

Kerr, B. (1994). *Smart girls two: A new psychology of girls, women, and gift-edness.* Dayton, OH: Ohio Psychology Press.

Larkin, J.H. (1994). Foreword. In K. McGilly (Ed.), *Classroom lessons: Integrating cognitive theory and classroom practice* (pp. ix–xiii). Cambridge, MA: The MIT Press.

Louis, B., & Lewis, M. (1992). Parental beliefs about giftedness in young children and their relation to actual ability level. *Gifted Child Quarterly, 36,* 27–31.

Lubinski, D., & Benbow, C.P. (2000). States of excellence. *American Psychologist, 55,* 137–150.

Lupart, J., & Odishaw, J. (2003). Introduction. *Exceptionality Education Canada, 13*(1 & 2). Special theme issue on pan-Canadian services for at-risk youth.

Lupart, J., & Webber, C. (2002). Canadian schools in transition: Moving from dual education systems to inclusive schools. *Exceptionality Education Canada, 12* (2 & 3), 7–52.

Matthews, D.J. (1994, March). *Program planning: Providing a range of options to address individual needs.* Paper presented at the National Association of School Psychologists' conference, Seattle, Washington.

(1997). Diversity in domains of development: Research findings and their implications for gifted identification and programming. *Roeper Review, 19,* 172–177.

McKeough, A., & Sanderson, A. (1996). Teaching storytelling: A microgenet-ic analysis of developing narrative competency. *Journal of Narrative and Life History, 6,* 157–192.

Meichenbaum, D., & Biemiller, A. (1998). *Nurturing independent learners: Helping students take charge of their learning.* Cambridge, MA: Brookline Books.

Neumeister, K.L., & Hébert, T.P. (2003). Underachievement vs. selective achievement: Delving deeper and discovering the difference. *Journal for the Education of the Gifted, 26,* 221–238.

New, R.S. (2001). Italian early care and education: The social construction of policies, programs, and practices. *Phi Delta Kappan, 83,* 226–236.

Paley, V.G. (1986). On listening to what the children say. *Harvard Educational Review, 56,* 122–131.

Perry, T. (2003). Up from the parched earth: Toward a theory of African-American achievement. In T. Perry, C. Steele, & A. Hilliard, III (Eds.),

Young, gifted and Black: Promoting high achievement among African American students (pp. 1–108). Boston: Beacon.

Porath, M. (1992). Stage and structure in the development of children with various types of "giftedness." In R. Case (Ed.), *The mind's staircase: Exploring the conceptual underpinnings of children's thought and knowledge* (pp. 303–317). Hillsdale, NJ: Erlbaum.

——— (1993). Gifted young artists: Developmental and individual differences. *Roeper Review, 16*, 29–33.

——— (1996). Narrative performance in verbally gifted children. *Journal for the Education of the Gifted, 19*, 276–292.

——— (1997). A developmental model of artistic giftedness in middle childhood. *Journal for the Education of the Gifted, 20*, 201–223.

——— (2000). Social giftedness in childhood: A developmental perspective. In R.C. Friedman & B.M. Shore (Eds.), *Talents unfolding: Cognitive and developmental frameworks* (pp. 195–215). Washington, DC: American Psychological Association.

——— (2001). Young girls' social understanding: Emergent interpersonal expertise. *High Ability Studies, 12*, 113–126.

——— (2002). Gifted education: Accomplishments, directions, and frameworks for debate. *Australasian Journal of Gifted Education, 11, 30–35.*

Project Zero & Reggio Children (2001). *Making learning visible: Children as individual and group learners.* Reggio Emilia, Italy: Reggio Children.

Reis, S.M. (2003). Gifted girls, twenty-five years later: Hopes realized and new challenges found. *Roeper Review, 25*, 154–157.

Renzulli, J.S. (2002). Emerging conceptions of giftedness: Building a bridge to the new century. *Exceptionality, 10*, 67–75.

Richardson, P. (2004, March 17). Personal communication.

Rinaldi, C. (2003). The teacher as researcher. *Innovations in Early Education: The International Reggio Exchange, 10*(2), 1–4.

Robinson, N.M. (1987). The early development of precocity. *Gifted Child Quarterly, 31*, 161–164.

——— (1993). Identifying and nurturing gifted, very young children. In K.A. Heller, F.J. Monks, & A.H. Passow (Eds.), *Research and development of giftedness and talent* (pp. 507–524). Tarrytown, NY: Pergamon Press.

——— (2000). Giftedness in very young children: How seriously should it be taken? In R.C. Friedman & B.M. Shore (Eds.), *Talents unfolding:*

Cognition and development (pp. 7–26). Washington, DC: American Psychological Association.

Robinson, N.M., Abbott, R.D., Berninger, V.W., & Busse, J. (1996). The structure of abilities in math-precocious young children: Gender similarities and differences. *Journal of Educational Psychology, 88*, 341–352.

Robinson, N.M., Abbott, R.D., Berninger, V.W., Busse, J., & Mukhopadhyay, S. (1997). Developmental changes in mathematically precocious young children: Longitudinal and gender effects. *Gifted Child Quarterly, 41*, 145–158.

Robinson, N.M., & Robinson, H.B. (1982). The optimal match: Devising the best compromise for the highly gifted student. In D. Feldman (Ed.), *New Directions for Child Development: Developmental Approaches to Giftedness and Creativity* (No. 17) (pp. 79–94). San Francisco: Jossey-Bass.

Robinson, N.M., Zigler, E., & Gallagher, J.J. (2000). Two tails of the normal curve: Similarities and differences in the study of mental retardation and giftedness. *American Psychologist, 55*, 1413–1424.

Scott, C.L. (1999). Teachers' biases toward creative children. *Creativity Research Journal, 12*, 321–328.

Shore, B.M., & Friedman, R.C. (2000). Introduction. In R.C. Friedman & B.M. Shore (Eds.), *Talents unfolding: Cognition and development* (pp. xv–xix). Washington, DC: American Psychological Association.

Snow, C.E. (2001). Knowing what we know: Children, teachers, researchers. *Educational Researcher, 30*, 3–9.

Southern, W.T., & Jones, E.D. (1991). *The academic acceleration of gifted children.* New York: Teachers College Press.

Sternberg, R.J., & Davidson, J.E. (1986). *Conceptions of giftedness.* New York: Cambridge University Press.

Sternberg, R.J., & Grigorenko, E.L. (Eds.). (2004). *Culture and competence: Contexts of life success.* Washington, DC: American Psychological Association.

Strozzi, P. (2001). Daily life at school: Seeing the extraordinary in the ordinary. In C. Giudici, C. Rinaldi, & M. Krechevsky (Eds.), *Making learning visible: Children as individual and group learners* (pp. 58–77). Reggio Emila, Italy: Reggio Children.

Struthers, R. (2003). The artistry and ability of traditional women healers. *Health Care for Women International, 24*, 340–354.

Terman, L.M. (1925). *Genetic studies of genius: Vol. 1. Mental and physical traits of a thousand gifted children.* Stanford: Stanford University Press.

Wentzel, K.R. (1993). Does being good make the grade? Social behavior and academic competence in middle school. *Journal of Educational Psychology, 85,* 357–364.

Willms, J.D. (1999). Quality and inequality in children's literacy: The effects of families, schools, and communities. In D.P. Keating & C. Hertzman (Eds.), *Developmental health and the wealth of nations: Social, biological, and educational dynamics* (pp. 72–93). New York: Guilford.

(2002). Research findings bearing on Canadian social policy. In J.D.

Willms (Ed.), *Vulnerable children: Findings from Canada's National Longitudinal Survey of Children and Youth* (pp. 331–377). Edmonton: University of Alberta Press.

Wilson, R.J. (1996). *Assessing students in classrooms and schools.* Scarborough, ON: Allyn & Bacon Canada.

Winner, E. (2000). The origins and ends of giftedness. *American Psychologist, 55,* 159–169.

CONTRIBUTORS

Marie Battiste is Coordinator of the Indian and Northern Education Program in the Faculty of Education, University of Saskatchewan.

Paula Cameron teaches in the Faculty of Education, Mount St. Vincent University.

Wendy Craig is a professor in the Department of Psychology, Queen's University.

Cameron Crawford is with The Roeher Institute, Toronto, ON.

Jim Cummins is Canada Research Chair in Language Learning and Literacy Development in Multilingual Contexts at O.I.S.E./ University of Toronto.

Blye Frank is Professor and Director of Faculty Education in the Division of Medical Education, Dalhousie University.

Clyde Hertzman is Director of the Human Early Learning Partnership and Canada Research Chair in Population Health and Human Development, University of British Columbia.

Lori Irwin is Deputy Director of the Human Early Learning Partnership, University of British Columbia.

Paul Kershaw is a professor in the Human Early Learning Partnership, University of British Columbia.

John R. Kirby is a professor in the Faculty of Education and cross- appointed to the Department of Psychology, Queen's University.

Ben Levin is Canada Research Chair in Educational Policy and Research at O.I.S.E./ University of Toronto.

Judy L. Lupart is Canada Research Chair in Special Education in the Faculty of Education, University of Alberta.

Debra Pepler is a professor in the Department of Psychology, York University, a senior executive member of the LaMarsh Centre for Research in Violence and Conflict Resolution and Senior Associate Scientist at the Hospital for Sick Children.

Marion Porath is a professor in the Department of Educational and Counseling Psychology, and Special Education in the Faculty of Education, University of British Columbia.

Vianne Timmons is President of the University of Regina.

Kate Trafford is a GIS analyst with the Rural and Environmental Research and Analysis Directorate, Government of Scotland.

T. Douglas Willms is Director of the Canadian Research Institute for Social Policy and Canada Research Chair in Human Development, University of New Brunswick.